THE FRIGHTFEST GUIDE TO VAMPIRE MOVIES

First published by FAB Press, August 2022

FAB Press Ltd.
2 Farleigh, Ramsden Road, Godalming
Surrey, GU7 1QE, England, U.K.

www.fabpress.com

Picture research and layout by Kevin Coward
FrightFest Guide original book design, layout and pre-press origination by Harvey Fenton
Film cast and crew credits, additional research and index by Francis Brewster
Thanks also to Alan Jones and the FrightFest image archive

Author's Dedication:
To Christopher Lee for awakening me to a lifetime of vampire movies, to my wonderful family for putting up with those same movies,
and to every fan out there keeping the fresh blood flowing.

Front cover illustration:
Cover design by Harvey Fenton, based on Spanish poster artwork for Salem's Lot (1979), and Japanese poster artwork for Dracula (1958)
Frontispiece illustration:
Collage by Kevin Coward and Harvey Fenton, based on original theatrical poster artwork for Vampyres (1974)

Printed in Czech Republic

A CIP catalogue record for this book is available from the British Library

hardcover: ISBN 978 1 913051 19 8
paperback: ISBN 978 1 913051 20 4

-THE DARK HEART OF CINEMA-

FRIGHTFEST ®
GUIDE

VAMPIRE MOVIES

Nathaniel Thompson

-THE DARK HEART OF CINEMA -
FRIGHTFEST ®

Throughout its 23 years of programming the cream of the horror, sci-fi, thriller and fantasy genres from around the world at its three hugely anticipated yearly mega-events (as part of the Glasgow Film Festival in Scotland every March, in London every late August Bank Holiday and its Halloween Shocktoberfest) and online too, FrightFest, the United Kingdom's biggest, best and most prestigious Party Central for fear fans has premiered thousands of movies.

And of course vampires, those fanged creatures of the blackest night, have featured quite strongly in our foremost choices being one of the most beloved staples of the genre. Given the instant popularity of Bram Stoker's classic tale of terror 'Dracula' in 1897, and Hungarian/American star Bela Lugosi imprinting on pop culture a depiction of the immortal Count that has lasted since the 1931 Universal movie classic bearing his iconic name, nocturnal blood-drinkers have evolved over the decades through many incarnations from comedy, sci-fi and lesbian interpretations to High School, Mexican and comic book settings. Yet those wooden stakes, crucifixes and garlic have had little effect because the vampire has remained central to horror's pantheon for 100 years now. Eternal revivals of Dracula or the near dark breeds of Lost Boys and Twilight girls has not closed the coffin on the undead as there will always be an audience for the Prince of Darkness and his lustful disciples.

"THIS IS A VAMPIRE MOVIE LIKE NO OTHER. (MESMERIZING)"

LET THE RIGHT ONE IN

A FILM BY TOMAS ALFREDSON

BASED ON THE INTERNATIONAL BESTSELLER NOW IN PAPERBACK

Looking back at past FrightFest programmes is very interesting from the vampire perspective. From the classic chiller **Let the Right One In** (2008) to the comedy shocker **Let the Wrong One In** (2021), it really encompasses every quirky blood-sucking concept you can imagine. And some you really shouldn't! How about Guy Maddin's extraordinary **Dracula: Pages from a Virgin's Diary** (2002), a ballet rendition of Stoker's bestseller stylized as an expressionistic silent film. I can still remember the audience shock turning to adoration as it unspooled. Then there was the Cannes art-horror **The Transfiguration** (2016) that caused as much puzzlement as acclaim. **Higanjima: Escape from Vampire Island** (2009) and **Vampire Girl vs. Frankenstein Girl** (2009) put a uniquely Japanese spin on the iconic fantasy figures. **Chuck Steel: Night of the Trampires** (2018) proved stop-motion animation perfection. **Lesbian Vampire Killers** (2009) probably found its best ever audience at FrightFest back in the day when James Corden wasn't a feline punchline. **Byzantium** (2012) gave FrightFest one of its starriest Q&A lineups when actors Saoirse Ronan and Gemma Arterton, together with director Neil Jordan, took centre stage. And let's hear it too for **Bloodsucking Bastards** (2015) and **Fanged Up** (2017), which provided cult enjoyment. I did mean cult, with an L, by the way!

But while FrightFest is always about premiering the newest titles gleaned from a year of trawling the main festival markets and other events, we have never forgotten to pay our respects to the past. That treasure trove known as The Hammer House of Horror ensured we could showcase resorations and retrospectives of such keynote delights as **Captain Kronos: Vampire Hunter** (1974), **Dracula Prince of Darkness** (1966), **The Vampire Lovers** (1970), **Countess Dracula** (1971) and **Twins of Evil** (1971), usually with attendant Hammer Glamour in the guise of the lovely Caroline Munro, Madeleine Smith and Ingrid Pitt.

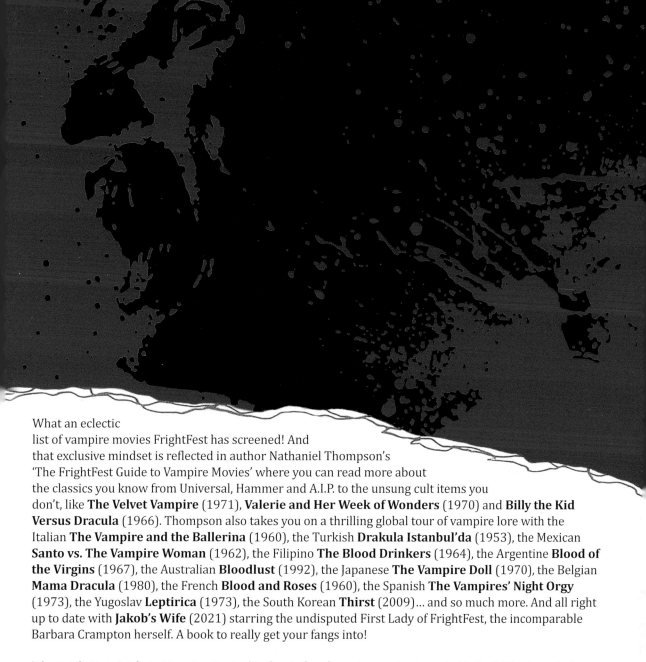

What an eclectic
list of vampire movies FrightFest has screened! And
that exclusive mindset is reflected in author Nathaniel Thompson's
'The FrightFest Guide to Vampire Movies' where you can read more about
the classics you know from Universal, Hammer and A.I.P. to the unsung cult items you
don't, like **The Velvet Vampire** (1971), **Valerie and Her Week of Wonders** (1970) and **Billy the Kid Versus Dracula** (1966). Thompson also takes you on a thrilling global tour of vampire lore with the Italian **The Vampire and the Ballerina** (1960), the Turkish **Drakula Istanbul'da** (1953), the Mexican **Santo vs. The Vampire Woman** (1962), the Filipino **The Blood Drinkers** (1964), the Argentine **Blood of the Virgins** (1967), the Australian **Bloodlust** (1992), the Japanese **The Vampire Doll** (1970), the Belgian **Mama Dracula** (1980), the French **Blood and Roses** (1960), the Spanish **The Vampires' Night Orgy** (1973), the Yugoslav **Leptirica** (1973), the South Korean **Thirst** (2009)... and so much more. And all right up to date with **Jakob's Wife** (2021) starring the undisputed First Lady of FrightFest, the incomparable Barbara Crampton herself. A book to really get your fangs into!

'The FrightFest Guide to Vampire Movies' is the sixth volume in a series intended to build the knowledge of the curious spectator and the cult connoisseur alike – the exact same maxim with which we meticulously produce our annual events that are globally famous, currently listed as one of the Top 25 greatest, and used by the international film industry as a litmus test for the future of the horror genre.

Enjoy this latest respected roundup of all things untold, bat-like, cloaked and dead and loving it written with the same passionate enthusiasm that sets Frightfesters apart from the mundane fest rest. But FrightFest is not just a film festival or the friendliest community you could ever wish to join. It's an ever-increasing brand that includes FrightFest Presents, our multi-platform/VOD entertainment label that has released such diverse and popular titles as **Some Kind of Hate** (2015), **My Father Die** (2016), **The Siren** (2019), **Videoman** (2018), **The Wind** (2018), **12 Hour Shift** (2020), the cultural phenomenon **The Love Witch** (2016) and the critically acclaimed **Relic** (2020) and **You Are Not My Mother** (2021).

~ Alan Jones, FrightFest co-director

NATHANIEL THOMPSON

Nathaniel Thompson was first bitten by vampire movie mania as a young child thanks to viewings of **The Kiss of the Vampire** and **Dracula Prince of Darkness** in a single weekend. An avid film viewer, he spread his enthusiasm for the horror genre with a high school fanzine, *Movies from Beyond the Grave*, and in early 1998 he launched one of the earliest comprehensive review websites devoted to genre films, Mondo Digital (which continues to this day). That site also served as the springboard for his four-book *DVD Delirium* series for FAB Press, a survey of notable home video releases around the world with a focus on horror and art house cinema. For 15 years he has been a regular contributing writer for Turner Classic Movies, and he was a weekly contributor to FilmStruck during its run from 2016 to 2018. For the past decade he has written regularly for the Academy of Motion Picture Arts and Sciences and has worked behind the scenes at every Oscar ceremony during that period, so he's worn more than his share of tuxedoes.

One of his earliest professional jobs was at DreamWorks SKG soon after its founding, where he was able to observe firsthand the circumstances behind the making of the 1999 remake of **The Haunting** as well as other films like **Gladiator** and **In Dreams**. For ten years he oversaw the production and marketing of many acclaimed genre releases on DVD and Blu-ray at Image Entertainment including **Alone in the Dark** (the good one), **Cannibal Apocalypse,** the Boris Karloff horror anthology series **Thriller**, **The House with Laughing Windows**, a three-disc edition of **Caligula**, **Devil Doll**, dozens of Shaw Brothers titles, the EuroShock series featuring films by the likes of Jess Franco and Jean Rollin, and the cult films of Ted V. Mikels, Nathan Schiff, Paul Morrissey, and Ulli Lommel. He also worked in conjunction with Something Weird Video on its DVD releases throughout that period and owes more to the late Mike Vraney than can possibly be expressed.

Since the early days of the DVD format, Nathaniel has been a regular contributor of audio commentaries and has now amassed over 150 credits to date with titles including **Child's Play**, **Opera**, **Sleepless**, **The Card Player**, **Willard**, **Beyond the Door**, **The Velvet Vampire**, **Bad Dreams**, **The Apple**, **Butcher Baker Nightmare Maker**, **Warlock**, **City of the Living Dead**, **The Church**, **Conquest**, **Emanuelle in America**, **eXistenZ**, **The Sentinel**, **Forbidden World**, **The Silent Partner**, **Grave of the Vampire**, **Humongous**, **The Little Girl Who Lives Down the Lane**, **After Midnight**, **The Unholy**, **Watch Me When I Kill**, **The Hunting Party**, **Mad Doctor of Blood Island**, **Shredder**, **The Mephisto Waltz**, **Red Scorpion**, and **Ticks**. Among others, his commentaries have been conducted with Howard S. Berger, Bruce Holecheck (who also proved invaluable in research for this book), Troy Howarth, Steve Mitchell, Tom Holland, Steve Miner, Catherine Mary Stewart, John Dahl, Larry Buchanan, Robert Downey Sr., Celeste Yarnall, Joseph Zito, Jeffrey Konvitz, Bruce Davison, Lee Montgomery, Michael Sopkiw, Jack Sholder, Tony Randel, Clint Howard, and Barbara Cupisti.

You can see Nathaniel in front of the camera in such documentaries as **King Cohen, It Was a Colossal Teenage Movie Machine: The American International Pictures Story**, and **1982: One Amazing Summer!**, and he has been involved in the video bonus features for such films as **Videodrome**, **Don't Answer the Phone**, **Silent Scream**, **The Visitor**, and **Stunt Rock**.

Over the years Nathaniel has conducted interviews with numerous genre figures including the likes of Jean Rollin, David F. Friedman, Jack Hill, and Herschell Gordon Lewis. An avid connoisseur and collector of film scores, he has also interviewed and profiled such composers as Pino Donaggio, Lalo Schifrin, John Cacavas, Carter Burwell, Christopher Young, and Patrick Doyle. He has presented numerous film screenings and conducted Q&As with everyone from Radley Metzger and Pia Zadora to Jeff Bridges and Julie Andrews, and his writing can also be found in multiple issues of the much-missed magazine *Video Watchdog* and the FAB Press compendium, *Fear Without Frontiers: Horror Cinema Across the Globe*. He currently resides in Los Angeles and still tries to take in as many films on the big screen as possible.

Nathaniel Thompson
© Blake Kuehn

FOREWORD BY KIM NEWMAN

In the early 1940s, RKO Pictures hired Val Lewton to head a unit tasked with the production of low-cost horror movies. Lewton, a man of taste and vision, saw this could be a plum gig and set out to make *excellent* low-cost horror movies. In preparation, he surveyed the current state of the genre and concluded that 'vampires and werewolves have been done to death' – though the Lewton unit's first production, Jacques Tourneur's **Cat People** (1942), was a werewolf movie in all but name, and Mark Robson's **Isle of the Dead** (1945), which forsakes the *nosferatu* of Transylvania for the *vorvolakas* of Greece, was a vampire variant.

Lewton's initial thought was understandable, but now seems odd. By 1942, there had been maybe *ten* proper vampire movies – a tally that has to include mysteries where deaths seem vampire-related but are actually caused by something else (cf: **London After Midnight**, 1927, **The Vampire Bat**, 1933, **Mark of the Vampire**, 1935) and three versions of (plus one sequel to) *Dracula* ... with the balance made up by oddities like Carl Dreyer's Euro artfilm **Vampyr** (1932) and the off-brand vampire-werewolf-Jekyll-and-Hyde movie **Condemned to Live** (1935). How done to death would Lewton think vampire movies if he were working in the early 1970s – when there seemed to be ten vampire movies every month – or considering the genre now, when every imaginable vampire has shown up on screen (if not always in mirrors)?

We have long since passed the point of vampire saturation, and the constantly reinvented Count Dracula has been jostled in the popular imagination by upstarts Barnabas Collins, Lestat de Lioncourt and Edward Cullen as the pale public face of vampirism. Notice how there are generally two major vampire characters and Dracula is always one of them? When Bram Stoker published *Dracula* in 1897, he drew on literary precursors like John Polidori and J. Sheridan Le Fanu, whose Lord Ruthven (from 'The Vampyre') and Carmilla Karnstein (from 'Carmilla') had their own metastatising and sometimes-resurgent franchises. In the mid-19th century, Ruthven – whose film career has been very spotty, though Polidori fans can gleam tiny comfort from references in **The Vampire's Ghost** (1945), **Countess Dracula's Orgy of Blood** (2002) and **Byzantium** (2012) – was the star of several competing stage versions, some of which made him a tartan-clad Scots vampire, including a couple of operas.

F.W. Murnau's **Nosferatu** (1922) and Tod Browning's **Dracula** (1931) present very different versions of their vampire villains – Max Schreck as the ratlike Count Orlok stitched into a tunic that gives him a stick insect profile and Bela Lugosi as the gigolo-like drawing room Dracula (essentially, the character of Lord Ruthven) with spotlit eyes, hypnotic gestures ("you have to be double-jointed and Hungarian", explains Martin Landau as Lugosi in **Ed Wood**, 1994) and a natty cloak. Screen vampires exist in the line of descent from both these Draculas. Feral, snarling, inhuman monsters often copy Schreck's classic make-up while romantic, doom-haunted predators ape Lugosi's seduction techniques. It's not often noted that the dry, dusty, repulsive Orlok dies for love – while the more purely evil Lugosi Dracula gets hunted down and impaled. Lugosi instantly had his ghostly doppelganger in Carlos Villarias of the Spanish version of the Universal **Dracula** shot on the same sets – slightly more interestingly photographed, far less well-acted, and (notably) not edited to pick up the pace the way the Lugosi film is. Schreck had to wait for Klaus Kinski in Werner Herzog's revisionist remake **Nosferatu the Vampyre** (1979) and Willem Dafoe in E. Elias Merhige's metafictional **Shadow of the Vampire** (2000) to be shadowed, though Nosferatu-look bald, rodentine spectres stalk through Jaromil Jires' **Valerie a týden divu/Valerie and Her Week of Wonders** (1970) and Tobe Hooper's TV version of Stephen King's Dracula-comes-to-Peyton Place novel **Salem's Lot** (1979). Still, the default Dracula imitation is a Lugosi voice – notice how no one echoes Christopher Lee's distinctive, sepulchral tones when they impersonate a vampire.

REVENGE OF THE VAMPIRE 'X'

THE UNDEAD DEMONS OF HELL TERRORIZE THE WORLD IN AN ORGY OF STARK HORROR

Starring: BARBARA STEELE · JOHN RICHARDSON

By now, we've had an infinity of Draculas – "how would you like to go around looking like a head waiter for seven hundred years?" whines George Hamilton in **Love at First Bite** (1979) – and the Count has suffered competition to the point of copyright infringement from Blacula, Spermula, Cannicula, Bunnicula, Deafula, Gayracula, Ejacula, Dragula and Duckula, plus sundry Counts and Barons from around the world. He has even been upstaged by his own brides. The drifting, etherial predators of the Browning version and Christopher Lee's peignoir-clad pearl-fanged concubines in the Hammer Films set a style followed by Carmillas, Millarcas and Elisabeth Bathorys, ranging from Barbara Steele's unrepentant Asa Vajda in Mario Bava's **La maschera del demonio/The Mask of Satan/Black Sunday/Revenge of the Vampire** (1960) through Delphine Seyrig's Dietrich-like Bathory in Harry Kumel's **Les lèvres rouge/Daughters of Darkness** (1971) and Mariclare Costello's unusual American Carmilla-type in John Hancock's **Let's Scare Jessica to Death** to Lina Leandersson's ambiguous Eli ("if I wasn't a girl would you like me anyway?") in Tomas Alfredson's **Låt den rätte komma in/Let the Right One In** (2008).

Still, however, vampire movies keep coming back round to Dracula, with Schreck, Lugosi and Lee still the Draculas to beat, though John Carradine, Udo Kier and (bizarrely, perhaps) Adam Sandler have their own little corner for takes on the role ... which has been essayed by a range of tall, domineering leading men that includes Jack Palance, Louis Jourdan, Frank Langella, Gary Oldman, Gerard Butler, Jonathan Rhys Meyers, Luke Evans and Claes Bang. Dario Argento's little-liked **Dracula 3D** (2012) is unique in casting as Dracula and Van Helsing actors who have also played the other key role – Thomas

Kretschman, Argento's Dracula, was Van Helsing in the 2013-14 TV series, and Rutger Hauer, a rare Dutch actor cast as Van Helsing, was Dracula in **Dracula III: Legacy** (2005). Also, we should take note of the many, many crap Draculas – some of the worst readings of the part have come from a wide range of talents including David Niven, Alex D'Arcy, Richard Roxburgh, Dominic Purcell, Andrew Bryniarski, Charlie Callas, Leslie Nielsen and Marc Warren. With all these indignities and humiliations, not to mention Sandler's 'blah de blah de blah', it's a wonder that Dracula keeps rising from the grave ... but, given the inherent power of the material, not surprising that even in the 21st century Bram Stoker's vision still dominates, even as pop culture juggernauts like **Dark Shadows**, Anne Rice's **Vampire Chronicles**, **Buffy the Vampire Slayer** and **Twilight** have their moments, then fade at the dawn of the next decade.

The novelist David J. Schow once remarked that vampires were "the **Star Trek** of horror". He didn't mean that entirely positively – but just as **Star Trek** (and **Star Wars** and the Marvel Cinematic Universe and a other mainstream manifestations) draws in a different, potentially wider fan following than the perceived-as-niche genre of science fiction, vampire stories have broken out of the ghetto of horror, thriving in all kinds of interesting genre-splice hybrids like **The Legend of the 7 Golden Vampires** (1974) – which fuses Shaw Brothers kung fu with Hammer

Black Belt vs. Black Magic!

You haven't seen Kung fu until you've seen the 7 BROTHERS and 1 SISTER take DRACULA

It's Dynamite!

"The 7 Brothers meet DRACULA"

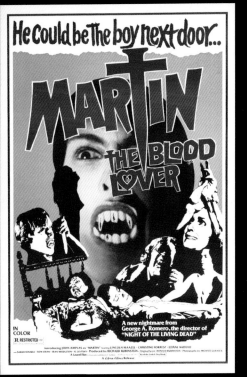

He could be the boy next door...

MARTIN THE BLOOD LOVER

IN COLOR
R RESTRICTED

A new nightmare from George A. Romero, the director of "NIGHT OF THE LIVING DEAD"

Introducing JOHN AMPLAS as "MARTIN" starring LINCOLN MAAZEL · CHRISTINE FORREST · ELYANE NADEAU
with SARAH VENABLE · TOM SAVINI · FRAN MIDDLETON · AL LEVITSKY · Produced by RICHARD RUBINSTEIN · Original Score · DONALD RUBINSTEIN · Photography by MICHAEL GORNICK
A Laurel Film   Based on and order & Roy Romero
A Libra Films Release

Dracula action, with a side order of Chinese hopping vampires – or such self-explanatory mash-ups as **Emmanuelle vs. Dracula** (2004), **The Batman vs. Dracula** (2005), and **Bonnie & Clyde vs. Dracula** (2008). The vampire movie has long since ceased to be purely a sub-genre of horror. Outside the parent genre, there are whole filmographies for sub-types like vampire romance, vampire comedy, vampire soap opera, vampire porn (yes, *of course* there are multiple films with titles like **Dracula Sucks**, **Intercourse with the Vampyre** and **Muffy the Vampire Layer**), vampire western, vampire Mexican wrestling movie, vampire art movies, vampire dystopia, vampire apocalypse, vampire action ... even vampire realism, from George Romero's **Martin** (1977) to Michael O'Shea's **The Transfiguration** (2016). Jean Rollin managed to scramble pretty much all of these sub-sub-genres into his whole unique and fascinating vampire filmography.

STRAND RELEASING PRESENTS

THE TRANSFIGURATION

Vampirism is a handy metaphor for all sorts of things – political oppression, sexual diversity, addiction, sexually-transmitted disease, human predation, coercive relationships, existential ennui, gender roles. Every one of these readings of the basic folklore has a clutch of films to bear it out. Plus, you know, meaningless entertainments that still seem to stick in the mind longer than more significant movies ... during his brief tenure as a studio head, Bryan Forbes was frustrated to find an unbreakable deal with Hammer Films in place that took up production slots and budget funds he'd rather have spent on other projects, but fifty years on who'd swap **Twins of Evil** (1971) for **The Raging Moon** (1971)?

For me, horror as a genre starts with Dracula – not in the sense of being first in an objective history, but being the first iterations I saw. So, whether it's Orlok looming out of the castle shadows, Lugosi surrounded by cowbebs, brides and an armadillo, or Lee turning on a sixpence from well-mannered host to bloody-fanged horror, Dracula makes the best entrance – and, as demonstrated by a longevity barely interrupted by stakes through the heart or dissolutions at dawn, sticks around at the party longest.

~ Kim Newman
London, 2022

*Kim Newman is a critic, author and broadcaster. He is a contributing editor to **Sight & Sound** and **Empire** magazines. His books about film include **Nightmare Movies** and **Kim Newman's Video Dungeon**. His fiction includes the **Anno Dracula** series and **Something More Than Night**. His website is www.johnnyalucard.com. He is on Twitter as @AnnoDracula.*

FRIGHTFEST GUIDE

VAMPIRE MOVIES

INTRODUCTION

I. I BID YOU WELCOME

The definition of a vampire may seem clear today: a member of the undead who feeds on human blood, ranging from a soulless predator to a tortured creature with some remnant of its humanity and even recalling its past life. The bloodsucking aspect is of course the primary trait, and more than any other monster out there, the vampire has accumulated a roster of ground rules that have evolved and been flagrantly broken over the years. Sunlight, crosses, holy water, and garlic are the most frequent talismans to ward off a vampire, whose mesmeric influence can manipulate potential victims into bending to its will. In some cases, the vampire can only wield its power after being invited into one's home, and the most surefire ways of dispatching it involve a combination of a stake through the heart and beheading. This dense mythology primarily sprang from European superstition-driven folklore that also begat tales of witchcraft and devil worship to explain the process of death and warn youngsters from straying off at night. Particularly with the application of transfusions as a life-saving measure for victims, the vampire myth also served a purpose

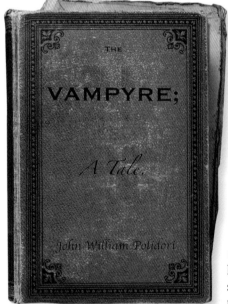

in rationalizing blood-borne and venereal diseases running rampant in many communities with normal people suddenly stricken with radical physical and mental maladies that appeared to defy explanation.

Vampires have always made for fine bloodcurdling story material, and though the Eastern European strain (which filtered from Serbia through surrounding countries) is the most influential in modern society, vampire variants have existed in most major cultures around the world. The exact etymology of the word has been debated by scholars for decades since the first English-language appearances of the term in the 1700s, but aspects of these blood-feeding beings appear all the way back to ancient Greek, Roman, Arabian, African, and Chinese myths. One constant is that these monstrosities are presented as a dangerous affront to the status quo, and particularly religious faith, with resuscitation from the dead serving as a particularly heinous blasphemy against humanity and its creator. As with the aforementioned witchcraft and demonism, the threat of the vampire provided all the more reason for average citizens to use holy symbols for protection and keep their homes safe from intrusive forces that would otherwise have to resort to feeding on animals to survive.

However, nothing has served to familiarize the world with vampires more than the written word. Though the subject matter has only been accepted as high literature in a handful of cases, the public has been regaled with poems, short stories, and eventually novels throughout the centuries, with the first bona fide English-language narrative work arriving courtesy of John William Polidori with his tale, 'The Vampyre.' This yarn about the aristocratic vampire Lord Ruthven and his tragic, years-long impact on the life of a young man named Aubrey famously sprang from the three-day summer story contest in 1816 between physician Polidori, Lord Byron (who was initially credited as author for the first publication in 1819), and Percy and Mary Shelley, a gathering that also

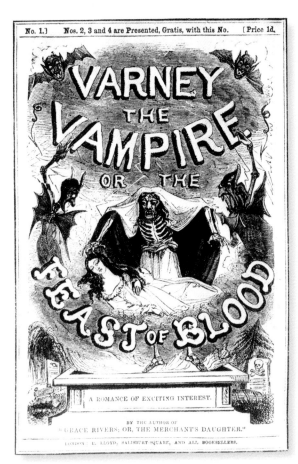

sparked the creation of Mary's revolutionary novel, *Frankenstein, or the Modern Prometheus*. Polidori's work capped off an escalating string of vaguely vampire-tinted poems, most famously Samuel Taylor Coleridge's fragment 'Christabel' (begun circa 1797), Johann Wolfgang von Goethe's 'The Bride of Corinth' (1797), and Gottfried August Bürger's 'Lenore' (1773), and in turn led to one of the most famous penny dreadful serials of the era, James Malcolm Rymer and Thomas Peckett Prest's erratic but influential *Varney the Vampire; or, the Feast of Blood*, begun in 1845. Among the key elements in the breathless hundreds of pages of adventurous exploits, that narrative introduces its titular character as a fanged vampire ultimately tormented by his cursed state, a device still with us today. Also influential is the French writer Paul Féval, a crime novelist who dabbled in vampirism in three novels, *Le Chevalier Ténèbre* (1860), *La Vampire* (1865) and *La Ville Vampire* (1874). Drawing inspiration from French serials of the era, his books place a strong emphasis on female characters, including what may be the first significant female bloodsucker, *La Vampire*'s Countess Addhema.

The theme of corrupted nobility continued with the most famous of all vampire serials, J. Sheridan Le Fanu's *Carmilla*, which first began publication in 1871 and appeared in novella form in the author's compendium *In a Glass Darkly* a year later. Told from the perspective of a young girl named Laura, the narrative follows the upheaval in her aristocratic home when a carriage accident delivers to them a new resident, Carmilla, who bears a striking resemblance to her legendary ancestor, Countess Mircalla Karnstein. The first significant lesbian vampire in fiction, Carmilla preys upon the young girl and ignites a retaliatory reaction from the men nearby, climaxing in a gruesome act of dismemberment. Though truly faithful adaptations of the story are few, the idea of an alluring female vampire with a penchant for women has never waned in popularity; furthermore, the character of Carmilla (or her previous guises as Millarca and Mircalla) has been repurposed dozens of times on film.

All of this activity throughout the 19th century was merely the prelude for the most enduring work of English-language vampire fiction, *Dracula*, written

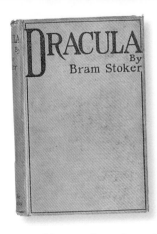

DRACULA By Bram Stoker

by Irish theatrical business manager and writer Bram Stoker, and first published in 1897. A ferocious page turner, the epistolary novel chronicles the nightmarish consequences when young solicitor Jonathan Harker travels to Transylvania to arrange the acquisition of Carfax Abbey in London for a Romanian nobleman, Count Dracula. After barely escaping with his life from Dracula's castle in the Carpathian Mountains, Harker returns to England where the blood-drinking menace has begun to prey on the populace, including Lucy Westenra, the best friend of Harker's fiancée, Mina. A team of impromptu vampire hunters is assembled by Abraham Van Helsing, including Harker, Arthur Holmwood (Lucy's betrothed), Dr. John Seward, and American adventurer Quincey Morris. With its vampire brides, implied baby sacrifice, castle wall crawling, and insect-eating minion Renfield, the novel was an immediate sensation, inspiring a posthumous companion story by Stoker entitled 'Dracula's Guest' (1914) and a 1924 stage adaptation by Hamilton Deane that became a major success in the United States three years later when it was significantly revised by John L. Balderston and arrived on Broadway starring Bela Lugosi and Edward Van Sloane. The drastically altered and streamlined play became the source for the 1931 Tod Browning film adaptation, which retained both of the leads and spawned a wave of popular monster films from Universal Pictures, including James Whale's **Frankenstein** later that same year.

Despite its groundbreaking status, Browning's **Dracula** was hardly the first vampire film. Two unauthorized adaptations had already fallen afoul of copyright issues in Europe, with Hungary's now-lost **Drakula halála** (1921) or **Dracula's Death**, directed by Károly Lajthay and co-written by a young Michael Curtiz, and far more famously, F.W. Murnau's **Nosferatu** (1922), which followed its literary

Drakula halála

Metro-Goldwyn-Mayer
LON CHANEY
LONDON AFTER MIDNIGHT

model closely enough to have its (unsuccessful) destruction ordered by Stoker's estate. Browning himself had dabbled in vampirism with the most legendary of all lost horror films, **London After Midnight** (1927), featuring Lon Chaney in chilling makeup as a presumed creature of the night who is actually an actor masquerading with his troupe to unmask a murderer. Browning and Lugosi would join forces again in 1935 for a remake of this film, **Mark of the Vampire**, though that has done little to quench the horror community's thirst to salvage the original film someday.

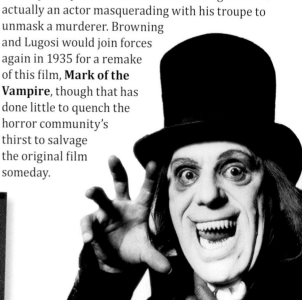

II. THE PRINCE OF DARKNESS

Even at the dawn of the sound era, a film's success was enough to spawn a sequel as quickly as possible. Universal had lost its monster at the end of the 1931 **Dracula**, but creative gears were turning to find a way to sate the public's appetite for further escapades involving the Count and his progeny. Though discussions started soon after the release of the Browning and Lugosi hit, a difficult, years-long process ensued to create **Dracula's Daughter** (1936) after multiple story overhauls. Two years later, Orson Welles launched his landmark radio series *The Mercury Theatre on the Air* on July 11, 1938 by essaying the title role in a production of *Dracula* that chilled viewers with its vivid sound effects, including a climactic staking achieved with a very squishy melon. Retaining more of the epistolary structure of Stoker's novel than its cinematic predecessors over its 55-minute running time, the production is still remarkable for its ambitious execution, including a soundscape of howling wolves, screams, shuddery musical stings, and a spooky evocation of the deadly oceanic trip on the ill-fated Demeter sailing vessel. A few months later that year, on October 30, Welles and company would escalate their assault on listeners' nervous systems with a production of *The War of the Worlds* that spawned increasingly elaborate stories of public panic.

Made at the height of World War II, the belated but inevitable **Son of Dracula** (1943) actually featured Lon Chaney Jr. as the Count himself heading off to Louisiana and reflected the very different climate of the time during World War II. That film would prove to be the last of Universal's standalone Dracula vehicles, with the character adopted into the monster mash framework of three subsequent films. Shot back to back by underrated director Erle C. Kenton, the phantasmagorical diptych of **House of Frankenstein** (1944) and **House of Dracula** (1945) features John Carradine as Dracula, and pulls together plot threads from both **Son of Dracula** and the popular **Frankenstein Meets the Wolf Man** (1943). Carradine's presence is limited in the first monster-laden film as the character is dispatched early in the story, but he returns for a more prominent role in the second as he takes on the identity of Baron Latos to ostensibly find a cure for his condition as cover

Some variation on the vampire film has existed at least as far back as a four-minute short film by Georges Méliès, **Le manoir du diable** (1896), which features a diabolic human creature transforming into a bat. Muddying the waters in the silent era is the rise of the vamp, a seductive woman who uses her wiles to manipulate those around her (often for criminal ends). Though bearing no characteristics akin to actual vampires, the sinister, sensual look appropriated by the vamp still betrays a shared aesthetic sensibility exploited by its most famous incarnation, actress Theda Bara, who portrayed 'The Vampire' in **A Fool There Was** (1915). Her role as a woman who lures an upstanding married lawyer to his doom was enough to inspire Fox to retain her for the next four years in a variety of vamp roles. 1915 also saw the start of Louis Feuillade's **Les Vampires**, a long-running, fast-paced French serial about a criminal gang whose black-heavy fashion choices are akin to those of the vamp. The cinematic origins of the vamp can be traced back a little further, to Robert G. Vignola's **The Vampire** (1913), which features the earliest vampire dance sequence, and similar imagery was also employed in the lost German film, **Nächte des Grauens** (1917), a.k.a. **A Night of Horror**. One of the most opulent of the vamp films arrived from Robert Wiene, who followed up his watershed masterpiece **The Cabinet of Dr. Caligari** (1920) later that same year with the fragmented and surreal **Genuine** (1920), about a frizzy-haired femme fatale whose presence in a painting inspires a dream involving murder and manipulation.

top left: **Le manoir du diable** (1896) by Georges Méliès.
opposite lower right: Lon Chaney in **London After Midnight** (1927).

for a more sinister agenda. Among its other Gothic thrills, **House of Dracula** employs a novel use of blood transfusion as a means to ward off vampirism and makes more substantial use of Carradine, who would go on to play Dracula in three subsequent features outside the studio system.

Though he stayed on at Universal for several years, including multiple pairings with Boris Karloff, Lugosi attempted to steer clear of typecasting and refused to reprise his Dracula role, albeit still accepting parts as Frankenstein's monster and Ygor among others. He would subsequently don his cape again for a very thinly disguised attempt to cash in on his Dracula fame with **The Return of the Vampire** (1943) for rival studio Columbia, after which he returned to Universal to portray the genuine Dracula for the second and final time in one of the most beloved films of the monster cycle, **Abbott and Costello Meet Frankenstein** (1948).

Though indisputably a comedy (and a very funny one), the film also functions as a superior monster film and provides Dracula with a particularly spectacular demise at the hands of Lon Chaney Jr.'s Lawrence Talbot in his Wolf Man mode.

After this last hurrah, the character of Dracula would lay dormant for a decade outside of the Stoker-inspired Turkish production **Drakula İstanbul'da** (1953). Attempts were made to bring back the Dracula formula with John Gilling's British sci-fi comedy **Mother Riley Meets the Vampire** (1952), which featured Lugosi in a role that proves to have no vampirism involved at all, and the worthwhile suburban-set **The Return of Dracula** (1958), geared for the American drive-in crowd. Dracula would make a roaring comeback and prove more popular than ever that same year when the legendary Hammer Film Productions mounted its own version of **Dracula** (1958) with Peter Cushing as Van Helsing and a ferocious, fang-baring Christopher Lee, a team already proven by director Terence Fisher with the earlier **The Curse of Frankenstein** (1957). Various combinations of Cushing and Lee would appear in numerous Hammer Dracula sequels over the following fifteen years, with the later entries only finding appreciation more recently. Lee's growing, vocal dissatisfaction with the role (particularly his decreasing amount of physical activity and dialogue) didn't prevent him from revisiting his vampire persona outside of Hammer with appearances including the French comedy **Dracula and Son** (1976), a wild ship-bound cameo in the all-star satire, **The Magic Christian** (1969), and a much-touted return to the original novel with Jess Franco's **Count Dracula** (1970).

above: Christopher Lee in **The Magic Christian** (1969).
opposite top right: Arthur Lucan and Bela Lugosi in
Mother Riley Meets the Vampire (1952).

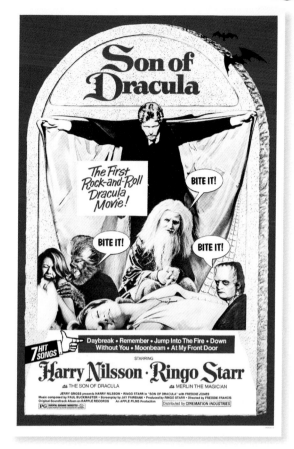

The success of Hammer's vampire rallies wasn't lost on American filmmakers, who quickly rushed to fill drive-ins with Drac-themed offerings of their own. Perhaps the strangest of these was one of the first, **Curse of the Undead** (1959), a quickie from Universal that became the first bona fide vampire western. Best known for the pulpy **Shack Out on 101** (1955), writer-director Edward Dein cooked up this script with his wife and frequent collaborator, Mildred, initially as a lampoon of two genres at once. The result is not only serious but also a fascinating exploration of vampire lore outside of the usual Stoker arena, with a clever gunslinging showdown far removed from the usual heart-staking solutions of the era.

With the rise of made-for-television films taking hold in the 1970s, the door was opened for new interpretations of the Stoker novel, with writer Richard Matheson offering an ambitious version,

Dracula (1973), starring Jack Palance and directed by Dan Curtis. Palance's Dracula follows suit by incorporating that old Universal horror chestnut, the undead monster infatuated with the reincarnation of a lost love, first used prominently in Karl Freund's **The Mummy** (1932) with Boris Karloff. That narrative device has since become a mainstay of vampire cinema, including another lovelorn take soon after in **Son of Dracula** (1974), the first vampire rock musical and the final release from Apple Films, a brief offshoot of The Beatles' profitable corporation derived from Apple Records. Cast as the sympathetic titular vampire is singer-songwriter Harry Nilsson, who longs to fall in love and walk in the sun, with Beatles drummer Ringo Starr appearing as his advisor, Merlin the Magician (!) Nilsson's earlier album, the controversial *Son of Schmilsson,* had already adopted a vampire theme with its cover photo (shot at George Harrison's house), and the singer had an ongoing friendship with the Beatles outside of Starr including notoriously rowdy activities with John Lennon in Alice Cooper's aptly named drinking club, The Hollywood Vampires.

above: Jack Palance in **Dracula** (1973).
opposite lower left: John Carradine in **House of Dracula** (1945).

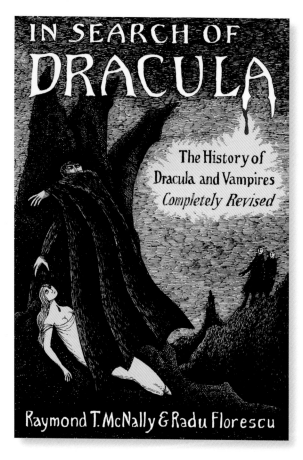

III: VLAD TIDINGS

The Jack Palance adaptation capped off what had been a year-long ascendance of vampire fascination in popular culture, ranging from the introduction of the beloved Count von Count of TV's **Sesame Street** on November 13, 1972, to the publication of the surprise bestselling book *In Search of Dracula: A True History of Dracula and Vampire Legends* by Raymond T. McNally and Radu Florescu. Despite a questionable thesis, the book (which was released to coincide with the 75th anniversary of Stoker's novel) has cast a long, powerful shadow over subsequent Dracula-related adaptations with its proposal of a connection between Stoker's character and ruthless 15th-century Romanian ruler Vlad Tepes, more infamously known as Vlad the Impaler, or Vlad III Dracula. Though existing documentation confirms little more than the appropriation of the Dracula name and the Romanian setting by Stoker, the

Vlad-vampire connection was firmly cemented in the public consciousness as part of a growing worldwide fascination with the paranormal throughout the decade that also extended to ESP, UFOs, Bigfoot, and hauntings. The book was swiftly adapted into a documentary, **In Search of Dracula** (1975), complete with solemnly intonated narration from Christopher Lee about the Carpathian Mountains' most famous literary progeny scattered among a potpourri of film clips and travelogue footage.

Vlad mania became familiar to monster kids of the 1970s and early '80s, with Forrest J. Ackerman's *Famous Monsters of Filmland* and its sister Warren Publishing magazines hawking "Genuine Soil from Dracula's Castle" pendants for several years beginning in 1979. In fact, 1979 is arguably the apex for international vampire cinema, at least in terms of quantity and box office prominence, with offerings including John Badham's **Dracula** from Universal, Werner Herzog's **Nosferatu the Vampyre**, the overachieving disco-laced comedy **Love at**

First Bite, the underachieving disco sex comedy Nocturna, the made-for-TV chiller Vampire, from none other than Mary Tyler Moore's MTM Productions, and a tangentially connected vampire bat yarn in the American Southwest, Nightwing. West Germany even chimed in that year with an amusingly ridiculous disco comedy option of its own, Dracula Blows His Cool, originally entitled Graf Dracula in Oberbayern. Thanks to Italian financial subsidies, they even brought in spaghetti western veteran Gianni Garko to slip on a cape and fangs to terrorize an intrusive gaggle of scantily clad models and photographers in his castle. Incredibly, first-time director Carl Schenkel (credited here as "Carlo Ombra") would later go mainstream with fare like the Denzel Washington vehicle The Mighty Quinn (1989). Aiming to balance out the escalating association in the public consciousness between Vlad Tepes and Dracula, Romania chimed in with its own 1979 feature, Doru Nastase's historical epic Vlad Tepes, which received only minimal international play. It's hardly coincidental that this decadent, delicious wallowing in cinematic vampirism coincided with the last full-throttle year of New Hollywood directorial excess and omnipresent disco, all of which would diminish significantly in 1980.

The fusion of Vlad the Impaler and Dracula has been reaffirmed over the years numerous times, most famously in Francis Ford Coppola's flamboyant Bram Stoker's Dracula (1992), which not only adds a prologue explicitly denoting the Count as Vlad himself but also grafting on the reincarnated love

aspect of the Dan Curtis film for good measure. The success of Coppola's film ensured an ongoing wave of subsequent variations on the Romanian leader (with wildly varying degrees of bloodsucking) including the German documentary Dracula: The True Story (1997), Dark Prince: The True Story of Dracula (2000), Vlad (2003), Dracula the Impaler (2013), Dracula Untold (2014), the Turkish production Deliler (2018), and Vlad's Legacy (2018).

Blurring the bloody line further between fiction and historical fact are the many reports of those claiming to be real-life vampires, mainly as a sexual blood-drinking fetish in certain circles, and the crimes of serial killers that echo vampiric activity. One of the most notorious of these was Fritz Haarmann, who preyed on at least two dozen young men and underage boys in Germany from 1918 to 1924. A former military officer and police informant despite his extensive criminal record, he earned his nickname (along with others such as the Butcher of Hanover) due to his repeated biting and tearing into his victims' throats. A partial inspiration for Fritz Lang's M (1931), he would most directly inspire Ulli Lommel's harrowing Tenderness of the Wolves

opposite top right: Vlad the Impaler woodcut by Ambrosius Huber (1499).
opposite bottom: Count von Count (Sesame Street).

(1973), the most explicit depiction of his crimes to date, despite subsequent attempts like **Der Totmacher** (1995). Four years after Haarmann's execution, Germany experienced another blood-drinking string of murders at the hands of Peter Kürten, the so-called Vampire of Düsseldorf, whose homicidal activities may have begun at the age of nine and continued through adulthood with numerous murders and sexual assaults including repeated attempts at blood consumption. His story would go on to inspire the haunting multinational true crime thriller **The Vampire of Düsseldorf** (1965), with Robert Hossein directing and even starring as Kürten. The story was later fictionalized as the three-character 1991 play *Normal: The Düsseldorf Ripper* by Anthony Neilson, which in turn was filmed as a Czech production, Julius Sevčík's **Angels Gone** (2009).

Of course, the most famous real-life murderer associated with vampirism existed much earlier: Elizabeth Báthory, the Hungarian noblewoman reputed to have imprisoned numerous young women and bathed in their blood to maintain her youthful appearance, with claims that Elizabeth and her cohorts were responsible for the deaths of hundreds of victims. The veracity of these claims has been seriously called into question, though

she was indisputably arrested and sentenced to be imprisoned within her castle, where she remained until her death in 1614; in any case, her story is a vivid springboard for horror ideas and has gone on to inspire numerous films like **The Legend of Blood Castle** (1973). This Spanish-Italian depiction of the Hungarian countess (played by Lucia Bosé, a onetime Miss Italy and mother of pop star Miguel Bosé) depicts her habit of standing nude in a bath, her appearance being rejuvenated as she is splashed by the blood of her victims. Numerous different edits of this film exist, with varying degrees of female nudity, including clothed and unclothed takes of multiple scenes. In addition to the original Spanish title of **Ceremonia sangrienta**, it has also circulated as **The Female Butcher** and simply **Blood Castle**. Later the same year, audiences saw a far more impressionistic depiction of the countess' antics as embodied by Paloma Picasso in one segment of Walerian Borowczyk's scandalous anthology, **Immoral Tales**, and the Báthory story has since been revisited again with actresses like Anna Friel in **Bathory: Countess of Blood** (2008) and Julie Delpy in **The Countess** (2009).

Other notable films depicting serial killers have delved into the forensic aspects of how a real 'vampire' might behave, including the grim Swiss

top right: **Bathory: Countess of Blood** (2008).

film **Mosquito der Schänder** (1977) by Marijan Vajda, also shown in English as **Bloodlust**. A mute accountant played by Werner Pochath harbors a sanguinary fetish that drives him to consume blood from fresh corpses with a sharp glass straw, including one sequence so queasy it hampered the film's international distribution in some territories. However, the most famous film in this vein is easily George A. Romero's **Martin** (1977), with a possibly delusional young man using razor blades to bleed his victims while operating under the belief that he is actually a vampire afflicted with an ancient family curse.

IV. THE VAMPIRE RENAISSANCE

Along with Vlad Tepes mania, vampirism experienced another seismic shift in the 1970s with the proliferation of blockbuster horror novels that increasingly populated both hardback shelves and paperback racks across the globe. The publication of first-time novelist Anne Rice's *Interview with the Vampire* in 1976 introduced readers to a new kind of tragic undead who form a makeshift family over the decades in New Orleans, including the tortured Louis, the charismatic Lestat, and eternally childlike Claudia. The book's success spawned a cycle of sequels collectively known as *The Vampire Chronicles*, comprised of thirteen additional canon novels and a variety of ties to other Rice works. After numerous aborted attempts, the first novel was filmed by Neil Jordan in 1994 and spawned a less noteworthy sequel, **Queen of the Damned** (2002). The series' strong LGBT overtones would also cement the connection in vampire lore for subsequent generations with other writers including Poppy Z. Brite and Whitley Streiber. Preceding Rice's novel by one year was Stephen King's second

novel, *'Salem's Lot*, which took the opposite approach by painting its vampires as a soulless pestilence. Followed by a short story sequel, two miniseries adaptations, and a quirky movie sequel, King's novel remains something of an outlier among the more common modern treatment of vampires as monsters with a melancholy romantic streak. That aspect was presented most successfully by Stephenie Meyer's *Twilight* books for young adults and the many works of Mississippi-born Charlaine Harris, who kicked off the *Southern Vampire Mysteries* series in 2001 with *Dead Until Dark* and followed it with 13 official novels as well as several short stories and offshoots. The classical treatment of vampirism has also remained a strong factor in horror literature, including Kim Newman's *Anno Dracula* series begun in 1992, which also incorporates numerous Stoker characters and offshoots along with Jack the Ripper lore; other series by J.R. Ward, Sherrilyn Kenyon, Christopher Moore, Mary Jane Davidson, and Jeaniene Frost, among many others, have offered their own takes on the modern day vampire concept as well as novel spins on hunters, extermination, and blood subsistence.

Though the vampire mythos may have originated in its Western form in Continental Europe, the tide moved slowly bringing it to the screen in the majority of countries. A hotbed of cinematic horror in the 20th century, Italy dove in with the most gusto after a false start with its first significant genre film of the sound era, **I vampiri** (1957). Begun by Riccardo Freda and finished by Mario Bava, the low-budget production isn't a vampire film per se, but derives its title from the Parisian blood-draining murders that allow a scientist to rejuvenate an aging aristocratic noblewoman. The Italian flirtation with vampirism became more overt with Bava's first proper directorial credit, the censor-baiting **Black Sunday** (1960), originally released in Italy

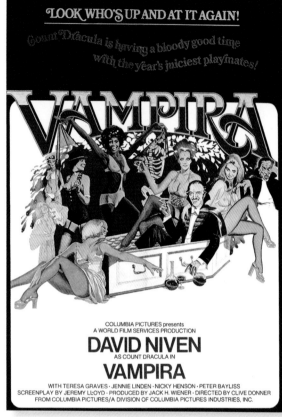

as **La maschera del demonio** before it underwent several title changes. Barbara Steele stars in dual roles as the wicked Princess Asa, who is executed for witchcraft then later resurrected by blood dripping on her tomb, and her descendant, the innocent Katia. Ostensibly derived from Nikolai Gogol's 1835 supernatural novella, *Viy*, Bava's film takes little from its source apart from the presence of a malefic sorceress revived from the dead; instead he delivers a succession of striking Gothic images including the famous slow-motion carriage arrival and explicit violence (for the time) including Asa's punishment via a spiked mask driven into her face. The opening narration explicitly identifies vampires as a factor in the story, though the execution blurs that definition beyond recognition by positing its villains as a mixture of witches, vampires, and zombies. Gogol's story would be filmed far more faithfully as **Viy** (1967) by Konstantin Ershov and Georgiy Kropachyov with delightfully inventive special effects by Aleksandr Ptushko, though the vampire connection is tenuous here as well, with the monsters embodying the Slavic association between *upyr* and occultism without any blood consumption involved. The Gogol story would be revisited again several times, most notably as Lamberto Bava's snowbound 1990 remake (also released as **La maschera del demonio** but circulated internationally as **Demons 5: The Devil's Veil**), a loose Korean interpretation called **Evil Spirit** (2008), the effects-crammed Russian production **Forbidden Kingdom** (2014), and the centerpiece of the three-part **Gogol** Russian series shown in theaters and on television between 2017 and 2018. As for Mario Bava, he would return to vampirism

in a more traditional sense on two occasions; both are covered in more detail later in this book, but the most notable is a segment of his phantasmagorical 1963 horror anthology, **Black Sabbath**, also inspired by Russian supernatural literature. Contrary to its title, Bava's influential science fiction-horror hybrid **Planet of the Vampires** (1965) is about alien possession and has nothing to do with vampirism except in the broadest sense of absorbing the life essence and identity of another.

top left: **Viy** (1967).
lower right: **Uncle Was a Vampire** (1959).

CRISTOPHER LEE IN

LA CRIPTA E L'INCUBO

AUDRY AMBER URSULA DAVIS JOSE' CAMPOS VERA VALMONT NELA CONJU'
JOSE' VILLASANTE - ANGEL MIDLIN
BILL CURTIS   JAMES BRIGHTMAN   CICELY CLAYTON
REGIA DI THOMAS MILLER   PRODUZIONE WILLIAM MULLIGAN
MUSICHE DI CARLO SAVINA - EDIZIONI MUSICALI BIXIC   DISTRIBUZIONE: M E C CINEMATOGRAFICA

In between the country's first two trailblazing horror films, Italy took time out to gently poke fun at cinematic vampirism by importing Christopher Lee to star in the broad comedy **Tempi duri per i vampiri** (1959), shown internationally as **Uncle Was a Vampire**. The film features Lee as the colorfully named Baron Roderico da Frankurten, who converts his nephew into a temporary creature of the night and unleashes pandemonium on their recently sold ancestral hotel. Amusing enough on its own terms, this is essentially the first modern vampire-centric comedy, paving the way for such later spoofs as **Dracula and Son** (1976), **Love at First Bite** (1979), and **Transylvania Twist** (1989). Of its progeny, the strangest must certainly be the British offering **Vampira** (1974) by Clive Donner, released abroad as **Old Dracula**. The idea of casting David Niven as Dracula proves to be the most conventional aspect of a tale that introduces an askew blaxploitation spin by

casting black genre staple Teresa Graves as his wife. Incredibly, the slapstick enterprise climaxes with our protagonist donning blackface in what amounts to a vampire movie first (and, mercifully, last).

Lee also had a more traditional Italian vampire role in **Terror in the Crypt** (1964), which was co-produced with Spain and used *Carmilla* as a springboard for the story of Count Ludwig Karnstein trying to stave off a family curse with the arrival of the mysterious Ljuba (Ursula Davis) at his castle. Famously rushed into production with a script written in as little as 24 hours (depending on reports) by genre heavyweights Ernesto Gastaldi and Tonini Valerii, it was released in Italy as **La cripta e l'incubo** and hints at the lesbian undertones in the story that would soon become box office gold. Italy and Spain also joined forces for **Malenka** (1969), the first horror film by Spanish fear maestro Amando de Ossorio of **Tombs of the Blind Dead** (1972) fame. Swedish leading lady Anita Ekberg, then a major international draw after a star-making turn in Federico Fellini's **La Dolce Vita** (1960), plays fashion-conscious socialite Sylvia, whose inherited countess title comes with a cursed German castle and a family history involving an executed sorceress. Famously edited down and retitled **Fangs of the Living Dead** as part of a much-ballyhooed "Orgy of the Living Dead" triple feature, the film was originally intended to rationalize away the vampire angle during the climax but was shot with two different endings that keep the film within the realm of the supernatural, more or less. Spain would continue to remain in the vampire game throughout the '70s with several titles covered elsewhere here, as well as the odd Spanish-U.S. co-production **Young Hannah, Queen of the Vampires** (1973), a.k.a. **Crypt of the Living Dead**, with Andrew Prine as an archeologist following the footsteps of his missing

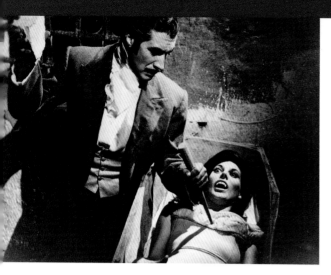

father on a remote island housing the tomb of Hannah (Teresa Gimpera), a centuries-old malefic blood feeder who was meant to be imprisoned until the next coming of Christ. Also among the cast are Mark Damon and Spanish horror regular Patty Shepard, both of whom had prior vampire experience elsewhere thanks to **Black Sabbath** and **The Werewolf vs. the Vampire Woman** (1971) respectively.

Widely exported fusions of fangs and pin-up style ogling were also profitable for Italy, starting with **The Vampire and the Ballerina** (1960) and **The Playgirls and the Vampire** (1960). The latter, directed by Piero Ragnoli under the title **L'ultima preda del vampire**, wrings pulpy thrills out of the premise of vampire Count Gabor Kernassy (Walter Brandi) obsessing over a burlesque dancer who bears a resemblance to his love two centuries earlier. That premise would be recycled in various forms in other related films (not to mention many other vampire films in general), but the high titillation factor made this an obvious draw for foreign export, with British distributor Richard Gordon making it a reliable programmer in dubbed form with various edits offered containing different amounts of striptease footage. **Slaughter of the Vampires** (1962) switches Brandi to a good guy role for his last starring appearance in the series as the target of vampires that have taken over a seemingly neglected castle, featuring German krimi stalwart Dieter Eppler cutting a memorable figure with a mean set of fangs. Extra points for having a Van Helsing-style vampire hunter named Dr. Nietzsche, played by none other than **The Beast in Heat** (1977) director Luigi Batzella under one of his many pseudonyms (in this case, 'Paolo Solvay').

Though its overall horror output has been smaller by comparison, France entered the vampire fray with Roger Vadim's **Blood and Roses** (1960, another variation on Carmilla), but largely stayed out of the game apart from the low-budget films of Jean Rollin (whose work was largely denigrated in his home country). France was a partner in several vampire films, most notably the Belgian-French-West German classic **Daughters of Darkness** (1971), but in general its impact has been far more limited. Odd Euro co-productions would pop up as well, like **Cave of the Living Dead** (1964), a product of West Germany and Yugoslavia originally released as **Der Fluch der grünen Augen** (or 'The Curse of the Green Eyes'). Despite its most famous English-language title, bestowed by producer Richard Gordon, the film has nothing to do with zombies and everything to do with vampires, as future **Mark of the Devil** (1970) writer-producer and Fassbinder regular Adrian Hoven is called in and finds suspicious activity revolving around a forbidding castle that serves as the headquarters of a sinister professor and a cave full of supernatural secrets. The film marked the one true foray into horror for Budapest-born director Ákos Ráthonyi, who had recently directed the krimi **The Devil's Daffodil** (1961) during the twilight of his career and would pass away at the age of 60 before the decade was out. Other nations like Turkey, Poland, Sweden, Czechoslovakia, Serbia, Japan, the Philippines, and South Korea have made significant contributions to the vampire on screen with some significant one-off titles, all covered in detail elsewhere in this book.

One country whose importance in vampire history came late in the game but, over time, has earned a strong international fan following

top left: **Slaughter of the Vampires** (1962).
top right: **Blood and Roses** (1960).

is Hong Kong, whose genre films drew upon the centuries-old Chinese legend of the *jiangshi* for inspiration. Containing zombie elements as well, these reanimated corpses often operate at the bidding of a sorcerer and differ from the Western vampire in many respects, despite the frequent presence of fangs. For example, items of wood or inscribed prayers can be used as repellents, and their distinctive hopping and lack of overt blood consumption have led to debates over whether they can even be considered vampiric at all. In local culture they first became familiarized through Pu Songling's mammoth 18th-century horror anthology, *Strange Stories from a Chinese Studio*, which also served as the basis for **A Chinese Ghost Story** (1987). Vampires turned up in minor capacities in Hong Kong films like **Encounters of the Spooky Kind** (1980) and even the much earlier **Midnight Vampire** (1936).

The *jiangshi* became cinematic superstars with **Mr. Vampire** (1985) and its numerous sequels and imitations over the years, introducing a genre-twisting sensibility that proved popular overseas as well. A comic by-product of the Hong Kong genre explosion inaugurated by the likes of **Zu: Warriors from the Magic Mountain** (1983), the series sparked a flood of vampire films frequently blended with a mixture of comedy and action for maximum popular appeal. These cinematic hybrids could be truly bizarre at times, like Chao Chung-Hsing's very silly instant cash-in **Hello Dracula** (1983) and its three sequels, the cheerful and bloody **The Vampire Who Admires Me** (2008), the knockabout action comedy **Taoism Drunkard** (1984), and the more traditional Westernized abstinent, cloaked vampire in Stephen Shin's **A Bite of Love** (1990).

V. GREY AREAS

The proliferation of vampire films over the past half century-plus has resulted in numerous borderline cases that incorporate elements of the lore, or bloodsucking behavior, without being strictly defined as part of the subgenre. For example, the Japanese chiller **Goke, Body Snatcher from Hell** (1968) is one of the most shocking titles from the venerable studio Shochiku, as it depicts a crashed planeload of survivors encountering an alien menace when their hijacker is invaded by a gelatinous monstrosity that infests through human foreheads. Both a stylish fever dream and a scathing depiction of human pettiness and selfishness, the film features much discussion of vampirism as a possible cause for their predicament and builds to one of the decade's grimmest climaxes.

In a similar vein, Canadian David Cronenberg has flirted with vampirism in his early films thanks to his obsessive theme of horror coming from biological transmissions or physiological transformations. The most relevant entry is his second film, **Rabid** (1977), which originated under the title *Mosquito* and casts legendary adult film star Marilyn Chambers as a hapless woman who undergoes an experimental scientific procedure following a motorcycle accident. Now imbued with a sharp, fang-like stinger in her armpit, she sets off a plague through Montreal that mixes elements of vampire and zombie horror while foreshadowing the popular contagion horrors in the wake of **28 Days Later** (2002). Equally difficult to pin down is one of the maddest vampire-associated films ever made, **Lifeforce** (1985), director Tobe Hooper's belated follow-up to his controversial

top left: **The Vampire Who Admires Me** (2008).
top right: Marilyn Chambers in David Cronenberg's **Rabid** (1977).

hit **Poltergeist** (1982). Essentially handed carte blanche by Cannon Films after first choice Michael Winner bowed out, the film was shot under the original title of its 1976 source novel, Colin Wilson's *The Space Vampires*, about energy-feeding alien beings that can transform into bats, and proceed to wreak havoc across London. Though financially unsuccessful at the time and heavily altered for its U.S. release (the original longer cut has since become standard), Hooper's lunatic spectacle has gone on to earn major cult status for its extravagant blend of science fiction and horror as well as its indelible lead 'vampire' played by a clothing-averse Mathilda May.

A more extreme transformation awaited another literary property with the release of Michael Mann's **The Keep** (1983), a famously turbulent but visually fascinating production whose compromises led it far astray from F. Paul Wilson's 1981 novel about Nazis infiltrating a castle only to unlock an ancient vampiric presence inside. The film instead presents a monster closer to the Golem in appearance, though its consumption of human energy and bestowing of youth upon an elderly Jewish professor still betray traces of the vampire elements in the original story.

Also drawing on the idea of energy consumption as a form of vampirism is **Doctor Sleep** (2019), Mike Flanagan's adaptation of the 2013 Stephen King novel depicting the adult life of his psychic child character Danny Torrance from *The Shining*. Here Danny (now Dan) crosses paths with The True Knot, a centuries-old band of roving psychic gypsies who fatally prey upon children with paranormal powers. The film makes the vampire parallels visually explicit with the members of the Knot displaying glowing eyes and hissing monstrously as they consume the "steam" of their victims, with Dan (played in the film by Ewan McGregor) and the young Abra Stone (Kyliegh Curran) recalling the intrepid generation-crossing vampire hunters of King's *'Salem's Lot*. In this case they face off against a female adversary, the ruthless Rose the Hat (Rebecca Ferguson), whose disciples are responsible for ensuring they have access to the nourishment they need to survive. Another King concoction with a dash of vampire flavour is an original screenplay he wrote with no prior literary basis, **Sleepwalkers** (1992), about a fading race of incestuous human-cat hybrids who move from town to town in search of virgin blood. Able to morph in and out of their fanged cat-faced guises, the sleepwalkers may not be King's most frightening creatures but they certainly rank among his oddest.

The definition of what constitutes a vampire film can get especially tricky when it comes to art house cinema, where elusive narratives and slippery genre classifications are more readily embraced by audiences. The all-time champion of this approach may be **La belle captive** (1983), the closest thing to a horror film in the cinematic output of avant-garde practitioner and kink pioneer Alain Robbe-Grillet.

top: **Lifeforce** (1985).
above left: **Sleepwalkers** (1992).

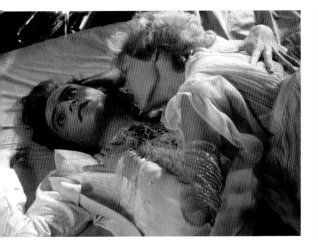

Drawing both its title and most prominent recurring visual motif from a 1931 painting of the same name by René Magritte, the film begins in fairly traditional territory as a government employee named Walter Raim (Daniel Mesguich) finds an evening assignment interrupted when a fetching mystery woman ushers him to a nocturnal party attended by blood-drinking revelers. After the night concludes with a bite on the neck, his entire sense of reality unravels as he attempts to parse out the nightmare encounter that has changed his life. Beautifully filmed, playful, and chilling, it's one of the best introductions to Robbe-Grillet's style, with more questions opened than answered by its elliptical, violent ending.

Also hailing from France is **Spermula** (1976), whose eyebrow-raising title conceals an arty fever dream from noted artist-turned-director Charles Matton, who continued to refer to it under his preferred original title, **L'amour est un fleuve en Russie**. "Certaines femmes vampires ne se nourissent pas de sang" ("Certain female vampires don't drink blood") promised the provocative French poster for this psychedelic reverie about a band of eternally young, iconoclastic artists and free thinkers who vanish from public life in the 1930s, relocating to South America where they concoct a radical plan to cure world aggression by draining so much male fluid at their castle headquarters that they can bring about a new age of world peace. Model Dayle Haddon cuts an imposing figure as the leader of the supernatural sect, whose nature is vague in the original French version, but who are transformed into aliens in the absurd, shortened English-dubbed version.

Published in 1911, Bram Stoker's final novel was a peculiar, obscure footnote in his career until it was very loosely adapted by Ken Russell as **The Lair of the White Worm** (1988), part of his gleeful four-film free-for-all at Vestron Pictures. Though this film is studded with familiar faces like Hugh Grant, Catherine Oxenberg, and a pre-*Doctor Who* Peter Capaldi, it's Amanda Donohoe who steals the show as Lady Sylvia Marsh, a pagan, pansexual priestess who sprouts enormous snake-like fangs and serves an enormous reptilian god lurking beneath the countryside. Packed with ripe, quotable dialogue ("You *have* been a good girl") and delicious visual flourishes, it's a vampire-flavored film for art deco lovers with Hammer influences at the forefront, too, including nods to **The Reptile** (1966) and the sexually charged Karnstein cycle.

The vampire gets name checked repeatedly in Philip Ridley's striking debut feature, **The Reflecting Skin** (1990), about Seth Dove (Jeremy Cooper), a young boy in 1950s Midwestern America who believes his neighbor, the improbably named Dolphin Blue (Lindsay Duncan), is a vampire intent on feeding off of Seth's recently returned soldier brother, Cameron (Viggo Mortensen). Though deeply sinister and studded with grotesque imagery, the film only skirts on the edges of the horror genre and uses Seth's (possibly misguided) belief in vampirism as a gateway to his own loss of innocence.

Falling more cleanly within the horror genre is **The Neon Demon** (2016), Nicolas Winding Refn's shimmering collage of transgressive imagery constructed around a Faustian pact made by the young Jesse (Elle Fanning) to rise in the modeling business, only to find its cutthroat nature more literally bloodthirsty than she imagined. The much-debated final act is a radical subversion of viewer expectations as it swirls vampirism, witchcraft, and cannibalism into a surrealistic stew that's difficult to forget. In particular, Refn lingers on the image of two nude models washing off the scarlet remnants from their previous evening's bloody bacchanal, a grisly and affectionate ode to the lesbian vampire classics of the 1970s. An earlier association between vampirism and modeling can be found in Fritz Leiber's enigmatic short story, *The Girl with the Hungry Eyes*, about a photographer whose two sessions with a beautiful but unsettling new model reveal that she has a dangerous appetite for human creative impulses and dreams. The story was later adapted as an episode of the TV series **Night Gallery** (with Joanna Pettet as the psychic predator) and again in much looser fashion as a feature film in 1995, with a more overt portrayal of a decades-old, resurrected vampire model.

Lingering between the art house and drive-in is the slippery **Let's Scare Jessica to Death** (1971), a masterful study in unease and madness about an ageless young woman and the supernatural contagion she spreads around the countryside via bloody gashes in the townspeople's necks. How much of it is real or imagined remains up in the air despite the misleading gaslight-implying title, with Zohra Lampert embodying the fragile Jessica, whose relocation to a farmhouse with friends turns into a nightmare thanks to a mystery girl who may have drowned nearby years before. Mixing vampire and ghost tropes, the film was intended to be a far more comical look at counterculture types playing house in the woods and fighting monsters but became one of the most haunting American films of the '70s under director John D. Hancock.

In some cases vampire elements can even be used for inanimate objects, such as the blood-guzzling auto in **Ferat Vampire** (1982) or the amusing British cult comedy **I Bought a Vampire Motorcycle** (1990), with the titular Norton Commando housing the spirit of a sorcerer bent on revenge against the gang responsible for his death. Even animals can get in on the bloodsucking action from time to time, with canines getting multiple options thanks to **Zoltan, Hound of Dracula** (1977) and the more family friendly Canadian curio, **Vampire Dog** (2012). There's even a leporine option with the children's book *Bunnicula* and its sequels, with the veggie-sucking title character adapted for the stage and a well-remembered animated TV version, 'Bunnicula, the Vampire Rabbit,' aired in 1982 as the part of the **ABC Weekend Specials** series.

top right: **Dr. Terror's House of Horrors** (1965).

VI. DRACULA'S GUEST STARS

Despite its long established cinematic pedigree, the vampire doesn't always take the spotlight in every film. The horror anthology in particular is conducive to weaving these fiends into broader narratives allowing for a variety of monsters, though the vampire often winds up stealing the show anyway. The beloved British studio Amicus, the closest thing to a rival for Hammer Films, proved to be vampire friendly right from its first successful omnibus feature, **Dr. Terror's House of Horrors** (1965), with the fifth and final of its stories, 'Vampire,' featuring a young Donald Sutherland as a physician who turns to a colleague when he suspects his new wife is a creature of the night. The most comical variation arrived in **The House That Dripped Blood** (1971), a literally bloodless but highly engaging and consistent anthology revolving around a cursed piece of property plagued by deadly misadventures. The last of the four tales, 'The Cloak,' is a comical offering with John Pertwee, TV's current Doctor Who at the time, as a spoiled thespian whose role in a vampire film takes a turn for the macabre when he acquires a very special costume accessory. The fanged capper with Ingrid Pitt, herself a vampire icon thanks to her roles in Hammer's **The Vampire Lovers** (1970) and **Countess Dracula** (1971), is a particular delight for horror fans despite being spoiled egregiously on the poster art.

In **The Vault of Horror** (1973), Amicus's grisly follow-up to its hit E.C. Comics compendium **Tales from the Crypt** (1972), the first story charts the horrific fate of murderous Daniel Massey, who dispatches his sibling (played by his real-life sister, Anna Massey) for financial gain, only to wander for a bite afterwards and discover

that her neighborhood isn't quite as genteel as it appears. This entry proved to be too gruesome for many censors and ended up having its ghoulish punchline blunted in most circulating prints with a strung-up, twitching Massey turned into a human blood tap. The demise of Amicus wasn't quite the end of the road though as one of its co-founders, Milton Subotsky, had one unofficial horror anthology left up his sleeve with **The Monster Club** (1981). Barely given a theatrical release and derided at the time for its parade of unconvincing dime-store creature masks in the title establishment, this music-packed, three-story collection adapted from the work of R. Chetwynd-Hayes has since been reevaluated and features an energetic turn by Vincent Price as the vampire Erasmus. In a meta turn, he puts the bite on none other than Chetwynd-Hayes himself (played by John Carradine) and welcomes him to the underground Monster Club for stories of beastly mayhem. This would mark Price's only big-screen turn as a vampire, though he would have a ball as the cape-wearing Count Sforza in the 1967 'V Is for Vampire' episode of TV's **F Troop**, and briefly

joined Kermit the Frog to slip on a pair of fangs on **The Muppet Show**. More recently, the horror anthology has kept the vampire alive and well (so to speak) with the likes of **Tales from the Hood 2** (2018), which depicts the ultimate Tinder date gone wrong in a bit of early #metoo retribution from beyond the grave.

Despite the abundance of slasher movies that ruled the horror box office in the 1980s, the decade proved receptive to vampires as well, with ensemble pieces in particular offering a showcase for the traditional bloodsucker. Lifting its jokey title from a 1963 vampire-centric Bugs Bunny cartoon short, **Transylvania 6-5000** (1985) is essentially an update on the 1940s formula of two reporters – in this case, Jeff Goldblum and Ed Begley Jr. – stumbling upon supernatural shenanigans in modern-day Transylvania (though shot in Yugoslavia). The vampire element here is provided by a fanged, scene-stealing Geena Davis (Goldblum's future wife for four years) as Odette, whose eye-catching, low-cut outfit is a randy throwback to the then-recent age of disco vampires. The most beloved ensemble title of the period has to be **The Monster Squad** (1987), Fred Dekker's affectionate love letter to Universal monster movies set within the world of an '80s kids' adventure. The springboard for the entire story is the ongoing feud between Van Helsing and Count Dracula, with a crucial amulet recovered in the modern day instigating a battle against a menagerie of monsters. Despite its title, Alan Clarke's **Billy the Kid and the Green Baize Vampire** (1987) isn't a horror movie at all but rather a (literally) dark musical about a snooker feud between the title characters, a cowboy and vampire locked in a tuneful duel of wits. Of course, the chance to see Royal Shakespeare Company fixture Alun Armstrong brandishing a pair of fangs is worth the time investment by itself.

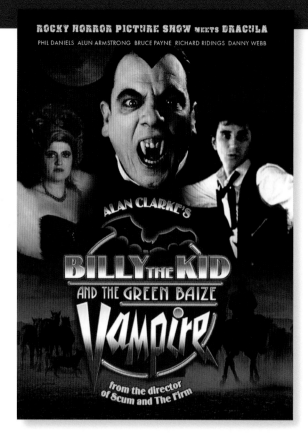

More recently, the vampire became a fixture for young audiences thanks to the animated **Hotel Transylvania** (2012) and its sequels, **Hotel Transylvania 2** (2015) and **Hotel Transylvania 3: Summer Vacation** (2018). Here Dracula (voiced by Adam Sandler) oversees a popular monster resort, tucked away from human eyes, whose business is thrown into disarray when his daughter falls for a human. The subsequent installments introduce an adversarial Van Helsing on a getaway cruise and the hotel's on-and-off policy against humans, which becomes complicated by the arrival of a human-vampire grandchild. Other kid-friendly viewing options include the stop-motion classic **The Nightmare Before Christmas** (1993), which counts a vampire among the monstrous denizens of Halloween Town, and the charming short film **Dear Dracula** (2012), with the world's most famous vampire lured into the limelight by a young boy's fan letter. Of course, the canine crime solver Scooby-Doo has tangled with vampires on multiple occasions as well, including the direct-to-video feature **Scooby-Doo! and the Legend of the Vampire** (2003), and the musical film **Scooby-Doo! Music of the Vampire** (2011).

VII. HORRIBLE SEXY VAMPIRES

At the opposite end of the spectrum, the eroticism inherent in vampire activity has been exploited with great potency in many films with a focus on nocturnal seductions, the consumption of bodily fluids, and the inherent link between sex and death that has fueled narratives since the days of Greek tragedies. After all, Bela Lugosi became an unlikely sex symbol thanks to his hypnotic eyes and elegant appearance, even if he was an intruder who would turn you into a walking corpse. Subsequent Dracula adaptations followed suit, along with female variants including the aforementioned **Blood and Roses**, but the advent of bona fide sexploitation in the early 1960s allowed filmmakers to run rampant with combinations of undressed performers and leering vampires aiming for the neck or a little bit lower. Filmmakers like Jean Rollin and Jess Franco created entire cottage industries out of highly erotic vampire films, particularly in the 1970s, though the extremes varied depending on the country of origin.

Despite the constraints of General Francisco Franco's controversial rule until 1975, Spain produced a number of key horror films with its own variations on classic movie monsters largely spurred by the international success of horror enthusiast Paul Naschy. That included shooting sexy and relatively chaste variants for the international and local markets, which continues to cause some confusion today depending on which version you see. One of the country's most surreal offerings is José Luis Madrid's **El vampire de la autopista** (1971), which was circulated in dubbed form later in the decade as **The Horrible Sexy Vampire**. Here the vampire is Count Oblensky, who preys on any woman who dares to remove her top in front of the camera. He also harbors a very persistent death wish and urges a quick staking from his confused descendant, both played by the indelibly named future Jess Franco player Waldemar Wohlfahrt. Venerable Spanish genre director León Klimovsky churned out several notable monster films, several of which we'll cover later on, but one of his more frequently overlooked curios is **Strange Love of the Vampires** (1975), also known as **Blutsauger, Night of the Walking Dead** (for some reason), and **El extraño amor de los vampiros**. More wistful

and contemplative than usual, the film involves a dying young woman (Emma Cohen) who finds an unusual new sense of motivation when she stumbles upon an entire vampire culture existing right under her nose.

In the United States, the eroticizing of vampire lore could go in outrageously absurd directions, as evidenced by the brain-melting **Dracula (The Dirty Old Man)** (1969), a patchwork wonder unleashed on the skin flick circuit by smut entrepreneur Whit Boyd. A nudie vampire film shot on the outskirts of L.A. with anonymous actors and no live sound, it was turned into a comedy during post-production by having a voice artist loop the whole thing with jokey schtick dialogue in the tradition of Jackie Mason or Henny Youngman. Thus you get Dracula luring a real estate agent named Mike to his cave and turning him into "Irving Jackalman," a snarling, wisecracking lycanthrope who tears off women's clothes. Sporting an early X rating, **Sex and the Single Vampire** (1970) features a pre-hardcore John Holmes as the irritated Count Spatula, whose coffin-dwelling rest is disrupted by the intrusion of a group of swingers eager to screw the night away in a spooky setting. That same period also saw the release of the more genteel **Guess What Happened to Count Dracula?** (1971) with Drac reinventing himself as a hip hotspot owner named Count Adrian who decides to make a new vampire bride out of his prettiest patron. Shot in 1969, the film was reputed to have been prepared in a number of variants by its distributor including the currently available PG-rated cut as well as a gay softcore variant briefly circulated as **Dracula and the Boys** and **Does Dracula Really Suck?**

opposite bottom: **Hotel Transylvania** (2012).
top right:, **Dracula (The Dirty Old Man)** (1969).

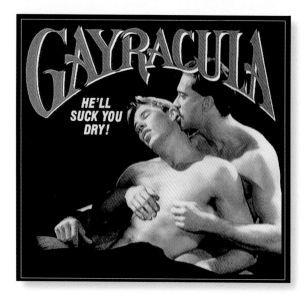

production **Suckula** (1974) pulls a bait and switch by providing a mad scientist Gothic romp with no vampire activity at all (but with graphic sex scenes that are stronger than you'd expect for something shot in Vancouver). Far more widely distributed and still capable of eliciting both confusion and astonishment is **The Bride's Initiation** (1973), with hammy porno actor Marc Brock donning a Dracula cape and nothing else to kidnap and terrorize various captives in his basement at the behest of his witch sidekick. Shot in Miami over the course of what appears to be a couple of afternoons, this was initially circulated as **The Demon's Brew** with ad art cribbed from Pier Paolo Pasolini's **Teorema** (1968) for no discernible reason.

More astoundingly, director Laurence Merrick went on to co-direct the controversial Oscar-nominated documentary **Manson** (1973) and ended up being murdered in 1977 by a prospective acting student who claimed to be under the influence of black magic. A bona fide gay sexploitation vampire film didn't really see notable distribution until much later with the goofy hardcore spoof **Gayracula** (1983), with late adult film actor Tim Kramer getting a rare leading role as Count Gaylord on the prowl in West Hollywood.

The advent of porno chic in the '70s proved to be a natural fit for vampire stories in the straight realm as well with the most famous entry, **Dracula Sucks** (1978), even getting toned down for mainstream theatrical and home video distribution. The earlier **Suckula** (1973) from Anthony Spinelli also featured the Count hunting for blood and other illicit action in L.A. while the identically titled Canadian

The tireless movie factory in the Philippines was a major force in drive-ins during the '70s, and its most indelible contribution to the sexy vampire film was the jaw-dropping **Vampire Hookers** (1978). John Carradine's second vampire film released that year, this harebrained horror comedy from prolific director Cirio H. Santiago splashes the screen with bright colors and stylized lighting to juice up the threadbare story about two American naval officers whose CPO goes missing during a night on the town. The mystery is tied to a series of nocturnal abductions in the area caused by a bevy of fanged seductresses (who don't seem to be involved in any kind of transactions for sex) overseen by the Shakespeare-quoting vampire daddy Richmond Reed (Carradine). Additional comic relief is provided by Filipino movie mascot Vic Diaz in a hammy turn as a flatulent member of the undead, and it all closes, as such a film must, with a catchy, twangy theme song featuring the useful warning, "She'll take you to the graveyard and try to ease your fears, but her friends out in the graveyard have been dead for a hundred years. They're vampire hookers, yeah, they're vampire hookers, and blood is not all they suck."

The home video boom that escalated in the latter half of the 1980s provided new opportunities for erotically-tinged vampire films, riding a wave of erotic thrillers that became a VHS tsunami in the '90s. The most successful of these was easily **Embrace of the Vampire** (1995), a heated supernatural romance starring Alyssa Milano, but it was hardly the first film to exploit that particular marketplace. Shot quickly for Roger Corman's Concorde Pictures, Katt Shea's **Dance of**

lower left: **Vampire Hookers** (1978).

the Damned (1989) is an enjoyable and resonant chamber piece about a suicidal exotic dancer (Jodi Hurtz) chosen by a vampire (Cyril O'Reilly) to share the experiences of being a human before he snacks on her at dawn. In record time, Corman commissioned a remake under the title **To Sleep with a Vampire** (1993) with **Family Ties**' Scott Valentine and brief horror it-girl Charlie Spradling taking on the leading roles for a fairly successful retread. Japanese director Shimako Sato made her debut with the British-Japanese production **Tale of a Vampire** (1992), which started off as an art film project but escalated into a mainstream

feature starring Julian Sands as a romantic but lonely nightwalker who becomes fixated on a young woman who reminds him of his long-lost love. Though falling outside the scope of sexually-themed genre fare, the direct-to-video wave also ushered in other films geared to the same audience, like Richard Elfman's **Modern Vampires** (1998), Jim Wynorski's **Vampirella** (1996), Jim McBride's **Blood Ties** (1991), Peter Flynn's **Project Vampire** (1993), Rick Jacobson's **Night Hunter** (1996), John Russo's **Heartstopper** (1989), J.R. Bookwalter's **Kingdom of the Vampire** (1991), a cheap family-friendly option with **My Grandpa Is a Vampire** (1992), and Gabriel Pelletier's quirky French-Canadian vampire comedy **Karmina** (1996).

VIII. SMALL SCREEN, BIG TEETH

Though our focus here may be on feature films, the history of vampirism on television is impossible to ignore considering how much give and take exists between the two formats over the years. Both **The Munsters** and **The Addams Family** launched in 1964 and couched vampirism within a family sitcom format, completely dodging the bloodletting aspects but bestowing its respective matriarchs, Lily Munster and Morticia Addams, with appearances unmistakably influenced by vampire cinema. **The Munsters** went the extra mile by making Grandpa (Al Lewis) a full-fledged vampire in Dracula mode and its youngest member, Eddie (Butch Patrick), a vampire-werewolf hybrid. Vampire fever didn't really hit TV until the Gothic afternoon soap opera **Dark Shadows**, which began as a straightforward melodrama from creator Dan Curtis but took a dramatic turn in its second season with the introduction of tortured, centuries-old vampire Barnabas Collins in the Spring of 1967. Portrayed by Jonathan Frid, he was first depicted as a violent menace and the true black sheep of the wealthy Collins family in a seaside Maine town; however, his popularity led to a far more complex past and personality involving a vindictive witch and lost love. Still popular and influential, the series sparked a merchandizing bonanza and led to vampire nods on other TV shows of the era. For example, Rod Serling's supernatural anthology **Night Gallery** began dropping vampires into its more comical segments, like 'Miss Lovecraft Sent Me,' 'A Midnight Visit to the Neighborhood Blood

top left: **Tale of a Vampire** (1992).
lower right: Al Lewis as Grandpa in **The Munsters** (TV series).

Bank,' 'The Funeral,' 'Smile, Please,' and 'How to Cure the Common Vampire,' as well as the far more serious 'Death on a Barge.' The short-lived 1977 UK series **Supernatural** featured a particularly chilling vampire story with 'Dorabella,' whose title character is a singer exerting a supernatural influence over a traveling hostel guest. Made-for-TV movies took notice of the vampire's popularity in the wake of Dan Curtis's massively popular **The Night Stalker** (1972), notable productions ranging from **I, Desire** (1982) to the cult monster party **The Midnight Hour** (1985) and on into the following decade with titles like **Blood Ties** (1991) and Stuart Gordon's **Daughter of Darkness** (1990).

Vampire fans were largely left thirsty for entertainment on TV for the bulk of the '90s, apart from occasional blips like the very brief urban vampire policier **Kindred: The Embraced** from 1996 and the enjoyable 1990-1991 Luxembourg-produced syndicated show **Dracula: The Series**, about teenagers trying to fend off the ongoing schemes of a certain famous vampire now known as Alexander Lucard. Running for seven seasons, **Tales from the Crypt** revived the horror anthology in 1989 and featured multiple standout relevant episodes, including 'The Reluctant Vampire' (with Malcolm McDowell as an abstinent blood bank employee), 'Comes the Dawn' (about poachers stalked by Alaskan vampires), and 'The Secret' (about a vampire couple making an unwise child

adoption choice). Less grisly is the 1996 episode 'Vampire Breath' from **Goosebumps**, in which two hockey-crazy kids encounter a vampire with dental issues. More substantial are multiple offerings from the long-running Canadian series **Are You Afraid of the Dark?** which featured bloodsuckers in 1991's 'The Tale of the Midnight Madness' (in which a screening of the original **Nosferatu** unleashes the title character into a movie house), 1996's 'The Tale of the Night Shift' (with hospital patients turning into late night snacks), and 1999's 'The Tale of Vampire Town' (about an adolescent Van Helsing in training who gets in way over his head).

The vampire, on both the big and small screens, changed forever in 1997 with the arrival of **Buffy the Vampire Slayer**, an unlikely rethinking of the 1992 film of the same title. Here Sarah Michelle Gellar stepped in as Buffy Summers, a seemingly normal high school girl who is actually a Slayer, a once-in-a-generation vampire hunter coached by Giles (Anthony Stewart Head), the school librarian and secret Watcher entrusted with her training. Along with her evolving "Scooby Gang" of friends and fellow fighters, she helps protect the California town of Sunnydale from vampires and other escalating supernatural threats – often at great personal cost. Creator Joss Whedon intended the show to be a celebration of female power, an aspect that became increasingly prominent as the show introduced a number of additional female protagonists and never defined its heroine solely by her romantic partners. The most popular of her temporary boyfriends was Angel (David Boreanaz), a vampire cursed with the possession of a soul and conscience after decades as a bloodthirsty killer known as Angelus. The character was spun off into the series **Angel** in 1999, which relocated him to Los Angeles where he starts a highly unorthodox detective agency. Despite a bumpy start, the series established its own identity and added a multitude of strong new characters to the so-called Buffyverse, which still continues to this day with comic books and conventions.

The success of Whedon's shows sparked a wave of new vampire series across the globe, many geared for younger audiences who had been bitten by the Buffy bug. The most enduring of these among the teen demographic was **The Vampire Diaries**, which ran for eight seasons starting in 2009. Based on the series of novels by L.J. Smith and created by **Scream**

top left: Buffy (Sarah Michelle Gellar) and Angel (David Boreanaz). opposite page top left: **The Vampire Diaries** (TV series).

scribe Kevin Williamson and Julie Plec, the show revolves around a turbulent love triangle between high schooler Elena (Nina Dobrev) and two very different vampire siblings, Stefan (Paul Wesley) and Damon (Ian Somerhalder). A spin-off series, **The Originals**, bowed in 2013 and widened the net further to encompass more of the history and family members with a focus on the first trio of vampires known to exist. In turn, another spin-off from that show was created by Plec in 2018, **Legacies**, which treads further into fantasy territory with another female heroine, Hope (Danielle Rose Russell), at a school catering to supernatural beings including various vampire descendants and hybrids.

Far more geared to adults, but similar in construction, was another blockbuster series adapted from a literary property, **True Blood**. Based on the aforementioned Charlaine Harris book series, the show, created by **American Beauty** (1999) Oscar-winning writer Alan Ball is also focused on a female protagonist, Sookie Stackhouse (Anna Paquin), a waitress with psychic abilities and sensitivity to the supernatural. She begins a very difficult relationship with the undead Bill Compton (Stephen Moyer) in a society where vampires have become commonplace thanks to the innovation of True Blood, a synthetic concoction that makes them more socially acceptable to their former food supply. Thanks to its platform on HBO, the series could indulge in depictions of sexuality and bloodshed unseen in any vampire series before it, and though the last stretch of the seven-season run (which ran from 2008 to 2014) became dangerously shaky, it remains a landmark in vampire-themed pop culture. A close competitor in the skin and gore sweepstakes could be found in **American Horror Story: Hotel**, the fifth incarnation of the FX anthology series; aired in 2015, its primary plotline involves a Hollywood hotel where the Countess Elizabeth (Lady Gaga) – what could that character name

possibly refer to? – holds sway over the guests and permanent residents including a coterie of eternally young vampire children and various pansexual orgy partners. Speaking of modern anthologies, the uneven but memorable 2005-2007 series **Masters of Horror** ventured into genuine vampirism only once, with Ernest Dickerson's 'The V Word,' about a pair of unwise funeral home intruders; however, there are also arguable elements to be found in additional episodes like Dario Argento's 'Jenifer,' Lucky McKee's 'Sick Girl,' and William Malone's 'Fair-Haired Child.' The show spawned a single-season successor, **Fear Itself**, which kicked off with vampires in its premiere episode, 'The Sacrifice,' about criminal interlopers hiding out at a fort in the wilderness that proves to be more dangerous than the police.

VAMPIRE MOVIES
top right: Lady Gaga in **American Horror Story: Hotel** (2015).
lower right: **True Blood** (TV series).
FRIGHTFEST GUIDE | 35

Originating as a clever BBC series in 2008, **Being Human** is one of the more successful attempts to work a vampire protagonist into a wider TV ensemble with Mitchell (Aidan Turner), another in the long line of monsters exercising control over the consumption of human blood, sharing a flat with a werewolf and a ghost. Due to the departures of key cast members, the show underwent significant overhauls and dissipated by its rocky fifth series; however, the concept and execution were strong enough to maintain a cult following, and to inspire a Canadian remake series of the same name that ran from 2011 to 2014. Also bearing some vampire elements is the 2013-2015 series **Hemlock Grove**, one of the first original genre series offered by

Netflix, which chronicles a variety of monstrous developments in a Pennsylvania town populated with an assortment of supernatural secrets. The comic book adaptation **Preacher**, which ran from 2015 to 2019, prominently features a vampire character in Joseph Gilgun's Proinsias Cassidy, an earthy Irish child of the night who accompanies the title character on a quest to find the literal God. Intermittent vampire characters also appear on the long-running American series **Supernatural**, particularly a four-episode thread involving belligerent vampire Gordon Walker (played by future **This Is Us** star Sterling K. Brown), who gets a taste of his own medicine. The show also introduces the concept of hidden vampire teeth emerging from the gums at feeding time, a memorably grotesque visual touch. More heavily focused on vampires, at least in its final stretch, is the Showtime series **Penny Dreadful**, which presents a mélange of Gothic literary characters drawing upon writers like Mary Shelley and Oscar Wilde. Its third and final season (of the series proper, not counting a later reboot) finally capitalized on the very vague vampire inferences of its initial narrative by bringing in numerous Bram Stoker characters including Dracula himself, here characterized as the brother of Lucifer and a key figure in the fate of the series' most compelling and tormented character, Eva Green's Vanessa Ives.

However, no Stoker-related series has inspired as much discussion or controversy as the BBC/Netflix production of **Dracula** in 2020. The brainchild of **Sherlock** team Stephen Moffat and Mark Gatiss, the three-part narrative is essentially a remix of the original novel with Danish actor Claes Bang

top left: **Being Human** (BBC, 2008).
lower left: **Supernatural** (TV series).

2007 series **Moonlight** with Alex O'Loughlin as a vampirized private eye; the Canadian sci-fi series **Sanctuary** (2008-2011) which posits the admittedly novel idea of Nikola Tesla as a vampire; the AMC series **NOS4A2**, an adaptation of Joe Hill's novel about a vampire and child predator named Manx (Zachary Quinto) matching wits with a resourceful artist (Ashleigh Cummings); the apocalyptic 2019 Netflix series **V Wars** depicting a viral outbreak and radical climate change turning the world into a breeding ground for human-vampire warfare; and more futuristic vampire adventures in the Syfy graphic novel adaptation **Van Helsing** (2016-2020) about a world where humanity can be salvaged from a vampire apocalypse.

amping up the title character's quips and sexual appetite. Featuring a reworked plight for Jonathan Harker and a murder mystery variation on the Demeter voyage, the series went a step too far for many viewers with an abrupt leap to the present day for its final installment chronicling Dracula's effect on the tragic Lucy Westenra (Lydia West), here reinvented as a vain club kid. As divisive as the end result may be (including the now infamous wi-fi password gag), the series works in several fascinating ideas including Dracula's acquisition of languages and knowledge through his blood consumption, not to mention a compelling interpretation of Van Helsing as a Dutch nun (and her descendant) played by Dolly Wells.

If that isn't enough vampire TV viewing for you, here are some additional shows of interest: the animated streaming series **Castlevania** inspired by the popular video game franchise; the romantic vampire fantasy **A Discovery of Witches** adapted from the writing of Deborah Harkness; the Disney Junior animated series **Vampirina** about a young vampire girl adapting to life in Pennsylvania; the four-season series **The Strain** adapted by Guillermo Del Toro and Chuck Hogan from their books about a vampire-like contagion tearing through modern civilization; the gay-themed **The Lair** about an island sex club controlled by a centuries-old vampire enclave; the '90s Canadian series **Forever Knight** about an ancient vampire paying for his sins by working as a cop (played by Geraint Wyn Davis following a Rick Springfield pilot film in 1989 entitled **Nick Knight**); a similar vampire cop concept in the 2007 Canadian variant **Blood Ties**; the short-lived but interesting

IX. ONE LAST BITE

The current millennium may be dominated by a barrage of zombies and a variety of plague-induced terrors, but the vampire shows no signs of dying any time soon. Hollywood managed to strike gold by going for action and teenaged audiences with the profitable **Underworld** and **Twilight** series, not to mention several game-changing international classics that revolutionized the depiction of vampirism on screen. We'll dive into those here of course, but for a quick primer, things kicked off on a mainstream note with **Dracula 2000** (2000) and, soon after, **Jesus Christ Vampire Hunter** (2001), an indescribable Canadian stab at a nouveaux midnight movie complete with musical numbers, wrestling, and martial arts as Jesus returns to combat the forces of evil including lesbian vampires. Only slightly less absurd and definitely in a similar vein is the later **Lesbian Vampire Killers** (2009), Phil

VAMPIRE MOVIES
opposite page top right: **Penny Dreadful** (Showtime series).
this page top left: **Dracula** (BBC, 2020).
FRIGHTFEST GUIDE 37

Claydon's British monster comedy about a small English town where the still-living Carmilla gobbles up all the female residents one way or another – until two hapless young amateur vampire hunters are sent in to stop her.

Widely reviled but certainly never dull, German director and perpetual provocateur Uwe Boll delivered one of the better entries from his cycle of video game adaptations (how's that for damning with faint praise?) with **BloodRayne** (2005), a pulpy vampire action film with a game Kristanna Loken heading a wildly overqualified cast as a human-vampire mutation (and daughter of vampire royalty) who sets off on a familial quest for vengeance. Say what you will, but any film featuring Meat Loaf, Udo Kier, Michael Madsen, Michael Paré, Michelle Rodriguez, and a very puzzled-looking Ben Kingsley (long past his Oscar win) deserves credit for sheer chutzpah. Boll followed it with two sequels, **BloodRayne: Deliverance** (2007) and **BloodRayne: The Third Reich** (2011), both essentially sent straight to video for good reason.

Vampire comedies enjoyed a resurgence of sorts in recent years, though the results have ranged from the unwatchable **Vampires Suck** (2010) and **Stan Helsing** (2009) to the genuinely charming and underrated **Vamps** (2012), which reteamed director Amy Heckerling and star Alicia Silverstone after the classic **Clueless** (1995) for a romantic comedy about two vampire best friends dealing with undead life and love in the modern Big Apple. The craze for young adult fantasy fare ignited by Harry Potter and his ilk had to produce a vampire option as well, which materialized with an adaptation of multiple books in Darren Shan's line of supernatural novels, **Cirque du Freak: The Vampire's Assistant** (2009). The condensed narrative follows a teenager (also named Darren Shan, in keeping with the novelist's pen name and played here by Chris Massoglia), who uncovers a freak show's vampire secret in the true identity of one of its star performers, Larten Crepsley (John C. Reilly); after going on the road, he must decide whether to become at least a partial monster himself. Though the film was indifferently received and had all of its prospective sequels scrapped, it makes for a reasonable introduction to vampire films for young viewers who might not be ready for any bloody trauma.

The streaming revolution not only gave a platform to many newer indie vampire productions but also blurred the line between what constitutes feature films, miniseries, and TV series. Chief among these is **Midnight Mass** (2021), part of gifted filmmaker Mike Flanagan's series of multi-episode horror sagas for Netflix. You never hear the 'v' word once (and the marketing gave no clue about its bloodsucking content), but this is one of the most thought-provoking takes on the mythos, mingled here with Catholicism itself along with faith in general from the perspectives of agnostics and Muslims. After killing a young woman while drunk-driving, Riley Flynn (Zach Gilford) returns to his family home on the desolate Crockett Island, a community soon to be held in thrall to its new priest, Father Paul (Hamish Linklater), who is far more than he seems. The result is an epic work of intelligent horror with a tense, cataclysmic finale capped off with a hauntingly bittersweet 'happy' ending.

As any die-hard horror fanatic knows, there's a perverse joy to be found in mining the depths of genre titles that received little to no theatrical distribution and instead wound up directly on video shelves, a move that has more recently transformed into direct-to-streaming offerings as well. For example, intrepid vampire movie hunters may have sifted around and uncovered pleasures minuscule or major from such wide-ranging titles as **The Last Sect** (2017), **Vampire Clan** (2002), **Hunted** (2015), **Aaron's Blood** (2017), **Manhattan Undying** (2017), **Nocturna** (2015), **Kiss of the Vampire** (2009), **Apostle of Dracula** (2017), **Blood Cure** (2013), **Bitten: Victoria's Shadow** (2001), **The Blood Queen** (2015), **Blood Kisses** (2017), **Bathory: Countess of Blood** (2008), **Revamped** (2012), **Blood + Roses** (2015), **Renfield the Undead** (2016), and **Shadowland** (2010). By this point we truly have thousands of vampire entertainments out in the world to be discovered, only a privileged selection of which can possibly be touched on here... but may you have many hours of happy hunting along the way.

right: **Cirque du Freak: The Vampire's Assistant** (2009).

A primal and popular part of monster lore to this day, the vampire fascinates whether it's a ghastly corpse freshly risen from the grave or a magnetic aristocrat suffering over the centuries.

Now prepare to spend an evening with some of the most notable bloodsuckers who have left their mark, including...

Dancing denizens of the undead holding unholy masquerade balls...

Hapless humans enslaved as plasma-pumping cattle...

Naïve Italian maidens trapped in a monstrous castle of death...

Melancholy French fiends drifting through empty beachscapes...

100-year-old high school students...

Centuries-old African princes unleashed on the streets of modern America...

Confused youngsters wielding razor blades to sate their bloodlust...

A supernatural pilot making nightly pit stops for a quick bite...

Drink deep as you enjoy this bloody bouquet of 200 delights ranging from world classics to outrageous oddities from the rich, full-blooded world of vampire cinema.

Just remember to be back in bed by dawn.

NOSFERATU

Germany, 1922
Director: F.W. Murnau.
Producers: Enrico Dieckmann, Albin Grau.
Screenplay: Henrik Galeen.
Cinematography: Fritz Arno Wagner,
Günther Krampf [uncredited].
Cast: Max Schreck, Gustav von Wangenheim,
Greta Schröder, Georg H. Schnell, Ruth Landshoff, Gustav Botz.

The first feature-length vampire film was threatened with almost immediate oblivion when this unauthorized adaptation of Bram Stoker's **Dracula** was contested by the author's estate and targeted for destruction. Fortunately, this uncontested masterpiece by F.W. Murnau survived and is now regarded as a high watermark of German Expressionist silent cinema as well as one of the most chilling horror films ever made. Titled **Nosferatu, eine Symphonie des Grauens** in its native country, the film altered the names of its characters to camouflage the source of inspiration but fooled no one; however, it also introduces numerous visual and narrative flourishes of its own, most notably a powerful climax that sends its vampire out on a far more dramatic and resonant note than Dracula himself. The uncanny performance of prolific actor Max Schreck as the bald, impressively clawed Count Orlok easily overshadows the rest of the participants and became the benchmark against which future cinematic vampires were measured. The film's legal troubles ensured the immediate downfall of its production company, Prana Film, co-founded by this film's producer, occult devotee Albin Grau; however, Murnau's career flourished afterwards and led to Hollywood before his untimely death. Many different versions of this film have circulated in the ensuing decades including one with a thundering score by regular Hammer Films composer James Bernard, and its influence continues to the present day with Schreck's appearance turning up in everything from subsequent vampire films and music videos.

DRACULA

USA, 1931
Director: Tod Browning.
Producers: Tod Browning, Carl Laemmle Jr. Screenplay: Garrett Fort. Cinematography: Karl Freund.
Cast: Bela Lugosi, Helen Chandler, David Manners, Dwight Frye, Edward Van Sloan, Herbert Bunston.

An instant sensation, Hollywood's first vampire film has become so absorbed in the public consciousness that most viewers now have no idea what a strange and troubled production it was. This radical distillation of the Bram Stoker novel by way of the 1924 hit stage play became one of the two flagship Universal monster classics from 1931 along with James Whale's **Frankenstein** (released later the same year), but in this case directed by Tod Browning and featuring star Bela Lugosi reprising his stage role. A major box office success and a touchstone for the modern sound horror film, **Dracula** made an icon of Lugosi but also provided seminal roles for Edward Van Sloan's Van Helsing and particularly Dwight Frye's wild-eyed Renfield, whose "Rats!" speech provides the film's most dramatic flourish. The hasty and reportedly maddening production, which necessitated partial directing duties given to cinematographer Karl Freund, resulted in a lack of traditional music underscore for the film proper, several continuity errors and scenes out of order (including the now-famous omnipresent piece of cardboard set dressing) and eccentric additions like castle wildlife including armadillos and possums. The soundtrack of the film was censored upon reissue, most notably the offscreen staking at the end, and was only restored during the home video era. Composer Philip Glass also mounted a divisive, high-profile reissue of the film with a specially composed score in 1999 performed by the Kronos Quartet, including several live engagements. Several generations of monster fans have derided the film for being too talky, but when seen on the big screen with an appreciative audience, the film remains suffused with a creeping dread that extends from Dracula's castle to the seemingly bright and safe London interiors of our heroes.

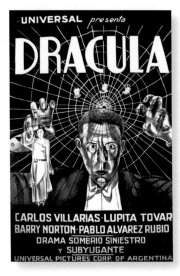

DRÁCULA

USA, 1931
Director: George Melford. Producer: Carl Laemmle Jr.
Screenplay: Baltasar Fernández Cué. Cinematography: George Robinson.
Cast: Carlos Villar [Carlos Villarías], Lupita Tovar, Barry Norton,
Pablo Álvarez Rubio, Eduardo Arozamena, José Soriano Viosca.

While Tod Browning was shooting his English-language version of the vampire classic at Universal, a simultaneous Spanish-language variant with different actors using the same sets and equipment was mounted at night under the supervision of director George Melford. Running half an hour longer than the Browning film, this alternative was a tantalizing mystery for decades due to the film's lost status and the frequent publication of dramatic still photographs in countless monster publications. The discovery of a print in the 1970s led to official distribution on home video that proved to be a revelation for Universal horror fans, many of whom consider this superior to its companion feature in terms of filmmaking craft. Though he can't help but come up short next to Lugosi, Carlos Villarías gives it his all as the title character and the plot is handled more coherently given the relative lack of studio interference. The future wave of Spanish-language vampire films from South America and Europe was also primed by this feature thanks to characters like Juan Harker and Lucía Weston, here delivered with a melodramatic intensity that stands in stark contrast to the staid approach of their English-speaking counterparts. This version also alters some of the more outré sexualized moments of the Browning version, particularly the climax's breast-clutching moment delivered by actress Lupita Tovar, mother of Hollywood actress Susan Kohner.

VAMPYR

Germany/France, 1932
Director: Carl Theodor Dreyer.
Producers: Carl Theodor Dreyer,
Nicolas de Gunzburg. Screenplay:
Christen Jul, Carl Theodor
Dreyer. Music: Wolfgang Zeller.
Cinematography: Rudolph Maté.
Cast: Julian West [Nicolas de
Gunzburg], Maurice Schutz, Rena
Mandel, Sybille Schmitz, Jan
Hieronimko, Henriette Gérard.

The first horror art film of the sound era marked a belated
return to the screen for legendary Danish director Carl
Theodor Dreyer after his powerful **The Passion of Joan
of Arc** (1928) and is cited as an adaptation of J. Sheridan
Le Fanu's 1872 short story collection *In a Glass Darkly*
(including *Carmilla*), but only in the very loosest sense.
The poetic, episodic narrative follows Allan Gray (Nicolas
de Gunzburg, the film's financier using the name "Julian
West") whose stay at a country inn leads to a sudden
murder, a trip to a castle inhabited by two peculiar
sisters, and the discovery of a vampire curse in the area
tied to a local doctor. The deliberate, dreamy pacing of
this film, the hazy lensing, and the subdued acting style
of the largely nonprofessional cast caused audience and
distributor problems when it was first shown, to such an
extent that it may have contributed to Dreyer's emotional
breakdown soon after. The film was significantly cut
in many countries and circulated in English under such
titles as **Castle of Doom** and **Not Against Flesh** with
poor public domain copies harming its reputation for
decades; however, the reinforcing of its copyright and a restoration have helped elevate its reputation as
one of Dreyer's finest films. The chilling nightmare in which Gray imagines himself being buried alive and
observed by the old female vampire is the most legendary sequence in the film (largely through its frequent
inclusion via stills in horror movie books over the years), but the entire film is filled with disquieting
details including Gray's first night at the inn and an unexpectedly harrowing climactic death in a flour mill.

MARK OF THE VAMPIRE

USA, 1935
Director: Tod Browning. Producer: E.J. Mannix
[uncredited]. Screenplay: Guy Endore, Bernard Schubert.
Cinematography: James Wong Howe.
Cast: Lionel Barrymore, Elizabeth Allan, Bela Lugosi,
Lionel Atwill, Jean Hersholt, Henry Wadsworth.

Bela Lugosi's second time donning a black cape on film
turned out to be his most unusual "vampire" role in this
sound remake of the most famous lost silent horror film,
London After Midnight (1927) starring Lon Chaney. The original film's director, Tod Browning, returned
to studio filmmaking for MGM here after nearly obliterating his career with the scandalous **Freaks**
(1932), and the result remains one of the more divisive classic horror films due to a twist ending that
some consider to be a total cheat. (Even the actors were unaware of it until late in the shooting process.)
Essentially a murder mystery dressed up in classic monster trappings, the film concerns a European village
convinced that recent murder and other uncanny events are due to a pair of vampires in the vicinity;
however, a call to help from Professor Zelin (Lionel Barrymore) reveals there's more than meets the eye.

Superbly shot by James Wong Howe
with a great deal of Hollywood
gloss, the film is an atmospheric
monster movie delight in its
strongest moments and packs
a great deal of entertainment
into its truncated one-hour
running time, though at least
20 minutes of footage was
reportedly excised from its
initial preview version.

DRACULA'S DAUGHTER

USA, 1936
Director: Lambert Hillyer.
Producer: E.M. Asher.
Screenplay: Garrett Fort.
Music: Heinz
Roemheld [uncredited].
Cinematography:
George Robinson.
Cast: Otto Kruger, Gloria Holden,
Marguerite Churchill, Gilbert Emery,
Edward Van Sloan, Irving Pichel.

The first American film to focus on a female vampire arrived at the close of the Carl Laemmle era at Universal, with the project undergoing numerous cast and story transformations for years on its way to the big screen. Bela Lugosi's high salary demands and issues with Bram Stoker's estate eventually led to this depiction of Dracula's deeply conflicted daughter (a reluctantly cast Gloria Holden), who arrives in London and introduces herself as Hungarian nobility, Countess Marya Zaleska. The recent enforcement of the United States' Production Code resulted in a film quite different from its predecessor, with a strong focus on comedy in the opening act softening up the censors to what remains a streak of daring lesbian content throughout the film. In addition to the much-discussed sequence in which Talbot seduces and feeds upon an undressing streetwalker during a nocturnal modeling assignment, the script is filled with suggestions of psychiatry (which was all the rage at the time) as a means of suppressing unwanted urges and repairing the human soul of our "dark, aristocratic" foreigner and her biologically inherited nature. As a result, this can be considered as the first bona fide lesbian vampire film, though its successors would be a long time coming.

THE RETURN OF THE VAMPIRE

USA, 1943
Director: Lew Landers. Producer: Sam White.
Screenplay: Griffin Jay. Music: Mario Castelnuovo-Tedesco.
Cinematography: L. William O'Connell, John Stumar.
Cast: Bela Lugosi, Frieda Inescort, Nina Foch, Roland
Varno, Miles Mander, Matt Willis.

With the actual Dracula character still controlled by
Universal at the time, Columbia Pictures found a tidy
workaround with this World War II-set slice of Gothic
horror starring Bela Lugosi as Armand Tesla, a mesmeric
member of the undead who bears more than a passing
resemblance to everyone's favourite bloodsucker. Here
he's revived from a stake-induced execution by a war
bombing and plots revenge on those responsible with the
aid of his unusually chatty werewolf sidekick, Andréas
(Matt Willis). Director Lew Landers had scored his first
hit with Lugosi thanks to **The Raven** (1935), and the
modern setting offers a notable change of pace for Lugosi
who was seen the same year donning monster makeup to
play one half of the Universal matchup in **Frankenstein
Meets the Wolf Man** (1943). The prolific Lugosi wouldn't
headline a straightforward studio horror release again
after this, but he did slip on his cape one more time for
his last genuine vampire appearance to portray Dracula
as part of the beloved monster mash ensemble in **Abbott
and Costello Meet Frankenstein** (1948) back home at
Universal. Though he doesn't appear on screen in this film
until nearly a third of the way in, Lugosi still makes for
a commanding presence and earned every penny of his
$3,500 salary.

SON OF DRACULA

USA, 1943
Director: Robert Siodmak. Producer: Ford Beebe.
Screenplay: Eric Taylor. Music: Hans J. Salter.
Cinematography: George Robinson.
Cast: Robert Paige, Louise Allbritton, Lon Chaney Jr.,
Evelyn Ankers, Frank Craven, J. Edward Bromberg.

With Bela Lugosi off playing Dracula in everything but name for another studio in '43, Universal soldiered on with its vampire series under the guidance of director Robert Siodmak whose future knack for film noir style is already in evidence here. Lon Chaney Jr. takes over starring duties here as Count Dracula (not his son), who arrives in New Orleans under the name "Count Alucard" (a device later repeated ad nauseum in other films). This time the Count is actually a patsy for the scheming Katherine Caldwell (Louise Allbritton), a femme fatale using her marriage to Dracula to control the estate of her late father and gain immortality she plans to share with her lover, Frank (Robert Paige). Hot off the success of **The Wolf Man** (1941), Chaney uses his bulky physicality and innate vulnerability to deliver a different kind of screen vampire who fits perfectly with the more fatalistic tone that was taking hold in Hollywood thrillers. The swampy, foggy Louisiana setting is also a clever American variation on the usual Eastern European formula courtesy of the original story written by Siodmak's brother, Curt. This would be the final Universal film centered around the Dracula character, though he would appear later as part of the ensembles in **House of Frankenstein** (1944) and **House of Dracula** (1945).

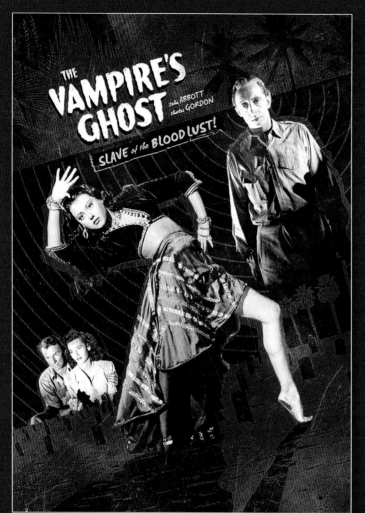

THE VAMPIRE'S GHOST

USA, 1945
Director: Lesley Selander.
Producer: Rudolph E. Abel.
Screenplay: John K. Butler, Leigh
Brackett. Cinematography: Robert
Pittack, Ellis Thackery [Bud Thackery].
Cast: John Abbott, Charles Gordon,
Peggy Stewart, Grant Withers,
Emmett Vogan, Adele Mara.

This early one-hour Republic Pictures
horror programmer is most notable
today as the first assignment for
trailblazing female screenwriter Leigh
Brackett, a young sci-fi writer who
would follow this with **The Big Sleep**
(1946) and go on to **The Long Goodbye** (1973) and **The Empire
Strikes Back** (1981). Here the narrative novelty lies in the setting of
an African seaside town, Bakunda, where drums pound away in the
background at all hours of the day. The white residents congregate
around a bar run by Webb Fallon (John Abbott), a hard-nosed
businessman who also happens to be a centuries-old vampire blamed
for a rash of killings in the area. Unexpected in many respects, the
script tweaks vampire lore throughout with clever touches involving
reflections in mirrors, daylight, and the toll taken by an immortal
existence as conveyed through the sad-eyed Abbott's multi-layered,
sympathetic characterization. The lengthy jungle adventure
section early on is a particularly refreshing wrinkle in vampire
cinema, and the oppressively humid
atmosphere throughout adds to the
ambience of a land where primal forces
and superstition feel more powerful
than our nominal heroes played by
Charles Gordon and Peggy Stewart.
Though never critically respected, the
film was a reliable double and triple
bill filler for years for Republic and
earned a fond place in the hearts of an
entire generation of monster kids.

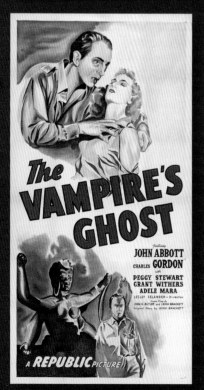

THE WHITE REINDEER

Finland, 1952
Director: Erik Blomberg. Producer: Aarne Tarkas.
Screenplay: Erik Blomberg, Mirjami Kuosmanen.
Music: Einar Englund. Cinematography: Erik Blomberg.
Cast: Mirjami Kuosmanen, Kalervo Nissilä, Åke Lindman,
Jouni Tapiola, Arvo Lehesmaa.

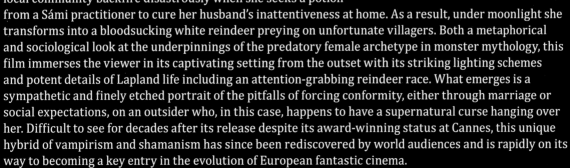

The shapeshifting aspects of vampirism take center stage in this pared-down Lapland folk tale about the daughter of a reputed witch, Pirita (Mirjami Kuosmanen, wife of first-time director Erik Blomberg), whose attempts to meld and marry within the local community backfire disastrously when she seeks a potion from a Sámi practitioner to cure her husband's inattentiveness at home. As a result, under moonlight she transforms into a bloodsucking white reindeer preying on unfortunate villagers. Both a metaphorical and sociological look at the underpinnings of the predatory female archetype in monster mythology, this film immerses the viewer in its captivating setting from the outset with its striking lighting schemes and potent details of Lapland life including an attention-grabbing reindeer race. What emerges is a sympathetic and finely etched portrait of the pitfalls of forcing conformity, either through marriage or social expectations, on an outsider who, in this case, happens to have a supernatural curse hanging over her. Difficult to see for decades after its release despite its award-winning status at Cannes, this unique hybrid of vampirism and shamanism has since been rediscovered by world audiences and is rapidly on its way to becoming a key entry in the evolution of European fantastic cinema.

DRAKULA İSTANBUL'DA

Turkey, 1953
Director: Mehmet Muhtar. Producer: Turgut Demirag.
Screenplay: Ümit Deniz. Cinematography: Özen Sermet.
Cast: Annie Ball, Cahit Irgat, Ayfer Feray, Bülent Oran, Atif Kaptan, Kemal Emin Bara.

Turkish cinema is widely known and beloved now for its vibrant repurposing of other countries' hits into eccentric new versions for local consumption, so it was inevitable that a variation of **Dracula** would be on its radar. That came to pass when the vampire film was at a particularly low ebb in the early 1950s when atomic monsters were more in vogue. Six years after F.W. Murnau's unauthorized take on the Stoker classic with **Nosferatu**, Turkish author Ali Riza Seyfioglu pulled off a similar copyright-flaunting feat with his short novel **Kazıklı Voyvoda**, now available in English as **Dracula in Istanbul**. Adapted to a modern-day Istanbul setting with Islam and general folklore swapped out for Christian iconography, the narrative of both the book and its film adaptation hews closely to the Stoker model, along with such innovations as prominent vampire fangs and an explicit connection to Vlad the Impaler whose savage behaviour had left a centuries-long mark on Turkey. Also notable are the inclusions of Dracula's wall climbing and Lucy's child-killing antics, elements played down in earlier versions (albeit with Lucy changed to Sadan here), as well as the tweaking of the Mina character (Güzin) into an alluring stage performer who captures the count's eye during her cabaret performances.

BLOOD OF DRACULA

USA, 1957
Director: Herbert L. Strock. Producer: Herman Cohen. Screenplay: Ralph Thornton [Aben Kandel].
Music: Paul Dunlap. Cinematography: Monroe P. Askins.
Cast: Sandra Harrison, Louise Lewis, Gail Ganley, Jerry Blaine, Heather Ames, Malcolm Atterbury.

There's no real Dracula connection here apart from a fleeting reference to the Carpathian mountains, but this teen horror follow-up to **I Was a Teenage Werewolf** (1957) from American International Pictures still delivers the vampire thrills with one of the era's most distinctive creatures thanks to her dramatic eyebrows, flurry hairdo and prominent canine fangs. Initially released in the United Kingdom as **Blood Is My Heritage** and paired up with **I Was a Teenage Frankenstein** (1957) on most double bills, this tale of adolescent angst gone very wrong involves young Nancy (Sandra Harrison) who's shuffled off to a girls' boarding school by her recently remarried dad. There she's taken under the wing of Miss Branding (Louise Lewis), a fledgling mad scientist trying to unlock human potential via hypnotism and a powerful amulet that turns Nancy into an intermittent blood drinker. Despite some very awkward action staging, the film makes for ideal drive-in fodder complete with an obligatory pop song, "Puppy Love." Film scholars have had a field day for decades analyzing the film's vague lesbian subtext, in particular its primary student-teacher relationship which not only plays on general fears of queerness at the time but points the way to the more overt lesbian vampire films to come just a few years later.

THE VAMPIRE

USA, 1957
Director: Paul Landres. Producers: Arthur Gardner, Arnold Laven,
Jules V. Levy. Screenplay: Pat Fielder.
Music: Gerald Fried. Cinematography: Jack MacKenzie.
Cast: John Beal, Coleen Gray, Kenneth Tobey, Lydia Reed,
Dabbs Greer, Herb Vigran.

"Half human, half wild animal, destroying beautiful women, out to satisfy its unholy lust for blood!" That sales pitch pulled in audiences as the vampire film fully entered the 1950s drive-in age with this United Artists release, part of its partnership with the production team of Arthur Gardner, Arnold Laven and Jules V. Levy. Set in the all-American suburbs with a sci-fi twist, the film follows the sorry fate of widower physician Paul Beecher (John Beal) who accidentally ingests experimental pills developed by a late mad scientist who's been experimenting with bats. As a result, Paul periodically transforms into a savage vampire beast who preys on the neighborhood, a secret he must keep from his innocent daughter, Betsy (Reed). You don't have to dig deeply to see this film as a metaphor for the darker secrets roiling beneath the façade of wholesome American fatherhood at the time including drug addiction, PTSD, and sexual deviation, all factors that would burst out in the open in later years. Shot at Hal Roach Studios in a mundane, flat style that adapted perfectly for TV broadcast, this quickie co-feature to the same team's **The Monster That Challenged the World** (1957) has gone on to a life of its own as a fascinating pulp horror spin on Nicholas Ray's domestic addiction study, **Bigger Than Life** (1956).

EL VAMPIRO

Mexico, 1957
Director: Fernando Méndez. Producer: Abel Salazar.
Screenplay: Ramon Rodriguez.
Music: Gustavo César Carrión.
Cinematography: Rosalío Solano.
Cast: Abel Salazar, Ariadna Welter,
Carmen Montejo, José Luis Jiménez,
Mercedes Soler, Germán Robles.

Mexico's ongoing love affair with homegrown monster movies (and vampire films in particular) began
in earnest with this influential Gothic yarn inspired by Universal's monster classics. Famous as the first
widespread feature with now-familiar vampire canine fangs, the film became a fast favourite when AIP
picked up K. Gordon Murray's English-dubbed edition for TV distribution in 1965 and inspired a decades'
worth of homegrown chillers. A family ailment brings Marta (Ariadna Welter) back home to her village
where she and the trepidatious Dr. Enrique Saldívar (Abel Salazar) realize a strain of vampirism is
afoot thanks the Hungarian stranger Duval, alias Count Lavud, played with a dashing and sinister air by
Germán Robles in a striking debut performance. The local and international success of this film ensured
Robles' status as a Mexican horror fixture for years to come in films like **The Brainiac** (1962), also
featuring producer Salazar as the titular creature, and **The Curse of Nostradamus** (1961), particularly
given that he steals this film with what amounts to a limited supporting performance. Vampire lore is
explored thoroughly and faithfully here from delightful bat transformations to the old no-reflection
gag, while the black-and-white cinematography by the very busy Rosalío Solano gives the production an
artistry far beyond the limitations of the tiny budget.

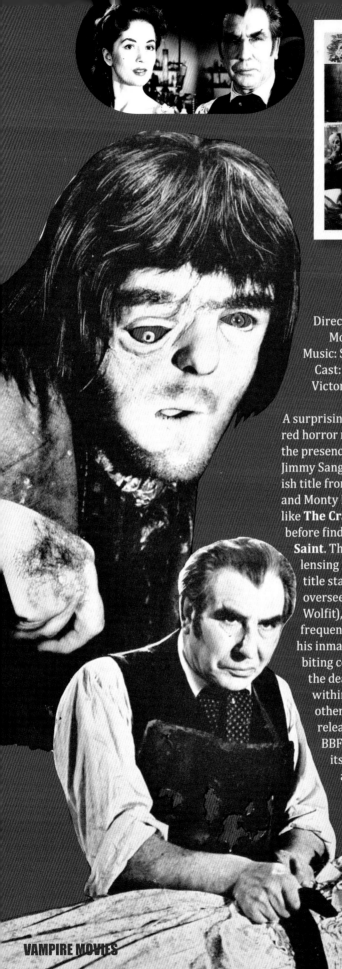

BLOOD OF THE VAMPIRE

UK, 1958
Director: Henry Cass. Producers: Robert S. Baker,
Monty Berman. Screenplay: Jimmy Sangster.
Music: Stanley Black. Cinematography: Monty Berman.
Cast: Donald Wolfit, Vincent Ball, Barbara Shelley,
Victor Maddern, William Devlin, Andrew Faulds.

A surprisingly dead-on attempt to copy Hammer's ruddy-red horror movie style during its infancy right down to the presence of star Barbara Shelley and screenwriter Jimmy Sangster, this period outing was the only vampire-ish title from the busy producing pair of Robert S. Baker and Monty Berman who struck gold with lurid favourites like **The Crawling Eye** (1958) and **Jack the Ripper** (1959) before finding their niche in ITC TV series like **The Saint**. The film takes advantage of its Eastmancolor lensing from the outset with a blood-gushing main title staking and an atmospheric asylum setting overseen by the nefarious Callistratus (Donald Wolfit), whose peculiar medical condition requires frequent transfusions and the enforced aid of one of his inmates, John Pierre (Vincent Ball). No fangs or biting come into play here, though the revival from the dead and quest for blood keep this marginally within the confines of vampire cinema. As with other Baker and Berman productions, this was released in several different variants with the BBFC mandating a draconian number of cuts on its initial release. Though put into production around the same time as Hammer's **Dracula** (1958) and released a mere three months after it, this film bears no resemblance to it in any form and cannot be considered an imitation.

Every night he rises from his coffin-bed silently to seek the soft flesh, the warm blood he needs to keep himself alive!

Dracula X

Adults only

DON'T DARE SEE IT ALONE!

DRACULA

UK, 1958
Director: Terence Fisher.
Producer: Anthony Hinds.
Screenplay: Jimmy Sangster. Music: James Bernard.
Cinematography: Jack Asher.
Cast: Peter Cushing, Christopher Lee, Michael Gough,
Melissa Stribling, Carol Marsh, Olga Dickie.

The importance of the first major British vampire film can't possibly be overstated. Already on the rise thanks to a string of notable science fiction and film noir programmers, Hammer Films was still new to the Gothic horror game after the recent success of **The Curse of Frankenstein** (1957), a bloody, colorful take on a literary horror classic from director Terence Fisher and writer Jimmy Sangster with career-making roles for Peter Cushing and Christopher Lee. That principal team reunited here for a highly compressed take on the Bram Stoker classic that cherry picks and switches around characters and plot elements with abandon into a kind of frenzied mosaic, with Lee's imposing, fang-baring, dialogue-deprived Count becoming an instant pop culture icon complete with his own dramatic signature theme provided by composer James Bernard. Also invaluable is the saturated cinematography of the great Jack Asher, who uses hues reminiscent of stained glass to give the film a dreamlike fairy tale quality. Drawing visual inspiration from swashbuckler films, the rousing Van Helsing versus Dracula climax (culminating in a still-jolting disintegration scene) became a classic Hammer moment and ensured a continuation of the story in eight sequels featuring Cushing and/or Lee over the next sixteen years. Released in the United States as **Horror of Dracula**, the film was subjected to different cuts in a variety of countries but has been reassembled (more or less) in recent years and still packs a punch with its perfectly timed frights including one immaculate graveyard jump scare.

THE RETURN OF DRACULA

USA, 1958
Director: Paul Landres.
Producers: Arthur Gardner, Jules V. Levy.
Screenplay: Pat Fielder. Music: Gerald Fried.
Cinematography: Jack MacKenzie.
Cast: Francis Lederer, Norma Eberhardt, Ray Stricklyn,
John Wengraf, Virginia Vincent, Gage Clarke.

The same year Alfred Hitchcock's **Shadow of a Doubt**
(1943) was remade as the now-forgotten **Step Down to
Terror** (1958), the storyline was given a thinly veiled
horror gloss for this second vampire release from United
Artists and the Gardner-Laven-Levy team behind **The
Vampire** (1957). Screenwriter Pat Fielder and director Paul Landres also return for the saga of Count
Dracula (Francis Lederer), who narrowly escapes from his crypt just before execution in Transylvania
and hides out in a sunny Carleton, California neighborhood as one of his victims: Bellac Gordal, a
European tourist visiting his American relatives for the
first time since childhood. However, young admiring Rachel
(Norma Eberhardt) suspects something's amiss with the
new arrival when a strange blood disorder strikes the
neighborhood. First shown in the UK under the baffling
title **The Fantastic Disappearing Man**, this black-and-
white film anticipates William Castle's gimmick
classic **The Tingler** (1959) by one year with
its brief blood-red color insert at the climax
and features one of the decade's more
intense vampire performances courtesy
of the Prague-born Lederer, who was
surprisingly dismissive of the project
in later interviews but appeared as
Dracula again in his final role in
a 1971 episode of **Night Gallery**,
'The Devil Is Not Mocked.'

THE MOST TERRIFYING NAME IN THE HISTORY OF THE WORLD NOW GIVES YOU THE MOST HORRIFYING THRILL IN THE HISTORY OF MOTION PICTURES!

THE RETURN OF DRACULA

Starring
FRANCIS LEDERER · NORMA EBERHARDT
with RAY STRICKLYN · JOHN WENGRAF · VIRGINIA VINCENT
Story and Screenplay by PAT FIELDER · Directed by PAUL LANDRES
Produced by JULES V. LEVY and ARTHUR GARDNER
Released thru UNITED ARTISTS

THE VAMPIRE'S COFFIN

Mexico, 1958
Director: Fernando Méndez. Producer: Abel Salazar.
Screenplay: Alfredo Salazar [uncredited]. Music:
Gustavo César Carrión. Cinematography: Víctor Herrera.
Cast: Abel Salazar, Ariadna Welter, Germán Robles,
Yerye Beirute, Alicia Montoya, Guillermo Orea.

Christopher Lee's first appearance as the Count courtesy
of Hammer arrived in between Mexican horror trailblazer
El Vampiro and this immediate sequel, but that had little effect on what amounts of a scrappier, stranger
revisit with most of the same cast and crew. Originally entitled **El ataúd del vampiro**, the story brings
back the beleaguered Marta (Ariadna Welter) and Enrique (Abel Salazar) for another round against the
bloodthirsty Count Lavud (Germán Robles) when he's revived by careless, graverobbing Dr. Mendoza
(Guillermo Orea) and his craven henchman (Yeire Beirute). The classic, timeless atmosphere of the prior
film gives way here to a very modern, urban setting that many viewers found jarring, though it does point
the way to the direction many vampire films would take in the 1970s with monsters born of superstition
contrasting against sterile concrete cityscapes. The film also marks an early use of the stake removal
gimmick to revive its marquee vampire, a tactic that would rear its head for decades to come, and includes
a sci-fi angle via Mendoza's attempts to study cell structure and variations as an underlying cause for
vampirism. Unfortunately, this film marked the end of the road for Count Lavud and company, but director
Fernando Méndez continued unabated with more Mexican horror classics including the excellent **The Black
Pit of Dr. M** (1959) and the genre-mashing horror western, **The Living Coffin** (1959).

BLOOD AND ROSES

Italy/France, 1960
Director: Roger Vadim. Producer: Raymond Eger.
Screenplay: Roger Vadim, Roger Vailland. Music: Jean Prodromidès.
Cinematography: Claude Renoir.
Cast: Mel Ferrer, Elsa Martinelli, Annette Vadim [Annette Stroyberg],
Alberto Bonucci, René-Jean Chauffard, Gabriella Farinon.

Following the scandalous international success of **...And God Created Woman** (1956), director Roger
Vadim exploited a successful formula by casting his then-wife, Brigitte Bardot, in sensuous melodramas
that found plenty of audience support overseas. After their divorce, he tried the same tactic with his new
wife, Danish-born Annette Stroyberg (briefly rechristened as Annette Vadim), and put her center stage
in this modernized, dreamlike variation on *Carmilla*, which was prepared in both English- and French-
language versions thanks to its two other bilingual stars, Mel Ferrer and Elsa Martinelli. The very wide,
voluptuous Technirama lensing and a glistening score by Jean Prodromidès make this one of the most

elegant, striking horror films of the 1960s, complete with a
Cocteau-style dream sequence and a surprising amount of overt
nudity even in the American version released by Paramount.
Vadim's original, longer French-language cut features a framing
device involving a psychoanalyst relating the story of poor
Carmilla to a fellow airplane passenger, with the reworked
English one adding narration and opting for an unambiguous
supernatural angle instead. Either way, it's essential viewing
and often considered the first irrefutable lesbian vampire film
thanks to an indelible, blood-tinged kiss between its two female
stars inside a rain-spattered greenhouse.

The most evil DRACULA of all !

THE BRIDES OF DRACULA

UK, 1960
Director: Terence Fisher. Producer: Anthony Hinds.
Screenplay: Jimmy Sangster, Peter Bryan, Edward Percy.
Music: Malcolm Williamson. Cinematography: Jack Asher.
Cast: Peter Cushing, Martita Hunt, Yvonne Monlaur,
Freda Jackson, David Peel, Miles Malleson.

The runaway international success of Hammer Films' **Dracula** (1958) virtually guaranteed a sequel, but only one of its stars returned for this second film in the two-decade cycle. This time Van Helsing (Peter Cushing) appears late in the story to combat a new vampire threat in the form of Baron Meinster (David Peel), who is freed from his chained confinement in the family castle by naïve French schoolteacher Marianne (Yvonne Monlaur). Far from rehashing the prior film's highlights, returning director Terence Fisher and a large crew of screenwriters inject the proceedings with several entertaining new wrinkles including a newly converted vampire coaxed from her grave through a particularly

macabre pep talk, a truly maniacal performance by actress Freda Jackson, whiffs of familial perversity within the Meinster household, and a new, grisly method of treating a nasty fang bite with impromptu cauterization. The absence of Dracula (or, more pointedly, Christopher Lee) had little detrimental effect on the film, which remains a Hammer fan favourite. In fact, Peel's ravenous performance coupled with his matinee idol blond looks makes him a striking contrast to his predecessor, coupled with the fact that he delivers a fine performance that capped off his short career before retiring to private life.

BLOOD-LUSTING FIEND WHO PREYS ON GIRLS!
VAMPIRE-QUEEN WHO FEEDS ON LIFEBLOOD OF MEN!

THE
Vampire
AND THE
Ballerina

A company of beautiful young dancers stranded in a lonely mountain village…as the horror legend two thousand years old comes alive!

HÉLÈNE REMY with MARIA LUISA ROLANDO · WALTER BRANDI · TINA GLORIANI
ISARCO RAVAIOLI · JOHN TURNER · Screenplay by RENATO POLSELLI · GIUSEPPE PELLEGRINI
ERNESTO CASTALDI · Directed by RENATO POLSELLI, A.C.I.P. Consorzio Italiano Film · Released thru United Artists.

THE VAMPIRE AND THE BALLERINA

Italy, 1960
Director: Renato Polselli. Producer: Bruno Bolognesi.
Screenplay: Ernesto Gastaldi, Giuseppe Pellegrini, Renato Polselli.
Music: Aldo Piga. Cinematography: Angelo Baistrocchi.
Cast: Hélène Rémy, Tina Gloriani, Walter Brandi, Isarco Ravaioli,
John Turner [Gino Turini], Pier Ugo Gragnani, María Luisa Rolando.

"Why don't you tell us a story about vampires?" The most erotically charged of the initial Italian 1960s vampire films, **L'amante del vampiro** (Anglicized as the kitschier **The Vampire and the Ballerina**) proved to be a breakthrough film for director Renato Polselli whose proclivity for outrageous, *fumetti*-inspired sex and violence found its first ideal match here.

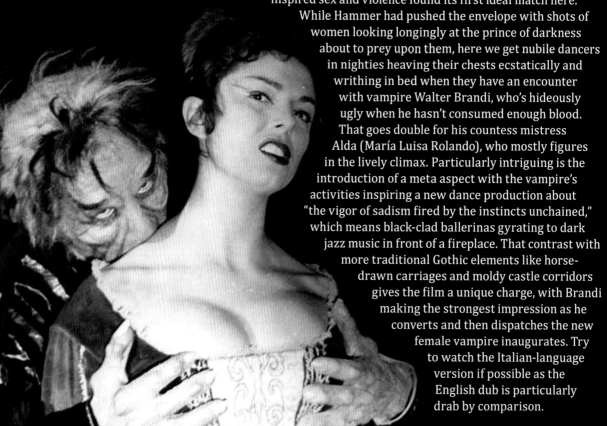

While Hammer had pushed the envelope with shots of women looking longingly at the prince of darkness about to prey upon them, here we get nubile dancers in nighties heaving their chests ecstatically and writhing in bed when they have an encounter with vampire Walter Brandi, who's hideously ugly when he hasn't consumed enough blood. That goes double for his countess mistress Alda (María Luisa Rolando), who mostly figures in the lively climax. Particularly intriguing is the introduction of a meta aspect with the vampire's activities inspiring a new dance production about "the vigor of sadism fired by the instincts unchained," which means black-clad ballerinas gyrating to dark jazz music in front of a fireplace. That contrast with more traditional Gothic elements like horse-drawn carriages and moldy castle corridors gives the film a unique charge, with Brandi making the strongest impression as he converts and then dispatches the new female vampire inaugurates. Try to watch the Italian-language version if possible as the English dub is particularly drab by comparison.

VAMPIRE MOVIES

HERCULES IN THE HAUNTED WORLD

Italy, 1961
Director: Mario Bava. Producer: Achille Piazzi.
Screenplay: Sandro Continenza, Mario Bava, Francesco Prosperi,
Duccio Tessari. Music: Armando Trovajoli.
Cinematography: Mario Bava.
Cast: Reg Park, Christopher Lee, Leonora Ruffo, George Ardisson,
Marisa Belli, Ida Galli [Evelyn Stewart].

After flirting with the idea of vampirism in his landmark proper
debut feature, **Black Sunday** (1960), Mario Bava explored it a bit
more directly with this wildly colorful sword and sandal fantasy.
Amid a spate of peculiar Continental productions, Christopher
Lee capitalizes on his sinister Dracula image as the villainous King Lico, who connives to send the strong
and heroic Hercules (Reg Park) to the underworld to save his true love. Along the way he encounters many
phantasmagorical threats, not least among them a squad of flying undead summoned from their tombs
by Lico (a sequence shown at the beginning of some prints). The bloodsucker factor depends on which
version of the film you see (and goes unmentioned on some language tracks) but either way the fiends are
so striking that this film was sometimes circulated under the title **Hercules vs. the Vampires** in countries
like Portugal, Austria, Belgium, France, and West Germany, with Lee's presence usually given the most
prominence to capitalize on the current Hammer Films frenzy. The film is also significant as Bava's first
feature in colour, using vivid lighting arrangements and inventive perspective tricks to make the film look
far more lavish than it is. That approach would serve him well when he made his next and most chilling
vampire film... but more on that in a moment.

THE WORLD OF THE VAMPIRES

Mexico, 1961
Director: Alfonso Corona Blake. Producer: Abel Salazar.
Screenplay: Alfredo Salazar. Music: Gustavo César Carrión.
Cinematography: Jack Draper.
Cast: Guillermo Murray, Silvia Fournier, Mauricio Garcés,
Erna Martha Bauman, José Baviera, Yolanda Margain.

Stepping outside the comfort zone of its two successful **El vampiro** films, Mexico went a little wider and wilder with this eccentric revenge potboiler originally released as **El mundo de los vampiros**. The irate Count Subotai (Guillermo Murray), who sports a particularly mean pair of fangs, tends to monologue about the unstoppable grudge he holds against the Colman family, whose descendants he intends to wipe off the earth. However, in a unique twist to vampire lore, he can be vanquished only by a special piece of music that works as a kind of exterminating incantation against the undead. Though the classic Universal influence can still be felt here (including the novelty of our vampire villain jamming away at an bone-constructed organ, **Phantom of the Opera** style), the inventive wrinkles in the usual vampire rules found here make this one stand out from the pack, and at least in its original Spanish-language form without the usual K. Gordon Murray English dubbing, this is one of the classiest Mexican horrors of its era. Complete with mutant bat servants, alluring vampire brides, enough skeletons to populate a dozen haunted houses, and cliffhanger scenarios like a deadly snake pit, this is prime south of the border pulp.

SANTO VS. THE VAMPIRE WOMEN

Mexico, 1962
Director: Alfonso Corona Blake.
Producer: Alberto López. Screenplay: Rafael García Travesi,
Alfonso Corona Blake. Music: Raul Lavista.
Cinematography: José Ortiz Ramos.
Cast: Santo, Lorena Velázquez, María Duval, Xavier Loyá,
Jaime Fernández, Augusto Benedico, Ofelia Montesco.

The silver-masked wrestling movie legend El Santo enjoyed one of the most lavish and memorable outings of his fifty-plus movie career with this seventh adventure, which places a strong emphasis from the outset on full-blooded supernatural horror as crusty-faced vampiress Tundra (Ofelia Montesco) awakens in her coffin and calls upon the lord of darkness to raise her undead sisters for a human blood banquet. Her main target is piano aficionado Diana (Maria Duval), part of a long-running bloodline of adversaries, but thankfully Santo is on hand to fulfill a prophecy foretelling his showdown with the forces of evil led by Queen Zorina (Lorena Velázquez). A big hit in its homeland, the film ensured the future of Santo's cinematic exploits and was one of the very few picked up by the busy K. Gordon Murray for an English-dubbed release (as **Samson vs. the Vampire Women**). Though the vampires take center stage here, to story also mixes in a bit of Satanism and even a werewolf sidekick who dons a mask to face off against Santo in the ring. Pure popcorn fun, the film would go on to earn a new legion of fans as a beloved 1995 installment of **Mystery Science Theater 3000**.

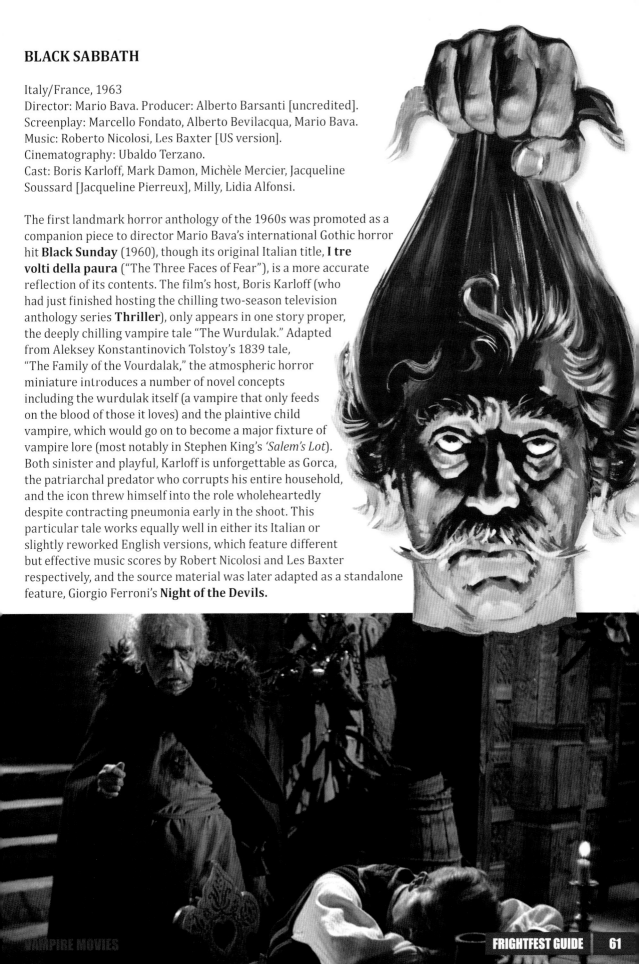

BLACK SABBATH

Italy/France, 1963
Director: Mario Bava. Producer: Alberto Barsanti [uncredited].
Screenplay: Marcello Fondato, Alberto Bevilacqua, Mario Bava.
Music: Roberto Nicolosi, Les Baxter [US version].
Cinematography: Ubaldo Terzano.
Cast: Boris Karloff, Mark Damon, Michèle Mercier, Jacqueline
Soussard [Jacqueline Pierreux], Milly, Lidia Alfonsi.

The first landmark horror anthology of the 1960s was promoted as a
companion piece to director Mario Bava's international Gothic horror
hit **Black Sunday** (1960), though its original Italian title, **I tre
volti della paura** ("The Three Faces of Fear"), is a more accurate
reflection of its contents. The film's host, Boris Karloff (who
had just finished hosting the chilling two-season television
anthology series **Thriller**), only appears in one story proper,
the deeply chilling vampire tale "The Wurdulak." Adapted
from Aleksey Konstantinovich Tolstoy's 1839 tale,
"The Family of the Vourdalak," the atmospheric horror
miniature introduces a number of novel concepts
including the wurdulak itself (a vampire that only feeds
on the blood of those it loves) and the plaintive child
vampire, which would go on to become a major fixture of
vampire lore (most notably in Stephen King's *'Salem's Lot*).
Both sinister and playful, Karloff is unforgettable as Gorca,
the patriarchal predator who corrupts his entire household,
and the icon threw himself into the role wholeheartedly
despite contracting pneumonia early in the shoot. This
particular tale works equally well in either its Italian or
slightly reworked English versions, which feature different
but effective music scores by Robert Nicolosi and Les Baxter
respectively, and the source material was later adapted as a standalone
feature, Giorgio Ferroni's **Night of the Devils.**

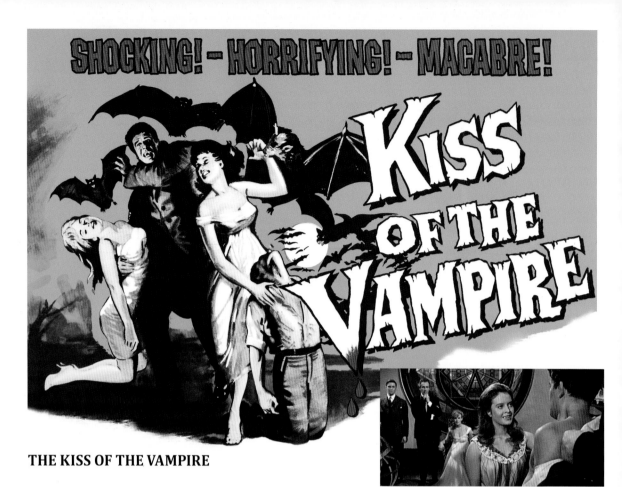

THE KISS OF THE VAMPIRE

UK, 1963
Director: Don Sharp. Producer: Anthony Hinds.
Screenplay: John Elder [Anthony Hinds].
Music: James Bernard. Cinematography: Alan Hume.
Cast: Clifford Evans, Edward de Souza, Noel Willman,
Jennifer Daniel, Barry Warren, Brian Oulton.

Hammer's first vampire film without a Dracula connection
also turned out to be one of its very best under the direction
of Don Sharp, a relatively new Australian filmmaker at
the time. The unusually tricky story concerns a stranded
honeymooning couple (Edward de Souza and Jennifer Daniel)
caught up in the macabre machinations of the aristocratic Dr.
Ravna (Noel Willman) and his vampire minions, including a
striking masquerade ball sequence that segues into a variation
on **The Lady Vanishes** (1938). James Bernard also provides
one of his most striking and restrained scores anchored by
a quasi-classical piano melody called "Vampire Rhapsody."
Featuring striking, expressionistic use of the colour purple and
surprisingly strong bursts of violence including a ferocious climactic bat attack, the film was considered
too strong for television later in the decade. Under the title **Kiss of Evil**, it lost most of its vampire elements
(including nearly the entire finale) and featured a jarring, newly-shot subplot about married villagers
and their daughter squabbling over Ravna's ball before delivering a baffling, cringeworthy conclusion
suggesting that women acting independently will only lead to wickedness. Fortunately, the original
theatrical version has remained the default one in more recent years, and this would be Hammer's only '60s
vampire one-off once Christopher Lee returned to the fold later in the decade.

THE BLOOD DRINKERS

Philippines, 1964
Director: Gerardo de Leon. Producer: Cirio H. Santiago.
Screenplay: Cesar Amigo. Cinematography: Felipe Sacdalan.
Cast: Ronald Remy, Amalia Fuentes, Eddie Fernandez,
Eva Montes, Celia Rodriguez, Renato Robles.

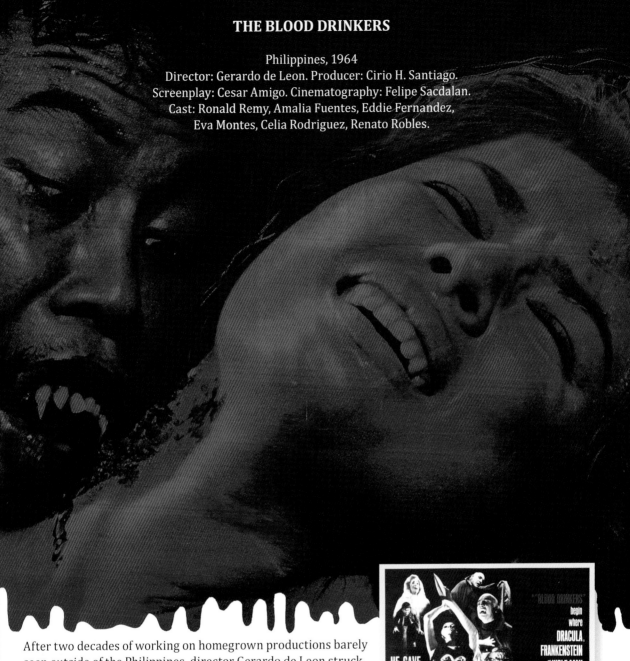

After two decades of working on homegrown productions barely seen outside of the Philippines, director Gerardo de Leon struck gold when he turned to horror with an uncredited spin on H.G. Wells' *The Island of Dr. Moreau* entitled **Terror Is a Man** (1959). This birth of the Filipino monster movie boom led to many projects by de Leon and compatriot Eddie Romero, with the early trailblazers released internationally by New York-based distribution outfit Hemisphere Pictures. The first hit Filipino vampire film, **The Blood Drinkers** (also released as **Vampire People**), takes its cues from years of digesting Universal and Hammer offerings to create the story of bald, sunglass-wearing Dr. Marco (Ronald Remy), who tries to save his dying beloved by finding a new blood supply from her sister (both played by Amalia Fuentes). Shot in a combination of color and cost-saving black-and-white film stock, it's a fog-enshrouded love letter to Gothic cinema with a heavy focus on local flavor (that nighttime serenade!) and the customs of local Catholicism, the latter playing heavily in the colorful nocturnal climax. As with the majority of Filipino cinema, this film was never safely preserved at home and now exists only in its English-language variant prepared for export.

THE LAST MAN ON EARTH

Italy/USA, 1964
Directors: Sidney Salkow (US version), Ubaldo Ragona (Italian version). Producer: Robert L. Lippert. Screenplay: US version: Logan Swanson [Richard Matheson], William F. Leicester. Italian version: Furio M. Monetti, Ubaldo Ragona. Music: Paul Sawtell, Bert Shefter. Cinematography: Franco Delli Colli.
Cast: Vincent Price, Franca Bettoia, Emma Danieli, Giacomo Rossi Stuart, Umberto Raho, Christi Courtland.

The path to realizing Richard Matheson's apocalyptic vampire novel *I Am Legend* on the big screen for the first time was a strange one, with Matheson initially going to England for six weeks to adapt it for Hammer Films at the behest of Anthony Hinds. Censorship concerns forced them to sell the project to American producer Robert Lippert, who announced the film would be directed by Fritz Lang. Instead the enterprise ended up with American TV director Sidney Salkow with a dissatisfied Matheson insisting on being credited by his pen name, Logan Swanson. Later a San Fernando Valley film teacher, Salkow brought aboard Vincent Price, the star of his previous film, the Nathaniel Hawthorne anthology **Twice-Told Tales** (1963), to play Robert Morgan, the sole unaffected human left in a city populated by the living dead. The film was shot in Rome with an awkwardly dubbed Italian cast apart from Price who noted, "The problem was that it was supposed to take place in Los Angeles and if there is a city in the world that doesn't look like Los Angeles, it's Rome." Despite divergent opinions about the finished result, this remains the most faithful screen version of the novel to date and was followed by the far less vampiric **The Omega Man** (1971), which features Charlton Heston fending off the infected who are now albinos suffering from a vicious blood disorder. Attempts to mount a third version began in the mid-'90s including an extensively developed attempt directed by Ridley Scott and starring Arnold Schwarzenegger, but it finally came to fruition as **I Am Legend** (2007) with a committed Will Smith battling extremely awkward CGI monstrosities closer to the pseudo-zombie contagion threats popularized by **28 Days Later** (2002).

VAMPIRE OF THE OPERA

Italy, 1964
Director: Renato Polselli. Screenplay: Ernesto Gastaldi, Giuseppe Pellegrini, Renato Polselli. Music: Aldo Piga. Cinematography: Ugo Brunelli.
Cast: Marc Marian [Marco Mariani], John McDouglas [Giuseppe Addobbati], Barbara Hawards, Albert Archet [Alberto Archetti], Carla Cavalli, Boris Notarenko [Aldo Nicodemi].

Following the international success of **The Vampire and the Ballerina** (1960), director Renato Polselli made his belated follow-up by pushing the level of hysteria through the roof for another saga about a dance troupe falling afoul of a member of the undead, in this case a vampire named Stefano (Giuseppe Addobbati) revived from his coffin slumber in an abandoned theater. Originally entitled **Il mostro dell'opera**, the film was plagued by financial issues during its long path to completion over three years which may account for the feverish, ragged nature of the final product including fang-gnashing nightmare sequences, jazzy dance numbers including the wildest dance of death finale this side of **Suspiria** (2018), a daring-at-the-time sapphic love scene (and implied threesome), and vampire-wielding pitchfork mayhem. Despite the title, this film bears no signs of inspiration from Gaston Leroux's *The Phantom of the Opera*; instead the film is a loose framework for peculiar visuals like skeleton-suited men leaping around with flaming torches and a fog-enshrouded torture chamber filled with manacled dancers. The film marked a turning point of sorts for Polselli, who dispensed with traditional narrative more in his subsequent films including, most famously, **Delirium** (1972) and **The Reincarnation of Isabel** (1973) at the expense of a commercially successful career.

DO YOU DARE IMAGINE WHAT IT WOULD BE LIKE TO BE ...THE LAST MAN ON EARTH...OR THE LAST WOMAN?

Alive among the lifeless...alone among the crawling creatures of evil that make the night hideous with their inhuman craving!

VINCENT PRICE

STARRING AS

The Last Man on Earth

CO-STARRING

FRANCA BETTOIA · EMMA DANIELI · GIACOMO ROSSI-STUART · Directed by SIDNEY SALKOW · Produced by ROBERT L. LIPPERT

Screenplay by LOGAN SWANSON & WILLIAM F. LEICESTER · From the novel "I AM LEGEND" by RICHARD MATHESON · AN AMERICAN INTERNATIONAL PICTURE

BILLY THE KID VERSUS DRACULA

USA, 1966
Director: William Beaudine.
Producer: Carroll Case.
Screenplay: Carl K. Hittleman.
Music: Raoul Kraushaar.
Cinematography: Lothrop B. Worth.
Cast: John Carradine, Chuck Courtney, Melinda Plowman
[Melinda Casey], Virginia Christine, Walter Janovitz, Bing Russell.

The small but memorable strain of horror westerns produced its most notorious entry (on the basis of its title alone) with this very cheap supernatural oater featuring John Carradine donning his Dracula cape again in a throwback to his Universal monster days. Something's amiss in a western town involving the bat-filed silver mine, slaughtered cattle, and the hypnotic James Underhill (Carradine) who just rode into town on a stagecoach; now it's up to Billy the Kid (Chuck Courtney) to face off against the menace who has designs on his fiancée, Betty (Melinda Plowman). Rapidly shot by Hollywood workhorse William Beaudine back to back with co-feature **Jesse James Meets Frankenstein's Daughter** (1966), this film was frequently badmouthed by indiscriminate workhorse Carradine (which is saying something) but offers plenty of novelty value with its mishmash of classic vampire and gunslinger tropes—not to mention dialogue like "This is the 19th century, not the middle ages!" and twangy lessons about driving stakes through vampires' hearts. This was also the debut feature for young Howard K. "Hawk" Koch as a producer's assistant, years before he became an AMPAS President and ushered in films like **Wayne's World** (1992) and **The Keep** (1983). Only in Hollywood...

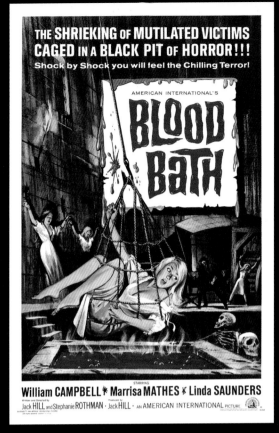

THE SHRIEKING OF MUTILATED VICTIMS CAGED IN A BLACK PIT OF HORROR!!!
Shock by Shock you will feel the Chilling Terror!

AMERICAN INTERNATIONAL'S

BLOOD BATH

STARRING
William CAMPBELL * Marrisa MATHES * Linda SAUNDERS

Written and Directed by Jack HILL and Stephanie ROTHMAN · Produced by Jack HILL · AN AMERICAN INTERNATIONAL PICTURE

BLOOD BATH

USA, 1966
Directors: Jack Hill, Stephanie Rothman.
Producer: Jack Hill. Screenplay: Jack Hill,
Stephanie Rothman. Music: Mark Lowry [uncredited].
Cinematography: Alfred Taylor.
Cast: William Campbell, Marissa Mathes, Linda Saunders
[Lori Saunders], Sandra Knight, Karl Schanzer, Biff Elliot.

No other vampire film has a lineage as utterly baffling as this patchwork creation originally shown to audiences as **Blood Bath** and then reworked into a rather different beast for TV broadcast as **Track of the Vampire**. Both sprang from remnants of a Yugoslavian art caper film called **Operation Titian** and its first American reworking from Roger Corman as **Portrait in Terror**, with various cooks including Jack Hill and Stephanie Rothman brought in to rework the material into the story of a Venice, California vampire artist (William Campbell) who murders his models and dunks them in melted wax when he isn't busy pursuing the reincarnation of his lost love. Rothman came up with the vampire stalking bits (using a rather different stand-in for Campbell), while additional scenes including a very protracted beach dance sequence were added to bring the film up to required TV length. In any form it's a fascinating jigsaw puzzle of a production with some striking location work and its fair share of eerie, macabre visuals thanks to Campbell's sinister beatnik appearance and the wax-coated corpses reminiscent of Corman's **A Bucket of Blood** (1959). Eventually all four versions were finally assembled for home video consumption by Arrow Video, though viewing all of them in quick succession is only recommended for the bravest of souls and could lead to permanent psychological damage.

CURSE OF THE VAMPIRES

Philippines, 1966
Director: Gerardo de Leon.
Producer: Amalia Muhlach [Amalia Fuentes].
Screenplay: Ben Feleo, Pierre L. Salas.
Music: Tito Arevalo. Cinematography: Mike Accion.
Cast: Amalia Fuentes, Romeo Vasquez,
Eddie Garcia, Johnny Monteiro,
Rosario del Pilar, Mary Walter.

Following the success of **The Blood Drinkers** (1964), director Gerardo de Leon and several of his cast members returned with this full-color refinement about the secret bloodthirsty curse upon the wealthy Escudero family, a Spanish-bred dynasty in the late 1800s. Its two youngest members are now of marrying age but fall under the influence of their parents, one of them dying and the other an outright creature of the night chained in the basement. The Gothic and religious elements remain at the forefront here, but the canvas is broadened with an approach closer to Roger Corman's Edgar Allan Poe films right down to

naming one key character Leonore, a letter removed from Lenore, and the device of having a primal, dangerous matriarch locked away for fear that she might contaminate the bloodline. Like its predecessor, this film (which was also circulated as **Blood of the Vampires** to cash in on Hemisphere Pictures' popular Blood Island cycle) proved to be a popular success on the drive-in circuit and provided a strong showcase for actor Eddie Garcia, also seen in **Beast of Blood** (1970), who undergoes an unusual character arc here and has now racked up one of the largest filmographies in Filipino cinema history.

DRACULA PRINCE OF DARKNESS

UK, 1966
Director: Terence Fisher.
Producer: Anthony Nelson Keys. Screenplay: John
Sansom [Jimmy Sangster]. Music: James Bernard.
Cinematography: Michael Reed.
Cast: Christopher Lee, Barbara Shelley,
Andrew Keir, Francis Matthews, Suzan Farmer,
Charles Tingwell, Philip Latham.

Christopher Lee's belated return to his most famous role as Count Dracula eight years after the groundbreaking **Dracula** (1958) finds him in fine hissing form, even with a relatively limited amount of screen time and no proper dialogue. Director Terence Fisher and writer Jimmy Sangster take the reins once again, this time in expansive Techniscope and delivering a particularly gory method of vampire resurrection here involving a slaughterhouse-style throat slashing and a sopping red reconstitution from Dracula's ashes. Though present to a degree before, religion takes a front seat here for the first time in the form of a priest (Andrew Keir) tasked with stopping the vampire menace in its tracks via particularly brutal means when two couples fall afoul of a plot by Dracula's manservant Klove (Philip Latham) to revive his master. Also noteworthy is the presence of Suzan Farmer as the default heroine, Diana, who is more proactive and shaded than usual for the era. However, the show is easily stolen by one of Hammer's finest stars, the auburn-haired Barbara Shelley, who could embody the conflict between the carnal and the repressive better than anyone – and sports a particularly fierce pair of fangs before her unforgettable (and surprisingly anti-patriarchal) final scene. The film proved to be a rousing success as part of Hammer's active partnership at the time with 20th Century Fox, ensuring that the Count's watery fate in this film would be far from his cinematic swan song.

Die Schlangengrube und das Pendel

BLOOD OF THE VIRGINS

Argentina, 1967
Director: Emilio Vieyra. Producer: Orestes Trucco.
Screenplay: Raúl Zorrilla [Emilio Vieyra]. Music: Víctor Buchino. Cinematography: Aníbal González Paz.
Cast: Ricardo Bauleo, Susana Beltrán, Gloria Prat, Walter Kliche, Rolo Puente, Emilio Vieyra.

Buenos Aires-born filmmaker and onetime actor Emilio Vieyra enjoyed a prolific career in a number of genres, but his international reputation will always be tied to a trio of outrageous sexy horror films starting with the lurid **Placer sangriento** (1967), a.k.a. **Feast of Flesh**, and continuing with the infamous **La venganza del sexo** (released in 1969 but shot earlier), which was spiced up in the United States as **The Curious Dr. Humpp**. The last of these to go into production was this flamboyant vampire saga, domestically titled **Sangre de virgenes**, which earned a theatrical release in Canada of all places in 1969. Taking advantage of the Spanish-language appetite for horror films that couldn't be made under Spain's restrictive Franco regime, this outing is a smorgasbord of go-go dancing teens, animated credits, a pair of blood-drinking undead lovers, and a substitution of seagulls for bats in its vampire lore, a tactic also adopted soon after by Jess Franco in multiple films. The striking Argentinian Alps locations also make for a refreshing change of pace for this tale of tourist youngsters terrorized by the forces of darkness, coupled with enough flesh-baring sex scenes to get the film banned in its native country.

THE FEARLESS VAMPIRE KILLERS

UK, 1967
Director: Roman Polanski. Producer: Gene Gutowski.
Screenplay: Roman Polanski. Music: Christopher Komeda
[Krzysztof Komeda]. Cinematography: Douglas Slocombe.
Cast: Jack MacGowran, Roman Polanski, Alfie Bass, Jessie Robins,
Sharon Tate, Ferdy Mayne.

Any doubts about acclaimed Polish filmmaker Roman Polanski's twisted sense of humor were quickly erased with the release of his fourth feature film and his first for a major studio. Half broad comedy and half chilling fairy tale, this intricate, snowbound ode to classic European and American horror films stars Polanski himself as Alfred, the jittery sidekick to an elderly vampire hunter, Professor Abronsius (Jack MacGowran). Every role here is vividly cast including Polanski's future wife Sharon Tate as the fetching village girl Sarah and a plummy Ferdy Mayne as the chief vampire, Count von Krolock, while gifted and tragically short-lived Polish jazz composer Krzysztof Komeda contributes a wonderfully vertiginous score that anticipates his iconic work on Polanski's **Rosemary's Baby** (1968). Comic embellishments involving Jewish and gay vampires were cutting edge for the time (to say nothing of the surprisingly apocalyptic ending), perhaps to the film's commercial detriment as it was heavily cut and redubbed for the American market by MGM (who also changed the film's original title from **Dance of the Vampires**). The restored version of the film has since become the standard, ensuring a loyal cult following and an opulent, idiosyncratic musical stage version launched in 1997 by Polanski and Jim Steinman that, like its inspiration, ended up reaching the United States in a radically butchered, degraded version of its original self with a fanged Michael Crawford howling "Total Eclipse of the Heart" to confused Broadway patrons.

THE LIVING CORPSE

Pakistan, 1967
Director: Khwaja Sarfraz. Producer: Abdul Baqi.
Screenplay: Naseem Rizwani. Music: Tassaduq Hussain.
Cinematography: Nabi Ahmed, Irshad Bhatti, Raza Mir.
Cast: Yasmeen Shaukat, Deeba Begum, Habibur Rehman,
Asad Bukhari, Allauddin, Nasreen, Rehan.

The world's only musical Pakistani adaptation of *Dracula*
is just as astonishing as it sounds. Originally titled
Zinda Laash and informally referred to as **Dracula in
Pakistan**, the stylish and still effective black-and-white
production gives its vampire villain (now called Tabani)
a Dr. Jekyll-inspired backstory as a scientist dabbling
in an immortality potion that backfires disastrously
by turning him into an undead fiend. From there the
action most closely follows the 1958 Hammer version, albeit with new character names and a batch of
peppy song and dance numbers (don't miss the groovy vampire bride interpretive dance scene) that were
likely instrumental in helping the film barely skirt by the local anti-horror censors, earning the country's
first "Adults Only" rating. In the role of Tabani, established stage and screen actor Rehan sports a truly
impressive set of vampire choppers thanks to multiple sets imported from Germany and customized by a
local dentist. Despite its box office success at the time (bucking great resistance from exhibitors who found
the project distasteful) and its landmark status at Pakistan's first successful horror release, the film was
considered lost for several decades until it was resuscitated for home video in 2003.

A TASTE OF BLOOD

USA, 1967
Director: Herschell Gordon Lewis.
Producer: Herschell Gordon Lewis.
Screenplay: Donald Stanford.
Music: Larry Wellington.
Cinematography: Andy Romanoff.
Cast: Bill Rogers, Elizabeth Wilkinson
[Elizabeth Lee], Thomas Wood [William
Kerwin], Lawrence Tobin, Ted Schell,
Otto Schlessinger.

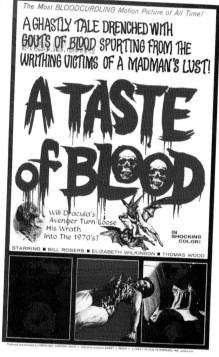

Made during the busiest frenzy in his entire career, director Herschell Gordon Lewis's only vampire film is just one of six features he cranked out in 1967 around the Miami, Florida area; at just under two hours, it's also his lengthiest effort and was, at the time, the longest vampire film ever released. Bouncing back and forth between Miami and a (very unconvincing) England, the story charts the odyssey of average guy John Stone (Bill Rogers) who turns into an undead avenger after consuming a shipment of brandy tainted with the blood of Dracula himself. Apart from the notable lack of intentional humour (a quality inherent in the script by Donald "Doc" Stanford devised as an overt sequel to Bram Stoker's *Dracula*), the usual Lewis trademarks are all here including a fixation on gaudy carpeting and furniture, a role for **Blood Feast** (1963) star William Kerwin, gobs of vivid stage blood, and even an outrageous cameo by Lewis himself sporting a very amusing quasi-Cockney accent that makes Dick Van Dyke's sound completely authentic by comparison. Though not for all, ahem, tastes due to Lewis's pacing and budgetary quirks, the colorful saga is notable as one of the earliest examples of the depiction of vampirism as a contagion and for the affliction's unique role as a disruptive force in the already tenuous relationship between our married protagonist and his wife, Helene (Elizabeth Lee).

DRACULA HAS RISEN FROM THE GRAVE

UK, 1968
Director: Freddie Francis. Producer: Aida Young.
Screenplay: John Elder [Anthony Hinds].
Music: James Bernard. Cinematography: Arthur Grant.
Cast: Christopher Lee, Rupert Davies, Veronica Carlson,
Barbara Ewing, Barry Andrews, Ewan Hooper.

The first Hammer Dracula outing without director Terence Fisher
(who was injured in an auto accident during preproduction)
fell into the hands of Oscar-winning cinematographer Freddie
Francis, who had been with the studio since shooting **Never
Take Sweets from a Stranger** (1960). Also known as a director
for his numerous Amicus contributions, Francis brings a potent
fairy tale approach here (especially the beautifully rendered
rooftop scenes) with Dracula (Christopher Lee as usual) now
donning a pair of fiery red contact lenses and cinematographer
Arthur Grant suffusing all of the vampire's scenes with an
unearthly red-amber hue in the style of Japanese horror films
at the time. The focus on religious faith (or lack thereof) is the
driving force here with the devout Rupert Davies locking horns
over the future of daughter Veronica Carlson with her atheist
baker boyfriend, Barry Andrews; no points for guessing how it
all turns out. The generational tensions that inform much of the
series are more clearly defined here than ever with Andrews
as the first of a string of youth culture stand-ins, allowing older
and younger viewers to project their own views onto the story
until the unambiguous Christianity-affirming finale, a tactic also
found in Hammer's **The Devil Rides Out** (also 1968). Incredibly,
the film managed to earn the very first G (all audiences) rating
in America despite a heavy amount of stage blood including a
memorable bell tower opener and Dracula's juiciest demise to
date. This would mark the end of Francis' tenure with Hammer,
for whom he also directed such films as **Paranoiac** (1963) and
The Evil of Frankenstein (1964), but just the beginning of his
increasingly bizarre contributions to vampire cinema.

THE RAPE OF THE VAMPIRE

France, 1968
Director: Jean Rollin.
Producers: Jean Rollin, Sam Selsky.
Screenplay: Jean Rollin.
Music: Yvon Géraud, François Tusques.
Cinematography: Guy Leblond.
Cast: Solange Pradel, Bernard Letrou, Ursule Pauly, Nicole Romain, Catherine Deville, Marquis Polho [Marco Pauly], Jacqueline Sieger.

At the height of the Paris riots in the Spring of 1968, a 29-year-old film editor, actor, and former theatre director named Jean Rollin threw gasoline onto the fire with his first feature film, **Le viol du vampire** or **The Rape of the Vampire**. Presented in black-and-white in two segments like the classic adventure serials Rollin adored, the film sports a pair of very loose narratives about a psychiatrist entangled in the possible delusions of a quartet of bloodsucking-obsessed sisters and a revolution brewing under the dominion of a bloodthirsty vampire queen played by the striking Jacqueline Sieger. Although critics accustomed to the more reputable French New Wave were

appalled at the time (especially given France's very meagre homegrown horror history to that point), the film found Rollin already in firm control of his cinematic trademarks like lonely beaches, beguiling young women of few words, stylized and borderline hypnotized performances, and a slow, meditative pace that becomes more hypnotic as the film progresses. Begun as a short film but expanded to encompass two stories to bring it up to feature length, Rollin's debut inaugurated a career that would yield some of the horror genre's most adventurous and lyrical vampire offerings.

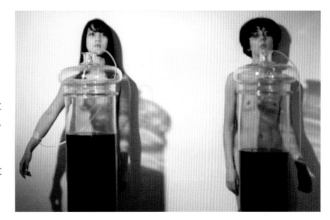

THE BODY BENEATH

UK, 1970
Director: Andy Milligan.
Screenplay: Andy Milligan.
Cinematography: Andy Milligan
[uncredited].
Cast: Gavin Reed, Jackie Skarvellis,
Berwick Kaler, Susan Heard,
Richmond Ross, Emma Jones.

Staten Island-based film and theater writer-director Andy Milligan was in the midst of a rapid six-film run in the U.K. when he made his one vampire-focused film, shot in such familiar London locations as Hampstead Heath and Highgate Cemetery. Divisive to be sure but highly endearing to those on the right wavelength, Milligan's 16mm wonders are quirky miniatures filled with theatrical dialogue, harsh lighting, bountiful costumes (designed by Milligan himself), softcore groping, and splashes of stage blood, all of which are found in abundance here. A "tomato juice"-sipping vampire clan run by the gregarious Reverend Alexander Algernon Ford (Gavin Reed) uses its recent relocation to an English abbey to resolve its growing inbreeding problems by targeting North American relatives, culminating in an extended psychedelic climax that may be the most ambitious sequence of the director's career. The story has fun dabbling with vampire conventions including unorthodox use of blood transfusions, new rules involving daylight exposure, and an amusing wrinkle by turning the vampire's familiar into a hulking hunchback played by Milligan repertory player Berwick Kaler. Despite his penchant for monster movies, Milligan would only revisit vampirism once more as an element in his berserk monster rally **Blood** (1973), shot back on his home turf.

COUNT DRACULA

West Germany/Italy/Spain, 1970
Director: Jess Franco.
Producer: Harry Alan Towers.
Screenplay: Peter Welbeck [Harry
Alan Towers]. Music: Bruno Nicolai.
Cinematography: Manuel Merino,
Luciano Trasatti.
Cast: Christopher Lee, Herbert Lom,
Klaus Kinski, Maria Rohm, Frederick
Williams, Soledad Miranda.

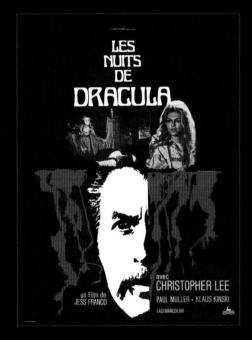

Christopher Lee's oft-stated ambition to portray an accurate rendition of Bram Stoker's Dracula character seemed to be within his grasp when Spanish filmmaker Jesús "Jess" Franco approached him for this version portraying the Count as an older, gray-haired nobleman who becomes younger over the course of the film as his bloodlust is sated. The resulting Barcelona-shot film, made at the end of Franco's fruitful association with producer Harry Allan Towers, was met with a muted response due to its deliberate pacing and very restrained bloodletting; it does have its charms though thanks to a stable of regular Franco actors including Herbert Lom, Soledad Miranda, Maria Rohm, Fred Williams, and Jack Taylor, not to mention a bug-eyed Klaus Kinski (by some reports having no idea he was in a vampire

film) offering his own take on Renfield. Reliable composer Bruno Nicolai provides able support with his jangling score, and as with many Franco productions, this one has benefited from considerable reassessment in recent years now that it can be placed more logically in context with the director's larger body of work. Perhaps more fascinating than the film itself is the feature-length "documentary" compiled from its monochrome behind-the-scenes footage shot by Pere Portabella, **Vampir Cuadecuc** (1971), an experimental repurposing of the Dracula narrative freed from the restrictions of dialogue and period setting.

COUNT YORGA, VAMPIRE

USA, 1970
Director: Bob Kelljan. Producer: Michael Macready.
Screenplay: Bob Kelljan. Music: Bill Marx.
Cinematography: Arch Archambault.
Cast: Robert Quarry, Roger Perry, Michael Murphy,
Michael Macready, Donna Anders, Judith Lang.

The 1970s got its first major original vampire courtesy of Count Yorga in two films released by AIP and starring American actor Robert Quarry, who was on track for a career as a new horror star until he was injured by a drunk driver. Originally conceived as a softcore erotic film but wisely changed along the way (the original negative still bears the odd title **The Loves of Count Iorga** and sexploitation star Marsha Jordan even makes an appearance), this modern day tale charts the supernatural consequences unleashed by the predatory count, who poses as a mystic and targets a group of Southern Californians including Michael Murphy and Donna Anders. Just gruesome enough to become a hit on the drive-in circuit, the film works up an effective sense of unease on the way to its chilling final shot. The film encountered significant resistance from the MPAA at the time and was released in a toned-down version, though more recent home video versions are complete. The film was quickly followed by the more violent and arguably superior **The Return of Count Yorga** (1971), with Quarry reprising his role for a nightmarish distillation of the American mindset after the turbulence of the late '60s including the crimes of the Manson Family (who are explicitly evoked in a vampire home invasion sequence). Both films effectively tap into the growing fascination with the occult that would become a major part of pop culture throughout the decade, proving that AIP could continue to flourish in a post-Roger Corman era.

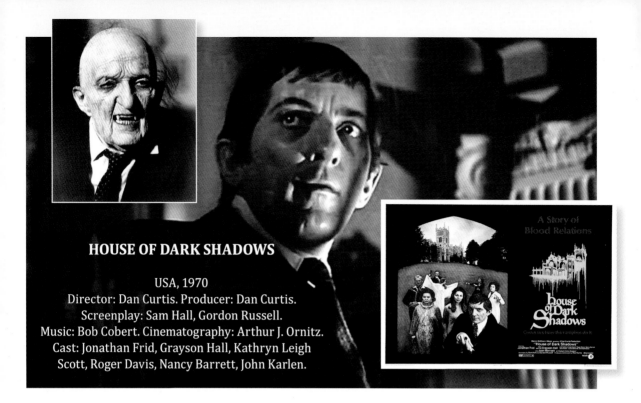

HOUSE OF DARK SHADOWS

USA, 1970
Director: Dan Curtis. Producer: Dan Curtis.
Screenplay: Sam Hall, Gordon Russell.
Music: Bob Cobert. Cinematography: Arthur J. Ornitz.
Cast: Jonathan Frid, Grayson Hall, Kathryn Leigh
Scott, Roger Davis, Nancy Barrett, John Karlen.

Even after a decade of Hammer titles, audiences were shocked when the goriest American vampire film to date turned out to be this fast and loose big-screen version of the popular daytime horror soap opera, **Dark Shadows**, which was still airing at the time. Series creator Dan Curtis and most of the principal cast appear here for a retelling of the story of centuries-old Barnabas Collins (Jonathan Frid), who's freed from his coffin imprisonment and wreaks havoc on his descendants. A time travel tangent on the TV series permitted the major players to take time off and appear here, with their storylines radically condensed and altered to sometimes jolting effect. A high body count and gruesome makeup effects by Dick Smith gave the film a very different feel from its small-screen source, with evocative real locations in upstate New York giving it far more production value as well. Though the film was financially successful, the TV series would end a year later and scuttle plans for an intended sequel with Barnabas; instead a very troubled non-vampire sequel, **Night of Dark Shadows** (1971), was quickly shot and released in a highly compromised version before fan interest died out. However, the saga of the Collins family has continued to live on including a TV series revival, numerous audio productions, and a flawed, comedic remake by Tim Burton in 2012 with Johnny Depp and fleeting cameos by the surviving original cast members.

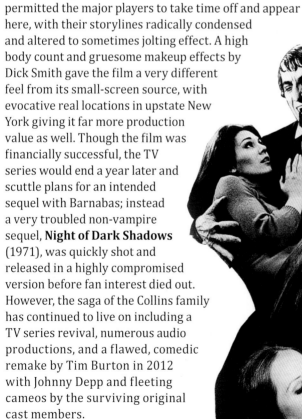

JONATHAN

West Germany, 1970
Director: Hans W. Geissendörfer. Producer: Hellmut Haffner.
Screenplay: Hans W. Geissendörfer. Music: Roland Kovac.
Cinematography: Robby Müller.
Cast: Jürgen Jung, Hans-Dieter Jendreyko, Paul Albert
Krumm, Hertha von Walther, Oskar von Schab, Ilona Grübel.

Though it boasts a nod to Bram Stoker in the opening
credits, this anti-fascist vampire allegory is a wholly
original work with some not terribly subtle commentary
about the nightmare that had plagued Germany during
World War II and the more current student protest
movement of 1968. Here we have a stylized 1700s German
town where vampires, now resistant to sunlight, have
become the ruling class complete with black-clad enforcers
and a coterie of young girls in pink
dresses and flower garlands.
As dogs dine on
human
remains
and rebels are shot in the back, Jonathan (Jürgen Jung)
is enlisted to take out the leader at a very high cost.
Mixing visual elements from fairy tales and
classic horror films, **Jonathan** was barely
shown outside of Germany apart from
minimal arthouse play up until 1973
and was notoriously difficult to
see for years. In its native country
it was a solid calling card for its
Bavarian-born, first-time writer
and director, 29-year-old Hans
W. Geissendörfer, who went on
to direct the Oscar-nominated
The Glass Cell (1978). It's also
shockingly gory at times, including
a small amount of real animal
violence that ensures this will never
get an uncut release in the U.K.

LES DISTRIBUTEURS ASSOCIÈS (films modernes) présent

THE NUDE VAMPIRE

France, 1970
Director: Jean Rollin. Producer: Jean Lavie.
Screenplay: Jean Rollin, Serge Moati.
Music: Yvon Gérault.
Cinematography: Jean-Jacques Renon.
Cast: Christine François [Caroline Cartier],
Oliver Martin [Olivier Rollin], Maurice
Lemaître, Bernard Musson, Jean Aron,
Ursule Pauly.

The same year directors like Claude Chabrol, Jean-Pierre Melville and Eric Rohmer were catapulting the French New Wave even further into the mainstream with some of their most successful films, director Jean Rollin was forging new ground of his own with the eye-scorching colors of **La vampire nue** or **The Nude Vampire**, a lurid pulp supernatural romance inspired by classic serials and comics. This was only Rollin's second feature, made in the wake of the stir caused by his experimental monochrome debut **The Rape of the Vampire** (1968); in many respects it feels like his first proper narrative film as it follows a sect of scientists holed up in a castle unleash nocturnal perils and exotic dance routines on the area, with a star-crossed love story at the center involving the naïve aristocrat Pierre (Olivier Martin) and an enigmatic young woman (Caroline Cartier) who might be the title character. Almost a candy-colored fashion show as much as a feature film, this fantasia of leopard skin and long fingernails is unmistakably a Rollin creation thanks to its lonely beach finale, aesthetic female nudity, and surreal use of animal masks. Also key here is the introduction of the mute and wildly photogenic real-life twins Catherine and Marie-Pierre Castel, who would become mascots in future Rollin films (either together or apart) as well as brief fixtures on the French adult film scene.

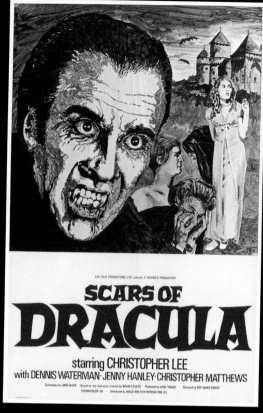

SCARS OF DRACULA

UK, 1970
Director: Roy Ward Baker. Producer: Aida Young.
Screenplay: John Elder [Anthony Hinds].
Music: James Bernard. Cinematography: Moray Grant.
Cast: Christopher Lee, Dennis Waterman, Jenny Hanley,
Christopher Matthews, Patrick Troughton, Michael Gwynn.

After the collapse of its long-running deals with American studios including Warner Bros., Hammer Film Productions found its budgets slashed considerably in the early '70s as it embarked on a batch of EMI Films projects. One of the first of these was **Scars of Dracula,** which dispenses with any previous series continuity and has Christopher Lee's undead count revived by a blood-slobbering rubber bat. Plot-wise this is much more simplistic than usual with Dracula terrorizing a village and two brothers in particular, but the violence quotient is amped up considerably here under the hand of director Roy Ward Baker including beatings, stabbings, post-mortem dismemberment, and the very gory aftermath of a mass bat attack. Critics were not amused with the film feeling particularly retrograde in the wake of more modern horror thrills coming out of Hollywood and the rest of Europe, and even today it tends to get lumped in the lower tier of the Hammer Gothics (more due to the obvious cost cutting than the gore). However, fans can still enjoy a larger, more active part for Lee than usual and the chance to see many members of the old gang (including Michael Ripper) together again one last time before Hammer hurtled Dracula into the 20th century.

VAMPIRE MOVIES

TASTE THE BLOOD OF DRACULA

UK, 1970
Director: Peter Sasdy. Producer: Aida Young.
Screenplay: John Elder [Anthony Hinds].
Music: James Bernard. Cinematography: Arthur Grant.
Cast: Christopher Lee, Geoffrey Keen, Gwen Watford,
Linda Hayden, Peter Sallis, Ralph Bates, John Carson,
Anthony Corlan [Anthony Higgins].

Made in the wake of Hammer's years-long partnership with the collapsed Warner Bros.-Seven Arts, this final Dracula salvo from the now transformed Warner Bros. stable stampedes away with the generational conflict from the prior **Dracula Has Risen from the Grave** into highly unsettling new territory. Here a trio of hypocritical upper-class gentlemen (Geoffrey Keen, Peter Sallis and John Carson) exploring the

extremes of London's seedy underground are lured by the dangerous Lord Courtley (Ralph Bates, in his Hammer debut) into a diabolical ceremony reviving Christopher Lee's Count Dracula, who repays his resurrectionists by putting them on an immediate death list that sends shock waves through their families. The first proper feature film directed by Hungarian-born Peter Sasdy inverts the previous Dracula entry by positing the older generation as fundamentally corrupt or weak, with the youth providing the only glimmer of hope against the forces of darkness. Considerably less gruesome than the two Hammer Draculas bookending it, this one instead pushes sexuality more aggressively in a lengthy Aubrey Beardsley-inspired brothel sequence whose unclothed activities were initially censored from circulating prints. The stylish and atmospheric film was originally written to spotlight Courtley as a vengeful vampire with Lee's Dracula nowhere to be found, but commercial demands prevailed and Lee was shoehorned in to count off the fates of his victims and glower inside an abandoned church.

VALERIE AND HER WEEK OF WONDERS

Czechoslovakia, 1970
Director: Jaromil Jires. Producer: Jirí Becka.
Screenplay: Ester Krumbachová, Jaromil Jires.
Music: Lubos Fiser, Jan Klusák.
Cinematography: Jan Curík.
Cast: Jaroslava Schallerová, Helena Anýzová,
Petr Kopriva, Jirí Prýmek, Jan Klusák,
Libuse Komancová.

Faithfully adapted from a 1935 surrealist novel by Vítezslav Nezval, this landmark of the late Czechoslovak New Wave is a heady brew of coming-of-age story, celebration of young female sexuality, delicate folk horror and fantastically freaky vampire imagery. The country was still unsettled in the wake of the Prague Spring of 1968 when director Jaromil Jireš mounted this production on the heels of his highly controversial film, **The Joke** (1969). Young Valerie (Jaroslava Schallerová) is the glue that holds his perverse daydream together as her small village life is upended by the arrival of a leering, sinister fiend (Jirí Prýmek) who seems to be converting her family to the dark side. More of a picaresque look at the process of passing into adolescence than a traditional horror film, **Valerie and Her Week of Wonders** (originally **Valerie a týden divů**)

draws from the same well of visual inspiration as decades' worth of European genre films from Murnau to Bava but veers in a radically different direction. Rather than providing a traditional monster-vanquishing finale, it's ultimately a sweet-natured box of cinematic treasures that benefits greatly from repeated viewings. The film also earned a new lease on life in 2007 when it toured internationally with new live musical accompaniment by its own specially formed group, The Valerie Project.

VAMPIRE MOVIES

THE VAMPIRE DOLL

Japan, 1970
Director: Michio Yamamoto.
Producers: Fumio Tanaka,
Tomoyuki Tanaka.
Screenplay: Hiroshi Nagano,
Ei Ogawa.
Music: Riichirô Manabe.
Cinematography: Kazutami Hara.
Cast: Kayo Matsuo, Akira Nakao,
Atsuo Nakamura, Yukiko Kobayashi,
Yôko Minakaze, Kaku Takashina.

This belated bid for a Japanese counterpart to Hammer's ongoing Dracula series took hold via a pitch by producer Fumio Tanaka to Toho, which would go on to spawn what is now referred to as the "Bloodthirsty Trilogy" or the "Legacy of Dracula Trilogy" due to the presence of vampires and the same director, Michio Yamamoto. Also known in English as **The Night of the Vampire** and originally entitled **Yūrei Yashiki no Kyōfu Chi o Sū Ningyō** (or **Fear in the**

Ghost House), the film stars Toho marquee star Yukiko Kobayashi as the titular vampiress, Yuko, who has seemingly died in a car accident – much to the consternation of her fiancé, Kazuhiko (Atsuo Nakamura), who comes to visit her after half a year away for work. When he goes missing for eight days, Kazuhiko's sister, Keiko (Kayo Matsuo), is haunted by foreboding dreams and decides to investigate only to uncover a family curse involving the "God of Death." Right from its dark and stormy night opener, this visually flamboyant opus is pure Gothic to the core and adds a few new spins to the vampire concept, most notably introducing a Poe-inspired hypnotism angle that accounts for the vampire's eerie golden eyes. This marked a major breakthrough for Japanese vampire cinema, which had included such earlier efforts as Nobuo Nakagawa's far more sedate **The Lady Vampire** (1959), or **Onna kyûketsuki**, which throws a few werewolf rules involving the full moon into the mix for variety.

THE VAMPIRE LOVERS

UK, 1970
Director: Roy Ward Baker.
Producers: Harry Fine, Michael Style. Screenplay: Tudor Gates.
Music: Harry Robinson [Harry Robertson]. Cinematography: Moray Grant.
Cast: Ingrid Pitt, Pippa Steel, Madeline Smith, Peter Cushing, George Cole, Dawn Addams, Kate O'Mara.

After multiple Continental stabs at J. Sheridan Le Fanu's vampire novella **Carmilla**, Hammer finally got around to its own version during a very busy year already crowded with a pair of Dracula entries. The real trump card here was the casting of Ingrid Pitt as Carmilla, a.k.a. Marcilla, the centuries-old lesbian vampire who invades well-to-do households and drains the young daughters of their blood supply while inducing feline-themed nightmares. Peter Cushing has a small but pivotal role as a military veteran involved in the gruesome, oft-censored opening and closing sequences, while Madeleine Smith and Kate O'Mara make for two of the period's most beautiful new Hammer stars. A co-production with American International Pictures, the film was particularly butchered in the United States but still made a fortune due to its titillating subject matter with atmospheric direction by Roy Ward Baker conducted back to back with the same year's **Scars of Dracula** (1970). It's really Pitt's show all the way though with the Polish-born star, born Ingoushka Petrov, etching a complex and sometimes sympathetic portrayal of a bloodthirsty outsider consuming her way through British society. The film would go on to spawn two official Hammer sequels in what is now known as the Karnstein trilogy, with numerous other imitations following for years to come.

COUNTESS DRACULA

UK, 1971
Director: Peter Sasdy. Producer: Alexander Paal.
Screenplay: Jeremy Paul. Music: Harry Robinson
[Harry Robertson]. Cinematography: Kenneth Talbot.
Cast: Ingrid Pitt, Nigel Green, Sandor Elès, Maurice Denham,
Patience Collier, Peter Jeffrey, Lesley-Anne Down.

Well over a decade after inaugurating its string of Dracula
productions, Hammer Films finally got around to tackling
the most famous female bloodletter in history, the Countess
Elizabeth Báthory. Perhaps even more remarkably, this
was the first (but far from the last) big screen depiction in
popular culture for the Hungarian noblewoman reputed
to have tortured numerous female victims and bathed
in their blood to sustain her youth, though those claims
appear to be dubious at best in real life. Here a needlessly
dubbed Ingrid Pitt follows up her role in **The Vampire
Lovers** as the fiendish countess (here given the last name
Elisabeth Nadasdy), who recruits military captain Nigel
Green to assist in her crimes and eventually adopt the
identity of her daughter, Ilona (Lesley-Anne Down). No
fangs or traditional bloodsucking are involved here, with
the vampirism instead involving the saturation of blood as
a means of temporarily restoring our leading lady's
youth. Returning to the Hammer fold just after the
stylish **Taste the Blood of Dracula** and back
to back with his last big-screen Hammer film,
Hands of the Ripper (1971), director Peter
Sasdy injects the film with a great deal of
style and achieves one of the stronger one-
off attempts by the studio in its attempts
to stretch beyond the confinements of its
Dracula cash cows. However, this wasn't the
only Báthory-themed film released that year...

DAUGHTERS OF DARKNESS

Belgium/France/West Germany, 1971
Director: Harry Kümel. Producers: Paul Collet, Henry
Lange, Luggi Waldleitner [uncredited].
Screenplay: Pierre Drouot, Harry Kümel. Music: François
de Roubaix. Cinematography: Eduard van der Enden.
Cast: Delphine Seyrig, John Karlen, Daniele Ouimet,
Andrea Rau, Paul Esser, Georges Jamin.

A high point in European horror of any era, **Daughters of Darkness** (originally entitled **Les lèvres rouges**) is a masterpiece of cinematic style from Belgian surrealist Harry Kümel and an unforgettable vehicle for arthouse star Delphine Seyrig, here drawing inspiration from past screen sirens including Marlene Dietrich. American actor John Karlen, himself familiar to vampire fans thanks to his work on TV's **Dark Shadows**, and French-Canadian softcore star Danielle Ouimet also appear as a recently married couple who stop off at a desolate, sprawling beachside hotel where they make the acquaintance of Elizabeth (Seyrig) and her companion, Ilona (the scene-stealing Andrea Rau), both of whom may be connected to recent blood-draining murders in the area. Sparkling, witty, and erotic, the film is propelled by an infectious score by the great François de Roubaix, Seyrig's cheerful and beautifully sinister central performance, and some of the genre's most impeccable locations choices including the Astoria Hotel in Brussells and the Thermae Palace Hotel in Ostende. Though often lumped in with the lesbian vampire trend of the era, this is a beast all unto itself and a rare vampire film that can appeal to the most highbrow critic or the most seasoned Euro-cult aficionado.

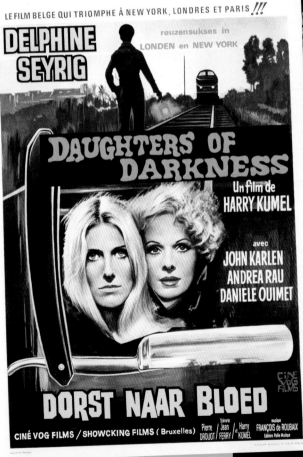

LAKE OF DRACULA

Japan, 1971
Director: Michio Yamamoto. Producer: Fumio Tanaka. Screenplay: Ei Ogawa, Masaru Takesue.
Music: Riichirô Manabe. Cinematography: Rokurô Nishigaki.
Cast: Midori Fujita, Chôei Takahashi, Sanae Emi, Shin Kishida, Kaku Takashina, Tatsuo Matsushita.

The same year Mario Bava used a lake as the focus to lay the groundwork for the slasher film with **Bay of Blood** (1971), Toho adopted a similar locale for the second in its trilogy of vampire films hot on the heels of the previous year's **The Vampire Doll** with returning director Michio Yamamoto, a onetime apprentice to Akira Kurosawa and Kihachi Okamoto. Originally titled **Noroi no Yakata Chi o Sū Me** (or **Cursed House: Bloodsucking Eyes**), the story involves the harrowing experience of young schoolteacher Akiko (Midori Fujita) when she returns to work by the same lake where she experienced a traumatic vampire sighting 18 years earlier while chasing her German Shepherd puppy, Leo. When a coffin is conveniently delivered nearby and Leo turns up violently murdered, she fears that the rash of blood draining in the area could be tied to her childhood trauma. Longstanding Toho actor Shin Kishida is a memorable, ferocious and pasty-faced bloodsucker here, sporting the same gold eyes as the prior film and getting a truly spectacular send-off that feels like all of Christopher Lee's Dracula demises rolled into one. The most widely seen film of the Yamamoto trilogy, this film also helped evangelize the idea of Japanese vampire cinema thanks to widely published stills of Kishida in action.

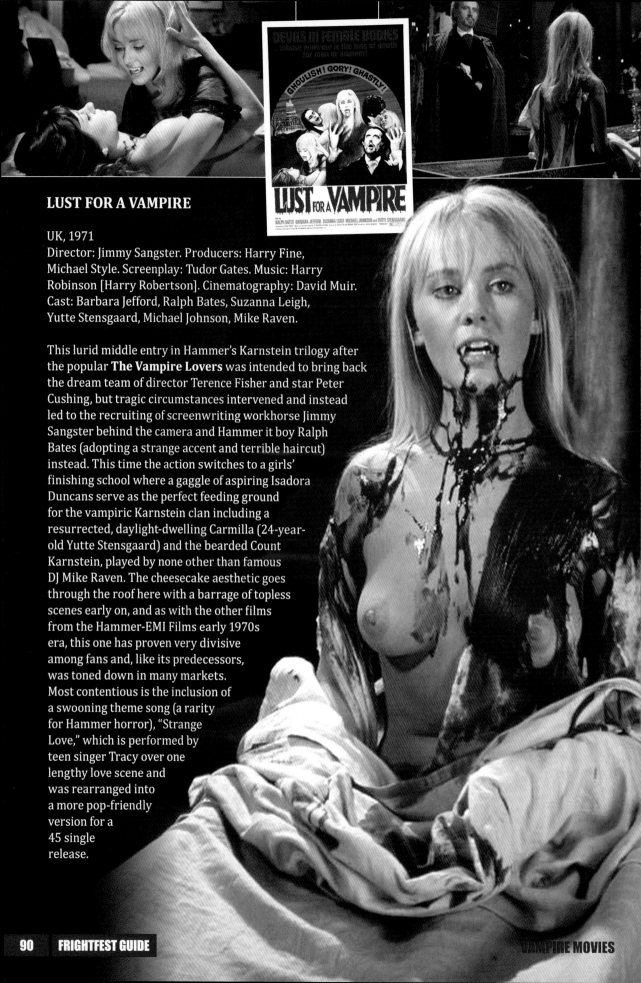

LUST FOR A VAMPIRE

UK, 1971
Director: Jimmy Sangster. Producers: Harry Fine,
Michael Style. Screenplay: Tudor Gates. Music: Harry
Robinson [Harry Robertson]. Cinematography: David Muir.
Cast: Barbara Jefford, Ralph Bates, Suzanna Leigh,
Yutte Stensgaard, Michael Johnson, Mike Raven.

This lurid middle entry in Hammer's Karnstein trilogy after
the popular **The Vampire Lovers** was intended to bring back
the dream team of director Terence Fisher and star Peter
Cushing, but tragic circumstances intervened and instead
led to the recruiting of screenwriting workhorse Jimmy
Sangster behind the camera and Hammer it boy Ralph
Bates (adopting a strange accent and terrible haircut)
instead. This time the action switches to a girls'
finishing school where a gaggle of aspiring Isadora
Duncans serve as the perfect feeding ground
for the vampiric Karnstein clan including a
resurrected, daylight-dwelling Carmilla (24-year-
old Yutte Stensgaard) and the bearded Count
Karnstein, played by none other than famous
DJ Mike Raven. The cheesecake aesthetic goes
through the roof here with a barrage of topless
scenes early on, and as with the other films
from the Hammer-EMI Films early 1970s
era, this one has proven very divisive
among fans and, like its predecessors,
was toned down in many markets.
Most contentious is the inclusion of
a swooning theme song (a rarity
for Hammer horror), "Strange
Love," which is performed by
teen singer Tracy over one
lengthy love scene and
was rearranged into
a more pop-friendly
version for a
45 single
release.

THE SHIVER OF THE VAMPIRES

France, 1971
Director: Jean Rollin.
Producer: Jean Rollin.
Screenplay: Monique Natan, Jean Rollin.
Music: Acanthus.
Cinematography: Jean-Jacques Renon.
Cast: Sandra Julien, Jean-Marie Durand,
Jacques Robiolles, Michel Delahaye,
Nicole Nancel, Dominique.

Jean Rollin's third and most colourful vampire film retains the comic strip influence of his earlier work but amps up the sexual content considerably, with the addition of a roaring psychedelic soundtrack by the band Acanthus firmly establishing this as a dramatic break from the cinematic vampire norm. The gossamer-thin plot involves a newly married couple going to a country castle to stay with some cousins, only to fall afoul of an ancient band of trendily dressed bisexual vampires who turn the honeymoon into a nightmare. Barely shown to English-speaking viewers upon its release, Rollin's film is an

unrestrained exercise in style with vivid splashes of red and blue lighting dousing the castle walls and even the screen itself, while the filmmaker uses the scenario to mount a string of isolated dreamlike visuals, most famously the enigmatic Dominique emerging from a grandfather clock. Several different variants of this film were prepared depending on the country of release, including a Spanish edition with some different music cues, a heavily cut American release as **Strange Things Happen at Night**, and a radically reworked West German version, **Sexual-Terror der entfesselten Vampire**, which replaces a significant amount of footage with new, fairly graphic softcore sex scenes featuring entirely different actors.

VAMPIRE MOVIES

TWINS OF EVIL

UK, 1971
Director: John Hough.
Producers: Harry Fine, Michael Style.
Screenplay: Tudor Gates. Music: Harry Robinson
[Harry Robertson]. Cinematography: Dick Bush.
Cast: Madeleine Collinson, Mary Collinson, Peter Cushing, Kathleen Byron, Dennis Price, Damien Thomas.

Hammer's third and final film in the **Carmilla**-inspired Karnstein vampire trilogy offers a refinement of its two predecessors, dispensing with the coy lesbian aspects and instead delivering a blood and thunder Gothic feast courtesy of director John Hough. Inspired by the likes of **Witchfinder General** (1968), Peter Cushing gives one of his most intense performances as Gustav, a fanatic bent on burning women at the stake and keeping a stern eye on his two nieces, Frieda and Maria (played by twin *Playboy* models Madeleine and Mary Collinson, both obviously dubbed). Of course, the undead residents of Castle Karnstein have other plans... A veteran of TV's **The Avengers**, Hough was one of the more visually adventurous young helmers of his generation and sets this one apart with its dark, ultra-saturated visual look achieved with veteran cinematographer Dick Bush, who performed similar miracles the same year with **The Blood on Satan's Claw** (1971) and such later films

as **Tommy** (1975) and **Phase IV** (1974). This would be the second of three Hammer vampire-themed films made in conjunction with The Rank Organisation, following **Countess Dracula** and preceding **Vampire Circus** (which recycled many of the same sets); the two studios would continue to collaborate on and off until Hammer's big-screen demise in 1979.

IL FILM PIÚ COMICO E DIVERTENTE DELL'ANNO

½ Litro di rosso per il CONTE DRACULA

BANCA DEL SANGUE RH+
imbottigliato da ANONIMA SUCCHIONI
Origine Controllata

PIA DEGERMARK · THOMAS HUNTER
con FERDIE MAYNE nella parte di "DRACULA", e IVOR MURILLO · INGRID VAN BERGEN · JOACHIM KEMMER · LYVA BAUER · DARIA DAMAR · KAY WILLIAMS
UN FILM DI FREDDIE FRANCIS
MUSICA DI JERRY VAN ROOYEN   PIER A. CAMINNECI per la AGUILA FILM   ATLAS INTERNATIONAL   MARMER CINEMATOGRAFICA

WIDESCREEN   TECHNICOLOR

THE VAMPIRE HAPPENING

West Germany/UK, 1971
Director: Freddie Francis. Producer: Pier A. Caminneci.
Screenplay: August Rieger. Music: Jerry van Rooyen.
Cinematography: Gérard Vandenberg.
Cast: Pia Degermark, Thomas Hunter, Ingrid van Bergen,
Yvor Murillo, Joachim Kemmer, Oskar Wegrostek, Ferdy Mayne.

In one of the more peculiar career paths following an international arthouse hit, Swedish actress Pia Degermark cashed in on her Cannes Film Festival award-winning performance in **Elvira Madigan** (1967) with only three more roles before retiring in the early '70s. Among these was the West German comedy **Gebissen wird nur nachts,** better known to English-speaking viewers as **The Vampire Happening**. Filled with nudity and strange sight gags, the film falls into the trend of goofy German softcore comedies of the era but also draws more than a passing bit of inspiration from **The Fearless Vampire Killers** thanks to Jerry van Rooyen's mod score, the animated opening titles and the presence of Ferdy Mayne as Count Dracula. Degermark stars as Betty Williams, a movie star who jets into Transylvania (complete with an in-flight sex film on the plane) to claim her inheritance, a family castle notorious for its history of ghastly tortures and other unspeakable practices performed by the diabolical Baroness Catali (also Degermark). The most shocking thing about this film is the identity of its director, Freddie Francis, who had previous vampire experience with **Dracula Has Risen from the Grave** and, inexplicably, made this in between **Trog** (1970) and **Tales from the Crypt** (1972). However, the result is still stylish, colorful, and certainly nothing to cause any shame. A far less engaging German vampire comedy followed with **Lady Dracula** (1977), which is mainly notable for featuring **Ben-Hur** (1959) star Stephen Boyd in his final role (as Dracula, of course) and for the unique experience of seeing **Mighty Peking Man** (1977) star Evelyne Kraft as his bride who gets revived in the present day only to resume her bloodsucking activities and find a bit of romance.

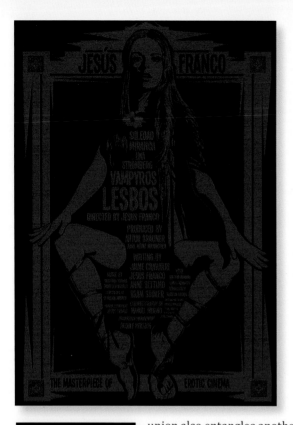

VAMPYROS LESBOS

West Germany/Spain, 1971
Director: Jess Franco. Producer: Artur Brauner
[uncredited]. Screenplay: Jess Franco.
Music: Manfred Hübler, Sigi Schwab.
Cinematography: Manuel Merino.
Cast: Susann Korda [Soledad Miranda], Dennis Price,
Paul Muller, Ewa Strömberg, Heidrun Kussin,
Michael Berling.

Jess Franco's most famous film from his West German
period is this psychedelic and borderline plotless
fever dream constructed around one of his most
unforgettable muses, Soledad Miranda (credited
here as Susann Korda), who had just appeared
as Lucy in Franco's subdued adaptation of **Count
Dracula**. Modern-day seaside Istanbul provides the
backdrop for the story of American transplant Linda
Westinghouse (Ewa Strömberg) whose intense dreams
revolve around Countess Nadine Corody (Miranda), a
Draculean descendant spreading visions of madness
throughout the female population. Their inevitable
union also entangles another Stoker-inspired character, Dr. Seward (Dennis Price),
as Linda falls under the sway of the dream invader. Shot and edited in a manner
anticipating music videos at least a decade away, this sun-blasted slice of art horror
paves the way for a wave of Franco films that equate vampirism with nautical
settings, lesbian sexuality, and romantic tragedy. It also features the Franco staple
of a stylized nightclub performance, in this case one of his finest with Miranda
performing a strip routine involving a candelabra to
the accompaniment of a now-classic psychedelic
score by Manfred Hübler and Siegfried Schwab.
That same duo would also score a companion
Franco-Miranda film, **She Killed
in Ecstasy** (1971); tragically,
Miranda would die from
injuries sustained in
a car accident just
after this film's
completion
in 1970.

THE VELVET VAMPIRE

USA, 1971
Director: Stephanie Rothman. Producer: Charles S. Swartz. Screenplay: Maurice Jules, Charles S. Swartz, Stephanie Rothman. Music: Clancy B. Grass III, Roger Dollarhide. Cinematography: Daniel Lacambre.
Cast: Michael Blodgett, Sherry Miles, Celeste Yarnall, Gene Shane, Jerry Daniels, Sandy Ward.

Roger Corman's New World Pictures was bound to take a stab at the lesbian vampire craze, but few could have predicted how eccentric and endearing the result would be. It's also the first directed by a woman, onetime USC film student Stephanie Rothman, who had just scored a big Corman hit with **The Student Nurses** (1970). Loaded with cheeky nods to Bram Stoker and J. Sheridan Le Fanu, the film is essentially a macabre love triangle between married couple Lee (**Beyond the Valley of the Dolls'** Michael Blodgett) and Susan (Sherry Miles) and the alluring, mysterious, and wealthy Diane (Celeste Yarnall), who invites them to the desert for a weekend of dune buggies, rattlesnakes, seduction, and bloodletting. A melancholy hangover from the previous decade's counterculture can be felt in the psychedelia-tinged visuals and music, but Rothman and company imbue the film with an air of timeless menace and longing even in modern settings like a bus station or a row of phone booths. The late Yarnall easily wins acting honours here, never baring fangs but eliciting both chills and sympathy as a pansexual carnivore who knows how to work a red dress to the hilt.

BLACULA

USA, 1972
Director: William Crain. Producer: Joseph T. Naar.
Screenplay: Joan Torres, Raymond Koenig.
Music: Gene Page.
Cinematography: John M. Stephens.
Cast: William Marshall, Vonetta McGee,
Denise Nicholas, Thalmus Rasulala, Gordon Pinsent,
Charles Macauley.

After tasting the bloody success of modern vampire cinema with **Count Yorga, Vampire**, AIP took the logical next step of combining the formula with the burgeoning blaxploitation craze ignited by **Sweet Sweetback's Baadasssss Song** (1971), **Shaft** (1971) and **Super Fly** (1972). The result was **Blacula**, whose title promises something far sillier than the full-blooded horror film unleashed on audiences. The real trump card here is the casting of theatre and TV actor William Marshall, whose powerful voice and physical presence create a new kind of tragic vampire in the form of undead African Prince Mamuwalde. Bitten by a racist Count Dracula and imprisoned Barnabas Collins-style in a coffin for decades, he's released on the streets of modern Los Angeles by an interracial gay couple and converts many of the locals to vampirism while pining for the lovely Tina (Vonetta McGee), the possibly reincarnation of his long-lost love. A crackling soundtrack by pioneering music great Gene Page adds an extra layer of excitement to the film, which became a major box office success for "Dracula's soul brother" (per the trailer) and quickly spawned a worthwhile sequel with Marshall and Pam Grier, **Scream Blacula Scream** (1973), as well as a brief wave of blaxploitation horror films including **Blackenstein** (1973), **Abby** (1974), **Sugar Hill** (1974) and **Dr. Black, Mr. Hyde** (1976).

THE BLOOD SPATTERED BRIDE

Spain, 1972
Director: Vicente Aranda. Producer: Jaime Fernández-Cid.
Screenplay: Vicente Aranda. Music: Antonio Pérez Olea.
Cinematography: Fernando Arribas.
Cast: Simón Andreu, Maribel Martín, Alexandra Bastedo,
Dean Selmier, Rosa M. Rodriguez, Montserrat Julió.

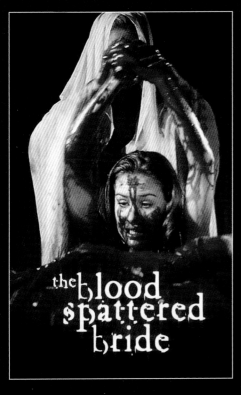

Best known on the arthouse circuit for films like **Lovers: A True Story** (1991) and **La pasión turca** (1994), Spanish director Vicente Aranda was already dealing with the war between the sexes when he made an international splash on the exploitation circuit with this jittery, modern-day reworking of **Carmilla**. With its nameless violent husband, duplicitous marriage and apocalyptic siege against womanhood itself, this now plays like a vampiric precursor to Lars von Trier's **Antichrist** (2009) as recently married Simón Andreu and Maribel Martín are disrupted by the arrival of the mysterious Mircalla Karstein (Alexandra Bastedo), first discovered buried nude on the beach. Beautifully shot and laced with shocking blends of sex and violence, this film (originally entitled **La novia ensangrentada**) was geared for the English-speaking market but ended up being heavily censored in many countries upon its release with several scenes shuffled dramatically out of order for the American version widely circulated on a notorious "Frenzy of Blood" double bill with **I Dismember Mama** (1972). Fortunately, the more coherent and savage full-length cut has since become the norm, cementing the film's position as one of the premiere Spanish horror films and a key entry in the lesbian vampire cycle of the early '70s.

DAUGHTER OF DRACULA

France/Portugal, 1972
Director: Jess Franco. Screenplay: Jess Franco. Music: René Sylviano,
Daniel White [uncredited]. Cinematography: Pepe Climens [José Climent].
Cast: Britt Nichols [Carmen Yazalde], Anne Libert,
Alberto Dalbés, Howard Vernon, Daniel White, Jess Franco.

Though not as well-known as some of Jess Franco's other stars like
Lina Romay and Soledad Miranda, the striking and earthy Portuguese
actress Britt Nichols (real name Carmen Yazalde) had a brief two-year
stint of glory with him starring in films like **A Virgin Among the
Living Dead** (1973) and **The Erotic Rites of Frankenstein** (1973).
Just after a nameless fanged supporting turn in Franco's monster jam
Dracula, Prisoner of Frankenstein (1972), she had her one starring
vampire role in this quirky fusion of Bram Stoker and J. Sheridan
Le Fanu as Luisa Karlstein, the heir to an ancient family whose crypt houses none other than Dracula
himself (Howard Vernon). Meanwhile the police are investigating murderous bathroom attacks on young
women in the area, a factor that makes this an unorthodox blending of traditional supernatural horror
and modern giallo thrills popularized in Italy at the time. Not for all tastes due to the slapdash assembly
and a sometimes-bumpy script aping the structure of his earlier **The Sadistic Baron Von Klaus** (1962),
this is still a valuable addition to the director's canon of vampire cinema and certainly memorable for the
carnal chemistry between Nichols and another unsung Franco siren, Anne Libert. Extra points for the novel
method of executing a vampire via a spike through the skull and immediate incineration.

VAMPIRE

DRACULA A.D. 1972

NEW FROM **HAMMER!**
THE TIME: NOW
THE PLACE: KINGS ROAD, CHELSEA
THE KILLER: COUNT DRACULA

UK, 1972
Director: Alan Gibson.
Producer: Josephine Douglas. Screenplay:
Don Houghton. Music: Michael Vickers.
Cinematography: Dick Bush.
Cast: Christopher Lee, Peter Cushing,
Stephanie Beacham, Christopher Neame,
Michael Coles, Caroline Munro.

Breaking continuity with its forerunners,
this mod entry in Hammer's Dracula
series begins with a newly fabricated, fatal
showdown between Christopher Lee's
creature of the night and Peter Cushing's
Van Helsing on a speeding carriage before leaping to the present day. A black mass conducted by dark
disciple Johnny Alucard (Christopher Neame) brings Dracula back to life in an abandoned church for a short-
lived revenge plot that spans across London. Complete with a funky score by Manfred Mann and library
music vet Mike Vickers, an amusing party sequence with the band Stoneground, and a small but vivid
appearance by Caroline Munro as Dracula's first modern
victim, this film has been derided frequently over the
years for its attempts to appeal to youth culture and its
instantly outdated "with-it" characters including a scarf-
fixated Stephanie Beacham. However, it's sumptuously
filmed and has its high points including a novel variation
on the rarely used running water method of executing
vampire, an unusually bloody climax, and a memorably
wicked turn by Neame who could have easily carried
villain duties by himself. Still grieving from the death of
his wife in 1971, Cushing lends gravitas with a haunted
performance that becomes a major asset in the final
third and marks a welcome return to the Dracula series
after a twelve-year absence.

GRAVE OF THE VAMPIRE

USA, 1972
Director: John Hayes. Producer: Daniel Cady. Screenplay: David Chase. Music: Jaime Mendoza-Nava. Cinematography: Paul Hipp. Cast: William Smith, Michael Pataki, Lyn Peters, Diane Holden, Kitty Vallacher, Jay Adler.

Designed to immediately grab the attention of anyone lucky enough to stumble across it, this downbeat, unabashedly gruesome entry in the '70s drive-in vampire revival offers numerous transgressive twists on the concept right from the beginning with bloodthirsty ghoul Caleb Croft (Michael Pataki) sexually assaulting and impregnating a young women out on a graveyard date. From there the "unwilling mother" (as she's credited) sacrifices her own blood supply to nourish her offspring, who grows up to be a vengeance-seeking college student James Eastman (William Smith). Veteran exploitation filmmaker, actor, and short film Oscar nominee John Hayes and screenwriter David Chase (future creator of **The Sopranos**, believe it or not, and author of the apparently unpublished source novel cited in the credits) pepper the story with the required number of bloody attack scenes, but it's the escalating conflict between the vampire father and son that forms the pitch-black heart of the film all the way to its bare-knuckle and bare-fang climax. This marked Hayes' second excursion into horror after the intriguing **Dream No Evil** (1970), which was marred by distributor interference, and it ended up played most widely on a double bill with another Hayes quickie, **Garden of the Dead** (1972). A bewildering number of different edits of this film exist ranging from virtually bloodless TV prints to an extra-bloody German VHS edition, but in this case the film manages to retain its impact no matter how you see it.

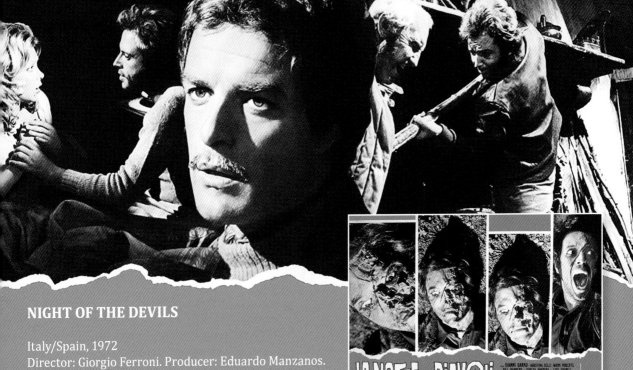

NIGHT OF THE DEVILS

Italy/Spain, 1972
Director: Giorgio Ferroni. Producer: Eduardo Manzanos.
Screenplay: Romano Migliorini, Gianbattista Mussetto,
Eduardo M. Brochero [Eduardo Manzanos].
Music: Giorgio Gaslini. Cinematography: Manuel Berenguer.
Cast: Gianni Garko, Agostina Belli, Mark Roberts [Roberto Maldera],
Bill Vanders, Teresa Gimpera, Umberto Raho.

Adapted from the same lengthy Aleksei Tolstoy short story that spawned
the vampire entry in Mario Bava's **Black Sabbath**, this chilling modern
fairy tale is the second of only two horror films directed by Giorgio
Ferroni, who had helmed the classic **Mill of the Stone Women** (1960)
but spent most of his time on spaghetti westerns and action films. This
rendition hews a bit closer to the Aleksey Tolstoy source material with
its framing device of our protagonist, Nicola (Gianni Garko, sporting
peculiar facial hair), locked away at a clinic as he rants about horrific
misdeeds after a car breakdown left him seeking shelter with an isolated
family in the Yugoslavian woods. The fact that everyone else in the area has
moved away should tip him off that a nightmare lies in waiting, albeit on a scale
he could never have imagined. In this case the afflicted undead dissipate into a pulpy mess when they're
staked, a Carlo Rambaldi invention that helps ratchet up the gore factor here (along with a few dollops of sex
and nudity). However, the film's strength lies in its uncanny atmosphere which reaches a fever pitch during
the forest attack climax, complete with unnerving cackling children, and a particularly downbeat twist
ending that diverges from both of its predecessors. Russia would go on to offer two later takes on the same
material, with the more successful being Gennadiy Klimov and Igor Shavlak's **The Vampire Family** (1980),
originally entitled **Semya vurdalakov**; the CGI effects-laden **Vurdalaki** (2017) bears only faint traces of
the original story. The Tolstoy source was also vaguely incorporated into Evgenly Yufit's experimental
Daddy, Father Frost Is Dead (1991), a.k.a. **Papa, umer Ded Moroz**, and Spanish television tackled its own
adaptation as "La familia Vourdalak" in 1975 as part of the horror anthology series, **El quinto jinete**. The
essential structure of the story was also borrowed for Larry Fessenden's "Skin and Bones" episode of the
single-season anthology series **Fear Itself**, with the expressive chameleonic actor Doug Jones making a
horrific impression as the undead patriarch. A different Tolstoy novella, *Oupyr* (1841), served as the basis
for the lavish Russian production **The Vampire** (1991), or **Pyushchye krovi**, about a large aristocratic
family of vampires; the unrelated Russian production **Upyr** (1997) is essentially a modern day variation on
the theme with a vampire feeding on a town with a very resistant local crime force.

THE NIGHT STALKER

USA, 1972
Director: John Llewellyn Moxey. Producer: Dan Curtis.
Screenplay: Richard Matheson. Music: Bob Cobert.
Cinematography: Michel Hugo.
Cast: Darren McGavin, Carol Lynley, Charles McGraw,
Ralph Meeker, Claude Akins, Simon Oakland, Barry Atwater.

A watershed moment in the history of made-for-TV horror,
this innovative modern-day vampire saga set in Las Vegas
introduced the world to world-beaten newspaper reporter Carl
Kolchak (Darren McGavin). A sardonic new kind of monster
hunter, he smells a local conspiracy involving the deaths of
numerous young women whose blood has been drained. The
trail leads him to the enigmatic Janos Skorzeny (Barry Atwater),
but collusion between politicians and his own higher ups make
it increasingly difficult to uncover the monstrous truth. The
paranoid, cynical nature of early 1970s thrillers by the likes of
Alan J. Pakula is a heavy influence on this film's pitch-perfect
script by genre legend Richard Matheson (adapting a then-
unpublished novel by Jeff Rice entitled *The Kolchak Papers*) in
the first of several TV collaborations with producer Dan Curtis
of **Dark Shadows** fame. In fact, the pair quickly mounted a
non-vampire sequel with McGavin, **The Night Strangler** (1973),
but were not involved in the single-season TV series, **Kolchak:
The Night Stalker**, which premiered a year later and featured a
sequel episode to this film, "The Vampire," aired just in time for
Halloween of 1974. This film and its offshoots have been cited
as influences on many subsequent genre shows, most openly
The X-Files, and went on to inspire more tie-in novels and comic
books as well as an ill-fated revamped TV series in 2005 that
tried to overhaul Kolchak as young, sexy reporter trying to solve
his wife's murder. Not surprisingly, it was scrapped after only
six episodes were aired.

REQUIEM FOR A VAMPIRE

France, 1972
Director: Jean Rollin. Producer: Sam Selsky.
Screenplay: Jean Rollin. Music: Pierre Raph.
Cinematography: Renan Pollès.
Cast: Marie-Pierre Castel, Mireille Dargent, Philippe Gasté,
Dominique, Louise Dhour, Michel Delesalle.

The fourth of Jean Rollin's run of vampire movies released between 1968 and 1972, this dialogue-light macabre cinematic poem received his widest distribution in the United States when it was snapped up by exploitation maven Harry Novak and retitled **Caged Virgins**. Following a robbery conducted in clown garb, the pigtailed Marie-Pierre Castel and Mireille Dargent wind up at a country castle where a vampire clan subjects them to a gauntlet of horrors and erotic encounters. Though more naturalistic in style compared to **The Shiver of the Vampires**, the similar narrative and fatalistic approach makes this both a refinement of Rollin's ongoing parade of bloodsucker features and a new variant on his ability to weave together commercial cinema (including the outrageous image of a vampire bat feasting on menstrual blood) with his more experimental artistic impulses. More jarring for regular Rollin viewers is the inclusion of a protracted S&M sequence involving tortured nude women in chains, which made the film easier to sell but also feels more sadistic than the rest of his vampire films. Also promoted under the title **Vierges et vampires**, this was the first Rollin film to cheekily credit his money-centric producer as "$am $elsky" as well as the premiere collaboration with composer Pierre Raph, whose minimal but distinctive and playful sound would also define Rollin's **The Iron Rose** (1973) and **The Demoniacs** (1974).

VAMPIRE CIRCUS

UK, 1972
Director: Robert Young. Producer: Wilbur Stark.
Screenplay: Judson Kinberg [Jud Kinberg].
Music: David Whitaker. Cinematography: Moray Grant.
Cast: Adrienne Corri, Laurence Payne, Thorley Walters,
John Moulder-Brown, Lynne Frederick, Elizabeth Seal,
David Prowse.

The most ferocious entry in Hammer Films' decades-long vampire film cycle is an offbeat revenge saga, a sort of ghoulish spin on "The Pied Piper," about a protracted plot against the residents of the German village of Schtettel whose execution of an undead nobleman is tied to a traveling circus with seemingly supernatural performers targeting the youngest residents (including John Moulder-Brown and Lynne Frederick). A surprising cast of character actors including David Prowse, Adrienne Corri, Anthony Corlan (a.k.a. Anthony Higgins), and midget Skip Martin are the highlights of this macabre gem, which features many striking visual flourishes like a sinister passage through a magical mirror, a ground-level

afternoon panther attack in the woods, and the circus performances themselves, a combination of the surreal and the erotic. Taking a cue from Robert Aldrich, the film also boasts a lengthy, memorable pre-credits sequence that even functions as a potent, shocking horror short on its own. The story can feel disjointed due to the slow production pace of first-time director Robert Young, who was pulled away before some key sequences could be shot, but this fragmentation also gives the film an irrationality new to the Hammer cycle. Anyone looking to fill in the narrative gaps will be stymied by the 2012 novelization by Mark Morris, which relocates the action to the present day with numerous changes to the original concept. Frequently censored upon its initial release, the film has since gone on to amass a significant cult following and is now regarded as one of the strongest Hammer films of the studio's final decade.

COUNT DRACULA'S GREAT LOVE

Spain, 1973
Director: Javier Aguirre. Producer: Francisco Lara Polop.
Screenplay: Javier Aguirre, Alberto S. Insúa,
Jacinto Molina [Paul Naschy].
Music: Carmelo A. Bernaola.
Cinematography: Raúl Pérez Cubero.
Cast: Paul Naschy, Rossana Yanni,
Haydée Politoff, Mirta Miller, Ingrid Garbo,
Vic Winner [Víctor Barrera].

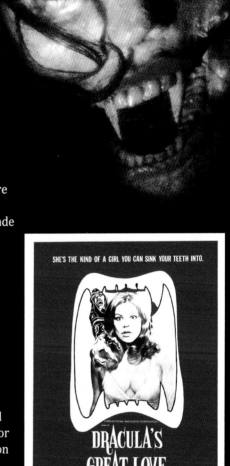

SHE'S THE KIND OF A GIRL YOU CAN SINK YOUR TEETH INTO.

DRACULA'S GREAT LOVE

PAUL NASCHY   HAYDÉE POLITOFF   ROSSANA YANNI
DIRECTED BY J AGUIRRE

After spending five years making six werewolf films as the beloved and tragic lycanthropic antihero Waldemar Daninsky, actor and co-writer Paul Naschy made the inevitable shift to playing a vampire with this flamboyant, gore-soaked offering made in tandem with another comparatively extreme vehicle, **Hunchback of the Morgue** (1973). Here Naschy stars as Dr. Wendell Marlow, who welcomes a quartet of nubile women and their guide to his neglected Carpathian Mountains sanitarium where, legend has it, the legendary Count Dracula met his final demise. However, as the title clearly gives away, the doctor isn't all that he appears to be... As usual with Naschy, he injects his monster with a large degree of pathos including a Shakespearean finale that only he could have pulled off despite such unsavory activities as murder and torture; the film is also laced with strong amounts of sex and violence, particularly in the export unclothed version prepared for audiences outside of General Franco's Spain. Particularly attention grabbing is the graphic curtain raiser, an axe to the face in full bloody color, which became one of the most reprinted and shocking movie stills well into the 1980s and a fixture in nearly every book on vampire cinema for years.

THE DEVIL'S PLAYTHING

Switzerland/Denmark, 1973
Director: Joe Sarno. Producer: Chris D. Nebe. Screenplay: Joe Sarno.
Music: Rolf-Hans Müller. Cinematography: Steve Silverman.
Cast: Marie Forså, Nadia Henkowa, Anke Syring, Ulrike Butz, Nico Wolf,
[Nico Wolferstetter], Flavia Keyt.

Also known under a variety of titles like **Vampire Ecstasy** and **Veil of Blood**, this dark Germanic fairy tale marks the sole pure horror project for American sexploitation director Joseph W. Sarno after the use of sparing macabre elements in some of his previous films like **Sin You Sinners** (1963). The wispy strand of a plot is a variation on the Hammer formula with a quartet of nubile young women becoming candidates for the resurrection of the bloodthirsty Baroness Varga, who was executed many years before but vowed to return. Though he didn't show a significant affinity for Gothic horror, Sarno was assigned the film by producer and distributor Christian Nebe who wanted to ride the wave of vampire films coursing through Europe at the time. The result is light on fang action but heavy on bare flesh, Jean Rollin-style atmosphere, and moody castle shenanigans, all at Sarno's usual deliberate, meditative pace. This would also mark the official screen debut of Stockholm-born actress Marie Forså among a cast mostly comprised of German sex comedy veterans; though her career would only last another six years, she makes a potent impression here and would serve as one of Sarno's greatest muses in future non-horror roles.

THE DRACULA SAGA

Spain, 1973
Director: León Klimovsky. Screenplay: Lazarus Kaplan
[Emilio Martínez Lázaro and Juan Tébar].
Music: Antonio Ramírez Ángel, Daniel White.
Cinematography: Francisco Sánchez.
Cast: Tina Sáinz, Tony Isbert, Narciso Ibáñez Menta,
Cristina Suriani, María Kosti, Helga Liné.

Ostracized by society, the bloodline of Count Dracula has only one chance at survival: a pregnant granddaughter named Berta (Tina Sáinz) raised outside of the pasty-faced family. She and her philandering husband find a visit to her ancestral home full of horrors, including a horrific deformed inbred offspring locked in a secret chamber. That's the premise for this nice of change of pace in the '70s Spanish horror sweepstakes from the always reliable León Klimovsky in one of two vampire offerings from 1973 (and both without signature star Paul Naschy) along with **The Vampires' Night Orgy**. A strong emphasis on European folklore and an unusual narrative gimmick that plays like a period vampire twist on **Rosemary's Baby** set **The Dracula Saga** (**La saga de los Drácula**) apart from the usual Spanish horror fare, with the particularly strong female cast highlighted by the always magnetic Helga Liné. As usual for Spain, some scenes were shot in both clothed and unclothed versions, the latter quite Hammer-like with an emphasis on bare breasts and gaping neck wounds in the same shot. Unfortunately, this film was subjected to one of the silliest English dub tracks in Euro horror history; be sure to watch the Spanish-language version with subtitles if possible.

LA SAGA DE LOS Drácula

TINA SÁINZ·TONY ISBERT·NARCISO IBAÑEZ MENTA
CRISTINA SURIANI·MARIA KOSTI·HELGA LINE·J.J. PALADINO
Director:
LEON KLIMOVSKY   eastmancolor

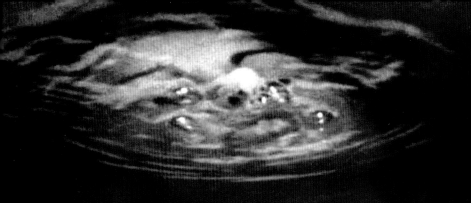

FEMALE VAMPIRE

Belgium/France, 1973
Director: J.P. Johnson [Jess Franco].
Producer: Marius Lesoeur. Screenplay: J.P. Johnson [Jess Franco], Gérard Brisseau [uncredited]. Music: Daniel White. Cinematography: Joan Vincent [Jess Franco].
Cast: Lina Romay, Jack Taylor, Alice Arno, Monica Swinn, Luis Barboo, Jean-Pierre Bouyxou.

Jess Franco's most extreme and delirious vampire film exists under a multitude of versions and titles (including **Erotikill, The Loves of Irina** and **The Bare-Breasted Countess**), but in any form it's an unforgettable showcase for his future clothing-averse wife, Lina Romay, as the mute and alluring Countess Irina Karlstein. She has a penchant for seducing and dispatching anyone in sight regardless of gender, though the manner of death varies depending on which version you see as she dispatches the cast either through blood drinking or fatally electrifying oral sex. The film crosscuts between her deadly escapades and a visiting writer (Jack Taylor) whose path is destined to cross with hers, leading to a literal blood bath finale. This would mark the first official collaboration between Franco (who also appears as a scientific investigator) and Daniel Lesoeur's company Euorciné, with whom Franco would continue to work on and off for the following decade. Those who hate Franco find plenty of ammunition here thanks to the ever-busy zoom lens and fixation on Romay's pubis, but those on his wavelength can find plenty to enjoy here thanks to the humid Mediterranean setting and lyrical score by regular Franco composer Daniel J. White, which was later recycled in the equally crotch-crazy **Zombie Lake** (1981).

"MOST IMPORTANT BLACK FILM SINCE "SWEETBACK" . . .
James P. Murray, Amsterdam News

"YOU WILL BE MOVED . . .   "BOUND TO BE MOST CONTRO-
YOU WILL RETURN . . ."   VERSIAL FILM OF THE YEAR . . ."
Terry Guerin, Andy Warhol's Interview Magazine   Lindsay Patterson Editor, Black Theatre Collection

Official selection of CANNES FILM FESTIVAL, "Critics Week"

Bad blood runs between them

GANJA & HESS

A FILM BY BILL GUNN

Starring DUANE JONES and MARLENE CLARK • Written and Directed by BILL GUNN
Produced by CHIZ SCHULTZ • Music Composed by SAM WAYMON
Executive Producers QUENTIN KELLY and JACK JORDAN
A Production and Release of KELLY-JORDAN ENTERPRISES, INC.

WORLD PREMIERE NOW

PLAYBOY
THEATER
57th St. West of 6th Ave. JU64448

GANJA & HESS

USA, 1973
Director: Bill Gunn. Producers: Allan Kelly, Chiz
Schultz. Screenplay: Bill Gunn. Music: Sam Waymon.
Cinematography: James E. Hinton.
Cast: Duane Jones, Marlene Clark, Bill Gunn,
Sam Waymon, Leonard Jackson, Candece Tarpley.

Vampirism infiltrated the 1970s American art film
world with this meditative study in cultural identity,
religious traditions, and addiction from director Bill Gunn, who turned out to be something far different
from the usual black exploitation fare of the time. That approach proved to be a major problem at first as
his original unmarketable 109-minute cut was drastically shortened and recut to play the horror circuit
under such titles as **Blood Couple, Double Possession** and **Black Vampire**. In its original form, the film
is a compelling depiction of a thirst for blood that passes through multiple characters and parallels the
suppression of African ancestry in the United States as experienced by anthropologist Dr. Hess Green,
played by Duane Jones of **Night of the Living Dead** (1968) fame, and Ganja Meda, played by **The Beast
Must Die** (1974)'s Marlene Clark, when they come into contact with an ancient dagger uncovered by
her husband (Gunn himself). With its casual depictions of bloodshed, Christian and African rituals, and
vulnerable bare bodies, the film is an intoxicatingly strange experience and has understandably eared
several generations of followers as well as a full-scale restoration from the Museum of Modern Art. In 2014,
Spike Lee mounted a very close Kickstarter-funded remake under the title **Da Sweet Blood of Jesus**, but
filmmaking craft aside, his lack of enthusiasm for the genre is evident throughout.

LEMORA: A CHILD'S TALE OF THE SUPERNATURAL

USA, 1973
Director: Richard Blackburn. Producer: Robert Fern.
Screenplay: Richard Blackburn, Robert Fern.
Music: Dan Neufeld. Cinematography: Robert Caramico.
Cast: Lesley Gilb [Lesley Taplin], Cheryl Smith,
William Whitton, Richard Blackburn, Steve Johnson,
Maxine Ballantyne.

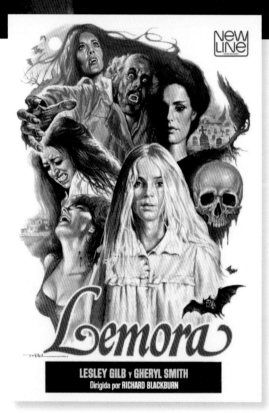

Inspired by a fondness for H.P. Lovecraft and the success of **Count Yorga, Vampire**, this Pomona, California-shot chiller remains the sole directorial effort by onetime film student Richard Blackburn. Equal parts monster movie and dreamy 1930s-set art film, this tale charts the perilous journey of teenager Lila Lee (future drive-in staple Cheryl "Rainbeaux" Smith) who goes to visit her injured gangster father and instead encounters a string of monstrous surprises in the countryside. Among the threats are the austere vampire queen Lemora (Lesley Gibb) and her minions, a combination of pasty-faced children and bloodsuckers who have devolved into irrational ghouls. Blackburn also appears in the film as a shifty preacher, an aspect that led to unsubstantiated claims that this film had been given a "Condemned" rating by the Catholic Church's National Legion of Decency. Blackburn himself describes the film as a meditation on the dark agenda adults have for children, an aspect sold by the delicate, ethereal presence of Smith (who was 18 years old at the time) and the spooky enchantment of the primarily nocturnal, Prohibition era setting. A severe financial disappointment upon its release and difficult to see for years (particularly in uncut form), the film has since undergone a major reappraisal and is now regarded as a key entry in the American independent horror movement of the 1970s.

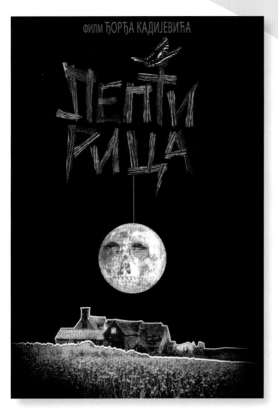

LEPTIRICA

Yugoslavia, 1973
Director: Djordje Kadijevic.
Screenplay: Djordje Kadijevic.
Cinematography: Branko Ivatovic.
Cast: Mirjana Nikolić, Petar Božović, Slobodan Perović,
Vasja Stanković, Aleksandar Stojković, Tanasije Uzunović.

Barely even qualifying as a feature at just over an hour, this Serbian-language production (originally shot for television broadcast) is an evocative horror fairy tale now renowned as one of the finest Eastern European genre films. Adapted from Milovan Glišić's novel *After Ninety Years,* the story delves into a mysterious country mill where, in the opening sequence, a man has been savaged by a cloaked creature with rows of razor-sharp fangs. A troubled romance between local man Strahinja (Petar Božović) and the stunning Radojka (Mirjana Nikolić) sends the former to work at the mill where he becomes embroiled in the tale of an ancient featured vampire named Sada. The major new twist here is using a vampire's shapeshifting abilities to transform into a

butterfly, a device used with potent but sparing effect here (and the justification for the film's odd alternate English title, **The She-Butterfly**). Slow but mesmerizing, the film also explores the rapport between the villagers more than the average monster film with religion intermingling into the daily working lives of the multigenerational labor force. The deliberate approach also pays off during the chilling climax, which not only ranks as one of the decade's most effective vampire attacks but immediately became legendary among children who happened to catch the film during one of its initial broadcasts.

THE SATANIC RITES OF DRACULA

UK, 1973
Director: Alan Gibson. Producer: Roy Skeggs.
Screenplay: Don Houghton. Music: John Cacavas.
Cinematography: Brian Probyn.
Cast: Christopher Lee, Peter Cushing,
Michael Coles, William Franklyn, Freddie Jones,
Joanna Lumley.

Christopher Lee and Peter Cushing's final
pairing as Dracula and Van Helsing was badly
treated upon its initial release in the wake of
Dracula A.D. 1972 with the same director, Alan

Gibson, at the helm. However, it has since undergone significant
reassessment for its transposing of classical horror conventions
in the modern setting of corporate malfeasance with Dracula
turned into a variation of the secretive Howard Hughes-inspired
figure from **Diamonds Are Forever** (1971). However, that's far
from the only peculiar twist here as the film mixes a Scotland Yard
investigation, an intense vampire bride basement attack, a catchy
pop-imbued score by **Kojak** and **Horror Express** (1973) composer
John Cacavas, and a few doses of nudity. This time Joanna Lumley
steps in for the absent Stephanie Beacham as Jessica Van Helsing,
with Cushing reprising his role as the Van Helsing descendent
Lorrimer. The initial advertising art gave away the Count's novel
demise here via hawthorn branches, a rarely utilized weapon
against vampirism, and despite the initial involvement of Warner
Bros., the film was given a belated, undignified rollout as **Count
Dracula and His Vampire Bride** from the short-lived indie
distributor Dynamite. At least wiser heads prevailed at Hammer
and rejected the film's original announced title, **Dracula Is Dead...
and Well and Living in London**.

VAMPIRE MOVIES

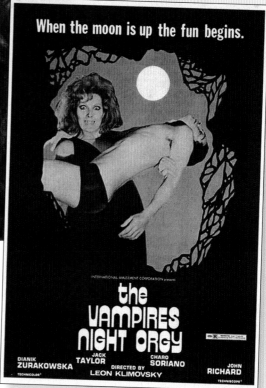

THE VAMPIRES' NIGHT ORGY

Spain, 1973
Director: León Klimovsky. Producer: José Frade.
Screenplay: Gabriel Moreno Burgos, Antonio Fos.
Cinematography: Antonio L. Ballesteros.
Cast: Jack Taylor, Dianik Zurakowska, José Guardiola,
Charo Soriano, Helga Liné, Manuel de Blas.

The other Spanish vampire film made in '73 by León Klimovsky along with **The Dracula Saga** is this evocative, orgy-free chiller with narrative echoes of the recent **The Devil's Nightmare** (1971). When a heart attack fells the driver of a bus filled with tourists, the hapless travelers are forced to take shelter in the closest village – which turns out to be populated entirely by vampires ruled by Spanish horror queen Helga Liné. The eerie, well-staged vampire group attacks recall the slavering hordes descending upon their victims in the same year's **Messiah of Evil** (1973), while the cannibalistic aspect of vampirism is emphasized here far more than usual including some sick gags involving the characters' mealtime mishaps. Cementing the film's Euro cult credentials is leading man Jack Taylor (as a solo traveler also stranded in the cursed town) in his second genre film that year along with **Female Vampire**, and as usual for the time given the stringent local censorship under General Franco, this film had some scenes shot in fully clothed and unclothed (female topless) options to satisfy audience demands around the world. Though still fairly tame, the latter option has since become the default one for most prints and home video releases.

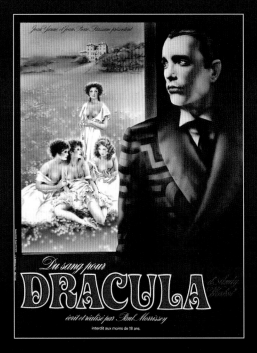

BLOOD FOR DRACULA

Italy/France, 1974
Director: Paul Morrissey. Producers: Andrew Braunsberg, Carlo Ponti, Andy Warhol, Jean Yanne.
Screenplay: Paul Morrissey, Pat Hackett [uncredited].
Music: Claudio Gizzi. Cinematography: Luigi Kuveiller.
Cast: Joe Dallesandro, Udo Kier, Vittorio De Sica, Maxime McKendry, Arno Jürging, Milena Vukotic.

Mixing black comedy splatter, twisted sexuality, and melancholy ruminations on ages past, this X-rated cult classic was director Paul Morrissey's immediate follow-up to his 3-D extravaganza of perversities, **Flesh for Frankenstein** (1973). In fact, this more subdued, lyrical film began shooting a day after that prior film wrapped, and much of the same cast returns here including an amusingly unlikely Joe Dallesandro as a Bolshevik-sympathizing stud handyman. An unforgettable Udo Kier headlines as the sickly Dracula, whose attempts to survive on virgin blood are thwarted in a crumbling Italian noble house of eligible young sisters overseen by none other than pioneering Italian filmmaker Vittorio De Sica. Roman Polanski makes a comical cameo as well, and the elegant, piano-driven score by Claudio Gizzi remains a fan favourite. Also released as **Andy Warhol's Dracula** (to the ongoing consternation of Morrissey), the film is well remembered for its imagery of Kier regurgitating contaminated blood on the estate floors and suffering a memorable demise that would lead Morrissey to cry copycat over **Monty Python and the Holy Grail** (1975). Italian prints and publicity materials erroneously credited Antonio Margheriti as the director among other substituted names, which led to legal proceedings in Italy over perceived tax shenanigans.

CAPTAIN KRONOS: VAMPIRE HUNTER

UK, 1974
Director: Brian Clemens.
Producers: Brian Clemens, Albert Fennell. Screenplay: Brian Clemens.
Music: Laurie Johnson. Cinematography: Ian Wilson.
Cast: Horst Janson, John Carson, Shane Briant, Caroline Munro,
John Cater, Lois Daine.

Hammer's efforts to inject new blood in its vampire titles paid off
with the unlikely new wrinkle on swashbuckling in the form of
this horror adventure written and directed by Brian Clemens, who
launched TV's **The Avengers** and penned Hammer's **Dr. Jekyll &
Sister Hyde** (1972). Intended as the start of an ongoing series, the
saga of Captain Kronos (Horst Janson) hunting down a clan of youth-draining vampires was a financial
disappointment at the time but has inspired a legion of fans as well as multiple comic book incarnations.
The ravishing Caroline Munro makes her second Hammer vampire appearance, and she would also appear
in the Clemens-penned **The Golden Voyage of Sinbad** (1973), which was shot after this film but released
before it. Despite the lack of overt bloodsucking, the film contains stronger violence than usual including
a protracted vampire execution that remains one of the most memorable moments. The skulking hooded
figures and fairy tale-inspired forest settings are also reminiscent of British occult horror films of the
period, most clearly **The Blood on Satan's Claw** (1971), and this was also one of the rare Hammers released
by Paramount Pictures who handled **Frankenstein and the Monster from Hell** (1974) the same year.

EVIL OF DRACULA

Japan, 1974
Director: Michio Yamamoto. Screenplay: Ei Ogawa,
Masaru Takesue. Music: Riichirô Manabe.
Cinematography: Kazutami Hara.
Cast: Toshio Kurosawa, Mariko Mochizuki, Mio Ôta,
Kunie Tanaka, Shin Kishida, Katsuhiko Sasaki.

Toho's stylish Bloodthirsty Trilogy wrapped up in wild style with this final entry, which rolled out three years after the previous **Lake of Dracula**. Director Michio Yamamoto returned once again along with actor Shin Kishida as the primary vampire, this time a shaggy-haired principal at a boarding school for young ladies. Newly arrived teacher Professor Shiraki (Toshio Kurosawa) finds the ailing principal stashing his recently deceased wife in the basement and urging the newcomer to take over leadership, only to uncover a supernatural plague afflicting the tennis-loving student body. The most Hammer-indebted of the trio (particularly **The Brides of Dracula**), this film was originally released as **Chi o Sū Bara** (or **Bloodsucking Rose**) and is the only one to feature the character of Dracula via a fascinating flashback about how the famed vampire ended up in Japan and spread his affliction outside of Europe. Adding to the fun is the wildest score from the series' regular composer, Riichirô Manabe, whose eccentric stylings are not only the most controversial aspects of these films but his handful of contributions to Toho's Godzilla cycle as well. Don't miss the knockabout climactic multiple vampire brawl, which features everything from axes to stools sent airborne as weapons against the undead.

THE LEGEND OF THE 7 GOLDEN VAMPIRES

UK/Hong Kong, 1974
Director: Roy Ward Baker.
Producers: Don Houghton, Vee King Shaw.
Screenplay: Don Houghton.
Music: James Bernard.
Cinematography: Roy Ford, John Wilcox.
Cast: Peter Cushing, David Chiang, Julie Ege, Robin Stewart, Shih Szu, John Forbes-Robertson.

Teaming up latter day Hammer Films and Hong Kong movie juggernaut Shaw Brothers sounds like a disastrous combination, but this candy-colored, action-horror hybrid defies the odds and sports a dedicated final Van Helsing appearance by Peter Cushing. A swan song in many respects, this was also the last Hammer Dracula film (or even vampire film in general), with the Count played here in bookend scenes by a dubbed John Forbes-Robertson after Christopher Lee decline to participate. It also features the last Hammer score by the great James Bernard and remains the best full-fledged vampire film (anthologies aside) directed by Roy Ward Baker in his seventh (and last) Hammer outing. This would be the first of a planned multi-film collaboration with Shaw Brothers (who also supplied uncredited director Chang Cheh and star David Chiang), though only one more title would come to fruition, the ill-fated actioner **Shatter** (1974). Though regarded with much affection now, the film (which also inaugurated a wave of modern Hong Kong horrors) did not fare well financially and didn't hit American screens until 1979 in a heavily reworked and much shorter version as **The 7 Brothers Meet Dracula**, emphasizing the martial arts and (fairly brief) nudity at the expense of coherence.

TENDER DRACULA

France, 1974
Director: Pierre Grunstein. Producers: Vincent Malle, Claude Berri [uncredited], Christian Fechner [uncredited].
Screenplay: Justin Lenoir. Music: Karl-Heinz Schäfer.
Cinematography: Jean-Jacques Tarbès.
Cast: Peter Cushing, Alida Valli, Bernard Menez, Miou-Miou, Nathalie Courval, Stéphane Shandor.

Originally entitled **La grande trouille** (or **The Big Scare**), this first of two French vampire farces with Hammer headliners features Peter Cushing as MacGregor, a famous actor who uses a medical dispensation to get out of his long-running popular role as a TV vampire. He'd rather do romantic soap operas instead so his two show runner writers (Bernard Menez and Stéphane Shandor) head to his foreboding castle for a weekend of increasingly surreal shenanigans during which they discover their star is a bona fide member of the undead who's devoted to his mysterious wife (Alida Valli). Extensive female nudity, bathroom taps pouring blood, musical numbers, chicken violence, silver face paint, and a dream sequence involving esteemed actress Miou-Miou sawed in half all figure in the bizarre proceedings, though the real attraction here is seeing Cushing (not known for playing monsters at all) donning fangs and a cape instead of wielding a stake. The entire film essentially works as an ode to the star with plentiful stills of his most famous roles and loving nods including a flashback explaining how he became a "high priest of horror." The film was prepared in both French and English-language versions (the latter with Cushing's real voice which makes it the more effective option), but it was barely shown outside of France and now ranks as the most curious and obscure footnote in Cushing's career.

VAMPIRE MOVIES

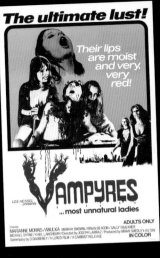

VAMPYRES

UK, 1974
Director: Joseph Larraz [José Ramón Larraz]. Producer: Brian Smedley-Aston.
Screenplay: D. Daubeney [José Ramón Larraz].
Music: James Kenelm Clarke.
Cinematography: Harry Waxman.
Cast: Marianne Morris, Anulka [Anulka Dziubinska], Murray Brown, Brian Deacon, Sally Faulkner, Michael Byrne.

Spanish-born director José Ramón Larraz closed out his mad flurry of British-shot horror titles like **Whirlpool** (1970) and **Symptoms** (1974) with this ferocious take on the erotic vampire film, which rockets into territory that was only hinted at in the envelope-pushing Hammer Karnstein cycle. Marianne Morris and Anulka make for the definitive lesbian vampire duo as they lure passing travelers to their sprawling country estate and drain their blood in a carnal frenzy, then dispose of the bodies in staged traffic accidents. A strong dash of poetic melancholia offsets the film's decidedly non-English indulgence in graphic sexuality and bloodletting, an approach that grabbed the attention of audiences at the time. Larraz's go-for-broke approach sat better with some actors than others; the two leading ladies have been highly supportive of the film with great affection shown to their director, while Brian Deacon and Sally Faulkner (who play a nearby camping couple in the biggest subplot) were less taken with the injection of unscripted sex scenes and rough violent sequences. Any production tensions aside, the final result, conceived as a British softcore exploitation item but turning out to be so much more, is one of the decade's pivotal vampire films and the inspiration for many later European productions including a considerably watered-down official Spanish remake by Victor Matellano in 2015.

LEONOR

France/Spain/Italy, 1975
Director: Juan Luis Buñuel. Producer: Michel Piccoli.
Screenplay: Roberto Bodegas, Juan Luis Buñuel, Clement
Biddle Wood, Bernardino Zapponi. Music: Ennio Morricone.
Cinematography: Luciano Tovoli.
Cast: Michel Piccoli, Liv Ullmann, Ornella Muti,
Antonio Ferrandis, José María Prada, José Guardiola.

The challenge of selling arthouse horror to audiences was never greater than in the case of this third and final film of writer-director Juan Luis Buñuel's uncanny 1970s trilogy that began with **Expulsion of the Devil** (1973) and continued with **The Lady with Red Boots** (1974). This one received the widest distribution of the trio thanks to distributor New Line (who cut 14 minutes and retitled it **Mistress of the Devil**) and a major prestige cast headlined by Michel Piccoli, Liv Ullmann, and Ornella Muti. The vampire element is so subdued here one could almost miss it entirely in the story of a nobleman whose grief drives him to make an unholy pact to revive his deceased wife, much to the misfortune of his newer bride. Ullmann makes for one of the era's more enigmatic and surprising vampires, with her child-murdering misdeeds kept offscreen and the horror element creeping into the story so slowly it's almost shocking when the story goes into pure Gothic territory in the final stretch. Complete with a haunting Ennio Morricone score and elegant cinematography by the great Luciano Tovoli (**Suspiria**), this medieval tragedy may not be to all tastes but will reward those who like their horror on the meditative side with a literary bent.

LIPS OF BLOOD

France, 1975
Director: Jean Rollin. Producer: Lionel Wallmann.
Screenplay: Jean-Loup Philippe, Jean Rollin. Music: Didier
William Lepauw. Cinematography: Jean-François Robin.
Cast: Jean-Loup Philippe, Annie Brilland [Annie Belle],
Natalie Perrey, Martine Grimaud, Catherine Castel,
Marie-Pierre Castel.

Jean Rollin's fifth vampire film, **Lips of Blood** (originally **Lèvres de sang**) is also perhaps his most beautiful thanks to its central device of a potent childhood memory that turns out to be the key to an entirely new identity. When Pierre (co-scenarist Jean-Lou Philippe) comes upon a photo of a castle familiar from his dreams and possibly his boyhood, he arranges a nocturnal liaison at a cinema with the photographer and stumbles into a vampire underworld connected to his past. The most hypnotic element here is presence of actress Annie Belle (here with her trademark close-cropped hair dyed dark brown) as his unearthly soulmate, Jennifer; under the name Annie Belle, she would go on to headline a string of Italian erotic and horror films including **Laure** (1976) and **House on the Edge of the Park** (1980) before retiring to private life as a social worker. Particularly memorable is the finale involving the beach and a pair of coffins, as pure a distillation of the Rollin vampire aesthetic as one could imagine. Unfortunately, commercial demands for dreamy erotic vampire cinema had largely dissipated by this point, so Rollin hedged his bets by reworking the footage into a silly pornographic variation entitled **Suce-moi vampire** with some of the same actors recruited for saucier new scenes.

MARY, MARY, BLOODY MARY

Mexico, 1975
Director: Juan López Moctezuma. Producers: Henri Bollinger, Robert Yamin.
Screenplay: Malcolm Marmorstein. Music: Tom Bähler. Cinematography: Miguel Garzón.
Cast: Cristina Ferrare, David Young, John Carradine, Helena Rojo, Arthur Hansel, Enrique Lucero.

Sandwiched in between the more frenzied freak-outs of **The Mansion of Madness** (1973) and **Alucarda** (1977), this second feature from Mexican director Juan López Moctezuma is a moody character study about – who else? – Mary (Max Factor model and onetime John DeLorean spouse Cristina Ferrare), a modernist painter who craves blood and draws it with a discreetly hidden hairpin. Combating loneliness as much as her blood hunger, she works her way through several casual encounters while avoiding another creature of the night (John Carradine) on her trail. Elements of Countess Báthory and *Carmilla* can be found woven into this tale, which has a woozy, painterly approach akin to cinematic fever dreams like **Messiah of Evil** and **Let's Scare Jessica to Death**. (Also, those opposed to animal cruelty in films should be warned that there is a sequence involving shark abuse that may not be simulated.) Like many female-centric projects around the same time, Moctezuma's film dispenses with most vampire conventions, instead focusing on Mary's isolation and seemingly endless need for companionship and sustenance. Ferrare is effective and unabashed in the role, though this would prove to be the final film of her short big-screen career as she moved on to become an author, jewelry designer, and frequent TV guest of Oprah Winfrey. Mexican vampire offerings from this point onward were few and far between, though curious viewers can find plenty of Gothic-style trappings in the rare but entertaining **La dinastía de Dracula** (1980) about a staked vampire being revived to embark on a vengeance crusade with the help of a very intense witch played by drive-in veteran Erika Carlsson.

She's a
beauty
She's a
beast
She's
Bloody
Mary

Mary, Mary,
Bloody Mary

R RESTRICTED BLOODY COLOR BLACK LION RELEASE

YOUNG DRACULA

Italy, 1975
Director: Lucio Fulci. Screenplay: Lucio Fulci,
Pupi Avati, Mario Amendola, Bruno Corbucci.
Music: Franco Bixio, Fabio Frizzi, Vince Tempera.
Cinematography: Sergio Salvati.
Cast: Lando Buzzanca, Rossano Brazzi, Moira Orfei,
Sylva Koscina, Christa Linder, John Steiner.

Basketball, gay panic, and Gothic horror collide
in this bizarre sex comedy from none other than
Italian horror maestro Lucio Fulci in a spiritual
follow up of sorts to his best comic effort, **The
Eroticist** (1972), both of which offer amusing takedowns of cultural
propriety and masculinity. That prior film's leading man, popular square-
jawed comic actor Lando Buzzanca, returns here as Costante Nicosia,
a boorish toothpaste factory magnate married in a socially convenient
arrangement to Mariù (Sylva Koscina). The uber-capitalist makes life
miserable for those around him, but after going one step too far and
incurring a curse from his gypsy aunt, he ends up spending a debauched
night in Romania with the leering Count Dragulescu (John Steiner).
Suddenly struck by simultaneous vampirism, homosexual tendencies, and
an urge to bite his wife on the rump, he starts to reassesses his worldview.
Fulci's ability to adapt to any number of genres has often been overlooked
in the wake of his gory '80s classics, but he always held a particular
fondness for his comedies including this one. It's certainly one of the
oddest vampire romps around all the way to the memorable twist ending

curtain dropper, but for Fulci followers it's also notable as one of the first features to unite him with his
dream team of cinematographer Sergio Salvati
and composers Franco Bixio, Fabio Frizzi
and Vince Tempera along with the same
year's **The Four of the Apocalypse**.

DRACULA AND SON

France, 1976
Director: Édouard Molinaro. Producer: Alain Poiré.
Screenplay: Alain Godard, Jean-Marie Poiré, Édouard Molinaro.
Music: Vladimir Cosma. Cinematography: Alain Levent.
Cast: Christopher Lee, Bernard Menez, Marie-Hélène Breillat,
Catherine Breillat, Mustapha Dali, Bernard Alane.

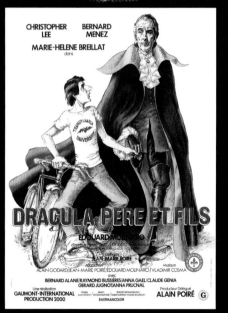

Three years after formally bidding adieu to his cape and fangs at Hammer, Christopher Lee got to show off his comedic chops in this lighthearted farce originally entitled **Dracula père et fils**. Famed French comedy director Édouard Molinaro of **La cage aux folles** (1978) fame helmed this tale about "the Count" (Lee) and his reluctant vampire son, Ferdinand (Bernard Ménez), driven out of Transylvania by political upheaval to find their new destinies as a TV star and a security guard respectively. Future arthouse provocateur Catherine Breillat and her sister, Marie-Hélène, play the principal female leads here in a story that plays like an amusing generational conflict / coming-of-age tale in its original French-language version. An uncut English-dubbed version was also offered to distributors, but in America it was butchered beyond recognition with a totally new script performed by voices in the style of TV's **Get Smart** by way of Woody Allen's **What's Up, Tiger Lily?** (1966). This was hardly the first time Lee had sent up his Dracula image, a trend going back to his role in the Steno comedy **Uncle Was a Vampire** (1959) and a caped cameo appearance during the climax of **The Magic Christian** (1969), though only this one has him putting the bite on an inflatable sex doll.

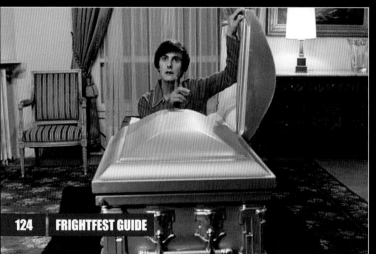

DRACULA

UK, 1977
Director: Philip Saville. Producer: Morris Barry.
Screenplay: Gerald Savory. Music: Kenyon Emrys-Roberts.
Cinematography: Peter Hall.
Cast: Louis Jourdan, Frank Finlay, Susan Penhaligon,
Judi Bowker, Jack Shepherd, Mark Burns.

The most accurate filmed rendering of Bram Stoker's novel to date came
from an unexpected source with this impressively mounted BBC production
originally aired as a single mammoth telecast in time for Christmas in 1977.
Since then it has been diced into two or three segments without doing significant
damage to the production, which was largely filmed on video (including some
endearing lo-tech effects work) with the usual 16mm film sections for some
outdoor sequences. Louis Jourdan makes for an urbane and subdued Dracula
who contrasts with a confident Frank Finlay as Van Helsing, not to mention a
fragile but perceptive Judi Bowker as Mina. Less effective is Richard Barnes'
Pythonesque American accent as composite character "Quincey P. Holmwood,"
but you can't win 'em all. The oft-adapted source material is made genuinely
frightening here using several seldom-filmed passages, most obviously the early
baby-feeding sequence (which was still slightly watered down by TV censors) and
a vivid presentation of Lucy's nocturnal behaviour. The production uses the video
format to its advantage as well with the atmospheric castle and crypt settings
given a queasy, unsettling immediacy that gives each sudden shadow a visceral
jolt. Even with some minor tweaks to the source, this should be one of the first
stops on any tour of classic Draculas.

MARTIN

USA, 1977
Director: George A. Romero.
Producers: Richard P. Rubinstein,
Ben Barenholtz [uncredited].
Screenplay: George A. Romero.
Music: Donald Rubinstein.
Cinematography: Michael Gornick.
Cast: John Amplas, Lincoln Maazel,
Christine Forrest, Elayne Nadeau,
Tom Savini, Sara Venable.

Just before he revolutionized horror cinema with **Dawn of the Dead** (1978), writer-director George A. Romero tackled vampirism for the first and only time in his career with this unforgettable character study of a troubled young man named Martin (John Amplas) who believes he is a vampire and drinks blood through the application of razor blades and syringes. Reflecting the ongoing generation gap of the 1970s, he's pitted against his hardline immigrant uncle (Lincoln Maazel) who believes in Martin's vampirism and swears to extinguish him if he acts on his bloodthirsty impulses. The film is deliberately ambiguous, an aspect enhanced by the fact that this was whittled down from a much longer 165-minute original cut, which was considered lost for decades. However, what stands now works perfectly as a queasy coming-of-age story with some of Romero's most startling stylistic touches, such as the dreamy black-and-white Gothic inserts that reflect Martin's possibly imaginary vampire persona. The film also marks the first teaming of Romero and innovative makeup artist Tom Savini, who also appears in the film as the boyfriend of Martin's cousin played by Romero's future wife, Christine Forrest. Though Savini's work is less elaborate here than his acclaimed zombie concoctions, he can still make viewers squirm with some of the most realistic bloodletting seen on screen up to that point including a jaw-dropping moment involving a tree branch and adult film actor Roger Caine. First screened at Cannes in 1977 but given an official release the following year, **Martin** was substantially reworked in Italy where it was retitled **Wampyr** and outfitted with a Goblin soundtrack mostly comprised of pre-existing tracks. Incredibly, the film was briefly swept up in the U.K.'s video nasty panic of the 1980s but didn't make it to the prosecution stage.

George Romero brings you the bloody, nightmarish tale of

MARTIN

Martin is a disturbingly thrilling film — for those strong enough in stomach, heart and mind to take it . . .

Starring JOHN AMPLAS as MARTIN
LINCOLN MAAZEL as CUDA •
CHRISTINE FORREST as CHRISTINA
ELAYNE NADEAU as ABBIE SANTINI •
Also Starring TOM SAVINI • SARA VENABLE •
FRAN MIDDLETON • AL LEVITSKY
Written and Directed by GEORGE A. ROMERO
Produced by RICHARD RUBINSTEIN

NIGHTMARE IN BLOOD

USA, 1977
Director: John Stanley.
Producers: Kenn Davis, John Stanley.
Screenplay: John Stanley, Kenn Davis.
Music: David Litwin.
Cinematography: Kenn Davis.
Cast: Jerry Walter, Dan Caldwell,
Barrie Youngfellow, John Cochran,
Ray K. Goman, Hy Pyke.

Host of the long-running San Francisco TV show **Creature Features** and author of the beloved horror reference guide of the same time, John Stanley made his one sojourn into feature film directing with this early entry in the depictions of horror fandom intersecting with bona fide monsters. Coming off of an abandoned project called *Dark Side of the Hunt* with collaborator Kenn Davis, Stanley is absolutely in his element here for a tale of a Bay Area horror convention besieged by a Malakai (Jerry Walter), star of such fictitious films as *The Crypt Ran Red* and a real vampire who can bare his fangs and prey on the guests with impunity until some amateur vampire hunters catch on. It took five years from initial shooting through post-production for this film to see the light of a projector, and despite its obvious technical shortcomings, Stanley's labor of love is a fascinating time capsule of the West Coast horror fan scene, a precursor to both the vampire wave of the late '70s and the bloodsucker actor concept of **Shadow of the Vampire**, and a sincere love letter to classic vampire cinema. Other delights include a brief opening appearance by a swashbuckling Kerwin Matthews (in his last role), fleeting glimpses of Fred Dekker and Kathleen Quinlan, a surprisingly rich look achieved through Techniscope lensing, and references galore to Universal, Hammer and Sherlock Holmes films peppered throughout the script.

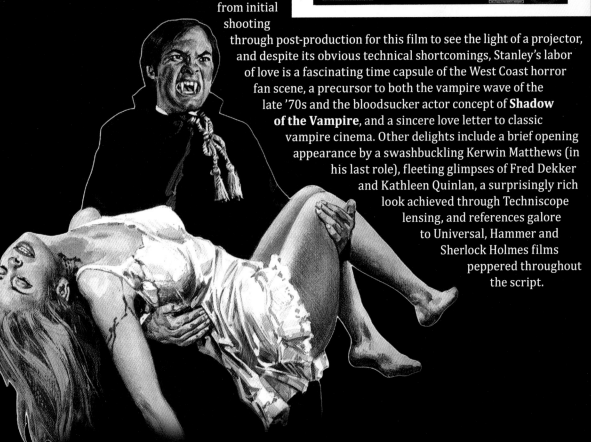

ZOLTAN, HOUND OF DRACULA

USA, 1977
Director: Albert Band. Producers: Albert Band,
Frank Ray Perilli. Screenplay: Frank Ray Perilli.
Music: Andrew Belling. Cinematography: Bruce Logan.
Cast: José Ferrer, Michael Pataki, Jan Shutan, Libby Chase,
John Levin, Reggie Nalder.

Also released as **Dracula's Dog**, this sixth feature by
drive-in veteran Albert Band took half a decade to bring to
the screen under the auspices of UK-based EMI Films after
he bought the Frank Ray Pirelli screenplay in 1973. Actor
Reggie Nalder makes his first (but hardly last) vampire
appearance here as Veidt, a disciple of evil who escorts
Dracula's recently revived canine from Romania to America
to track down the bloodline's last member, Michael Pataki, in
what amounts to a riff on his earlier **Grave of the Vampire**.
Oscar winner José Ferrer lends some degree of cachet to the
inherently silly premise, which is played mostly straight and
earned surprisingly solid reviews for what amounts to the
purest intersection of the 1970s craze for both vampire and
animal attack films. The box office potential wasn't lost on
Crown International, who snapped this up for American play
at the same time as the more typical '78 films **Malibu Beach**
and **Coach**. This was one of two supernatural doggie horror
films released that year along with Curtis Harrington's
made-for-TV epic **Devil Dog: The Hound of Hell** (1978),
though nothing can beat this film's outrageous curtain drop
of an ending that prompted Joe Dante to lament the missed
opportunity for a sequel called *Puppies from Hell*.

DOCTOR DRACULA

USA, 1978
Directors: Paul Aratow, Al Adamson.
Producer: Lou Sorkin. Screenplay: Paul Aratow,
Cecil Brown, Gary Reathman.
Cinematography: Gary Graver, Robbie Greenberg.
Cast: John Carradine, Donald Barry, Larry Hankin,
Geoffrey Land, Susan McIver, Regina Carrol.

A vampire film only created long after the fact,
this mind-melting cinematic crazy quilt from the
drive-in team of director Al Adamson and producer-
distributor Sam Sherman started life as a shelved
1974 production called **Lucifer's Women,** a modern-
day variation on the story of Svengali revolving
around a mesmeric occult researcher (played by
Larry Hankin) and his Satanist publisher (Norman
Pierce). The film was overhauled for its 1978 release as **Doctor
Dracula** complete with new scenes featuring John Carradine,
Regina Carrol and a bearded Geoffrey Land as Gregorio, a modern
incognito incarnation of Dracula who becomes locked in an
ongoing feud with the nouveaux Svengali. The end result is so
baffling and nonsensical it was sold off to American television, but
as an exercise in cinematic surgery there's a great deal to learn
here about how a vampire angle can be spun out of a thin air for
a film that was originally about something completely different.
Most notably, it's an example of Adamson and Sherman actually
anticipating a trend by noting the number of vampire films in
production that would hit in 1979, essentially beating them to the
punch by simply grafting a new subplot onto an occult oddity that
would have otherwise remained buried. Both versions have since
been salvaged and paired up on home video, an opportunity to
compare and contrast to your heart's content.

THIS TIME THE COUNT
IS NOT JUST GOING FOR THROAT!

DRACULA
Sucks

starring
JAMIE GILLIS ANNETTE HAVEN JOHN HOLMES SERENA JOHN LESLIE
executive producer   produced by   screenplay by   directed by
DAVID EMERICH DARRYL A. MARSHAK DAVID J. KERN, DARRYL A. MARSHAK PHILIP MARSHAK
A NEW CLASSIC FOR
ADULTS   A MR PRODUCTION LTD.. INC PRODUCTION   World Sales: KODIAK FILMS, INC.,
Los Angeles

DRACULA SUCKS

USA, 1978
Director: Phillip Marshak. Producer: Darryl Marshak.
Screenplay: Darryl Marshak, David Kern.
Music: Lionel Thomas. Cinematography: Hanania Baer.
Cast: Jamie Gillis, Annette Haven, John Leslie, Serena,
Detlef van Berg [Reggie Nalder], Kay Parker.

Existing in at least three distinctly different variants, this adults-only oddity from the porno chic era retains more of Bram Stoker's handiwork than the jokey title might lead you to expect. A bearded Jamie Gillis makes for an intense Count and headlines a cast of hardcore performers all dressed (or partially undressed) in chic 1930s garb including Serena, John Leslie, Seka, and Kay Parker. Still full of sharp fangs and bloody throats, the story of Dracula, Carfax Abbey, and his obsession with Mina (here played by Annette Haven) is relocated here to Death Valley, with most of the novel's major characters retained as well. Doing multiple vampire duties that year, **Salem's Lot** actor Reggie Nalder even turns up as one of

the strangest screen Van Helsings imaginable. A purely softcore version was initially released on mainstream home video, while an explicit hardcore one did the rounds under the title **Lust at First Bite**. However, the refurbished director's cut is the most rewarding one around, at least for those who don't mind a few bits of brief pornography sprinkled into their vampire action. Another hardcore Stoker-based film, **Dracula Exotica** (1980), was released soon after but isn't remotely as interesting.

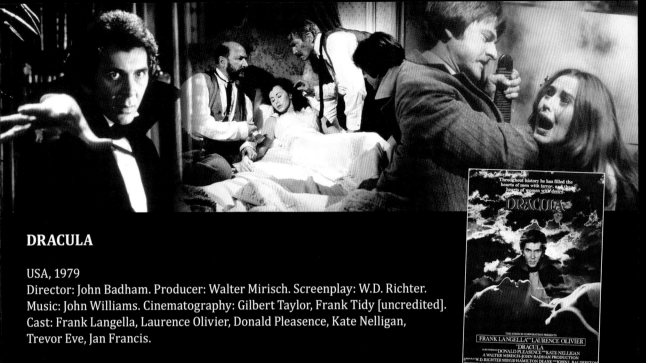

DRACULA

USA, 1979
Director: John Badham. Producer: Walter Mirisch. Screenplay: W.D. Richter.
Music: John Williams. Cinematography: Gilbert Taylor, Frank Tidy [uncredited].
Cast: Frank Langella, Laurence Olivier, Donald Pleasence, Kate Nelligan,
Trevor Eve, Jan Francis.

The most prestigious studio production in the 1979 big screen vampire
frenzy started life as an adaptation of the play by Hamilton Deane and John
L. Balderston, the source for Universal's original **Dracula** with Bela Lugosi, which had enjoyed a
successful, Tony Award-winning 1977 Broadway revival starring Frank Langella and featuring striking
monochromatic art designs by macabre humorist Edward Gorey. Hot off the success of **Saturday Night
Fever** (1977), director John Badham came aboard this version and retained many elements, such as the
Edwardian setting and the switch between Mina and Lucy's characters, while decking the film with
such commercial ornamentation as a sweeping, memorable score by John Williams, a formidable cast
(including Laurence Olivier, Kate Nelligan and Donald Pleasence), and a smoky, disco-friendly seduction
sequence by James Bond title designer Maurice Binder. Though the more gruesome elements of the story
have been played down, the film is notable for one of the most chilling sequences in all of vampire cinema
with Olivier's Abraham Van Helsing going underground to find his recently converted daughter, Mina (Jan
Francis) not exactly as he remembered her. Most controversially, Badham desaturated most of the once
vibrant film to a bland grayish sepia tone for home video release after the initial VHS editions, a decision
that outraged many fans until the original version was finally brought back into circulation in 2019.

FASCINATION

France, 1979
Director: Jean Rollin. Producer: Joe de Lara [Joe de Palmer].
Screenplay: Jean Rollin. Music: Philippe d'Aram.
Cinematography: Georgie Fromentin.
Cast: Brigitte Lahaie, Jean-Marie Lemaire, Franka Mai,
Fanny Magier, Evelyne Thomas, Muriel Montossé.

"Drink, my dear. It will bring back your color." After spending a decade exploring aspects of the traditional fanged, castle-dwelling vampire, director Jean Rollin ventured into new territory with this atmospheric chamber piece about an all-female blood cult operating in the French countryside. In typical fashion he mixes in a gun-toting criminal who seems to have the upper hand at first, but that's no match for one of Rollin's most iconic creations, the striking Brigitte Lahaie bloodily wielding a scythe while wearing nothing but a flowing black cloak. The entire film unfolds almost in real time over the course of a misty afternoon into a dark, bloody evening, with the erotic and violent proceedings finding Rollin delving far more thoroughly into the lesbian vampire concept than ever before. The sex scenes are integrated more smoothly into the overall film, reflecting the goals of the characters rather than serving as titillating window dressing. This also marks Rollin's first collaboration with composer Philippe d'Aram, whose dreamy synthesizer waltzes (including a Mellotron), coupled with the largest number of musicians in Rollin's career, imbue the film with an uncanny atmosphere right from the opening scene with a noblewoman sampling cow's blood, an idea that reoccurs in later vampire films as well.

VAMPIRE MOVIES

LOVE AT FIRST BITE

USA, 1979
Director: Stan Dragoti. Producers: Joel Freeman, Melvin Simon.
Screenplay: Robert Kaufman. Music: Charles Bernstein. Cinematography: Edward Rosson.
Cast: George Hamilton, Susan Saint James, Richard Benjamin, Dick Shawn, Arte Johnson, Sherman Jemsley.

The first vampire comedy to find genuine mainstream success arrived just before the collapse of the disco craze, with Dracula (George Hamilton) forced out of Transylvania and determined to win the heart of his true love, fashion model Cindy Sondheim (Susan Saint James), in the middle of sexually liberated, cocaine-fueled Manhattan. Against the odds, the broad humour, infectious dance music soundtrack, and committed performances created an audience pleaser buoyed by the strongest performance of Hamilton's career. Particularly indebted to Universal's original 1931 **Dracula**, the film frequently nods to Lugosi' interpretation as well as Dwight Frye's Renfield by way of Arte Johnson's cackling, bug-eating sidekick; in fact, that original film's makeup artist, William Tuttle, was brought back here after recreating the Universal look for Mel Brooks' **Young Frankenstein** (1974). One of the last successful films released by the beloved American International Pictures, the film has circulated in several alternate versions over the years with the majority of home video versions dropping the celebrated "I Love the Nightlife" song from the soundtrack and some TV prints adding a bizarre bonus scene with Dracula being pounced upon by a sexually aggressive subway passenger. However, this wasn't the only New York City disco vampire romantic comedy released in 1979...

DRACULA
Your favorite pain in the neck
is about to bite your
funny bone.

NOCTURNA

USA, 1979
Director: Harry Tampa [Harry Hurwitz]. Producer: Vernon P. Becker.
Screenplay: Harry Tampa [Harry Hurwitz].
Music: Norman Bergen, Reid Whitelaw. Cinematography: Mac Ahlberg.
Cast: Nai Bonet, John Carradine, Yvonne De Carlo, Tony Hamilton,
Brother Theodore [Theodore Gottlieb], Sy Richardson.

Usually seen as a belly dancer in a handful of
Hollywood films and TV shows, Vietnamese-
born Nai Bonet made an unorthodox bid for
leading lady stardom by partially self-financing
this lowbrow, very silly vampire comedy with
a wall-to-wall disco soundtrack aimed to cash
in on the recent **Saturday Night Fever** (1977)
craze. However, any possibility of luring in
young viewers was thwarted by Bonet's extended nude bathing
sequence, which in turn made this a popular VHS rental item before it vanished from the earth entirely.
In his umpteenth turn as Count Dracula, John Carradine seems disoriented and gets lines like "If I'm dead,
why do I have to wee-wee?" while Yvonne De Carlo nibbles on the scenery when it isn't in the hands of the
guttural, unforgettable Brother Theodore. Bonet's lack of thespian skills as the love-seeking title character
(Dracula's granddaughter) ensured that her career would end after just one more film, but the time
capsule value and sheer oddness here are compelling if one is dogged enough to track it down. Short-lived
distributor Compass International Pictures found little financial success with this film so soon after its
major success with **Halloween** (1978), though the wildly entertaining double-LP soundtrack (featuring the
likes of Gloria Gaynor and Vicki Sue Robinson) remains a strong favourite among discophiles to this day.

NOSFERATU THE VAMPYRE

West Germany/France, 1979
Director: Werner Herzog. Producers: Werner Herzog,
Michael Gruskoff [uncredited], Daniel Toscan du Plantier
[uncredited]. Screenplay: Werner Herzog. Music: Florian
Fricke, Popol Vuh. Cinematography: Jörg Schmidt-Reitwein.
Cast: Klaus Kinski, Isabelle Adjani, Bruno Ganz, Roland
Topor, Walter Ladengast, Dan van Husen.

A bizarre idea on paper and a marvel in execution, this remake of F.W. Murnau's 1922 silent horror classic
marked the second collaboration between audacious filmmaker Werner Herzog and his most famous and
tempestuous star, Klaus Kinski, here sporting a shaved head, rat-like fangs, and long talons as an updated
spin on Max Schreck's eternal nightmare figure. Equal parts Gothic horror and arthouse fever dream, the film
sticks to the essentials of the original film (albeit with the original Bram Stoker character names restored)
while cranking up its more eccentric elements, most famously the onslaught of plague-carrying rats achieving
by importing hordes of real ones from Holland under difficult circumstances. Kinski's haunted,
fascinating performance is offset by a nervous, fragile one by Isabelle Adjani, with Bruno
Ganz (as Jonathan Harker) figuring in the striking, ironic revisionist ending. However,
the most bizarre flourish may be the casting of the eccentric Renfield with avant garde
Panic Movement co-creator Roland Topor, whose novel *The Tenant* was filmed by
Roman Polanski in 1976 (with Adjani). In a rare but not unique practice, the film was
shot simultaneously in German and English-language versions with the multilingual
cast but the German version received far wider play and is preferred by its creator.

TWENTIETH CENTURY-FOX presents

KLAUS KINSKI ISABELLE ADJANI
in NOSFERATU THE VAMPYRE
(English Subtitles)
with BRUNO GANZ

MICHAEL GRUSKOFF presents A WERNER HERZOG FILM

PG PARENTAL GUIDANCE SUGGESTED ⬥
SOME MATERIAL MAY NOT BE SUITABLE FOR PRE-TEENAGERS

Written, Produced and Directed by WERNER HERZOG Color by EASTMAN

Now in paperback from AVON

© 1979 TWENTIETH CENTURY-FOX

SALEM'S LOT

USA, 1979
Director: Tobe Hooper. Producer: Richard Kobritz.
Screenplay: Paul Monash. Music: Harry Sukman.
Cinematography: Jules Brenner.
Cast: David Soul, James Mason, Lance Kerwin, Lew Ayres,
Bonnie Bedelia, Ed Flanders, Reggie Nalder.

Published in 1975, Stephen King's second novel, *Salem's Lot,* also became his second to go before the cameras following Brian De Palma's **Carrie** (1976). The two-part miniseries aired on CBS and became the talk of playgrounds around the United States thanks to countless traumatized young viewers who would have otherwise been unfamiliar with the work of director Tobe Hooper so soon after **The Texas Chain Saw Massacre** (1974). With its floating vampire children and depiction of a small town rotting from the inside out, the film was so successful it was released as a theatrical feature overseas, dropping some of the minor subplots but adding two stronger sequences (a shotgun in Fred Willard's mouth and a bloody antler impalement). Distinctive character actor Reggie Nalder makes a strong but silent impression as the head vampire, the **Nosferatu**-inspired Mr. Barlow (a far cry from the urbane and chatty antique store owner in the novel), with James Mason ideally cast as the enabling Mr. Straker. The casting of David Soul and Lance Kerwin as the main vampire hunters, Ben Mears and Mark Petrie, also pays off and paves the way for a new epilogue intended to set up a TV series that never materialized. Widely regarded as a high point of made-for-TV horror, Hooper's film would go on to inspire a bizarre satirical sequel by Larry Cohen, **Return to Salem's Lot** (1987), a less colorful 2004 miniseries remake starring Rob Lowe and Rutger Hauer, a **Chapelwaite** prequel series begun in 2021 starring Adrien Brody and based on King's "Jerusalem's Lot" short story, and a 2022 feature film directed by Gary Dauberman and starring Lewis Pullman and Alfre Woodard.

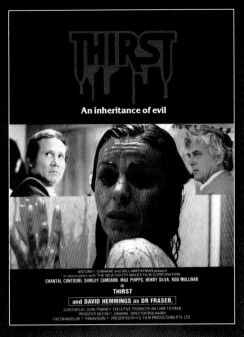

THIRST

An inheritance of evil

ANTONY I. GINNANE and WILLIAM FAYMAN present
in association with THE NEW SOUTH WALES FILM CORPORATION.
CHANTAL CONTOURI, SHIRLEY CAMERON, MAX PHIPPS, HENRY SILVA, ROD MULLINAR
in
THIRST
and DAVID HEMMINGS as DR FRASER.
SCREENPLAY JOHN PINKNEY EXECUTIVE PRODUCER WILLIAM FAYMAN
PRODUCER ANTONY I. GINNANE DIRECTOR ROD HARDY
EASTMANCOLOR • PANAVISION ® PRESENTED BY F.G. FILM PRODUCTIONS PTY. LTD.

THIRST

Australia, 1979
Director: Rod Hardy. Producer: Antony I. Ginnane.
Screenplay: John Pinkney. Music: Brian May.
Cinematography: Vincent Monton.
Cast: Chantal Contouri, David Hemmings, Henry Silva,
Max Phipps, Shirley Cameron, Rod Mullinar.

Though a vampire figured prominently in the comedy **Barry McKenzie Holds His Own** (1974), Australia didn't get a full-fledged bloodsucker film of its own until this remarkably prescient look at industrialized blood consumption, an element that would become commonplace in 21st century takes on the subject. Chantal Contouri stars as Kate, a descendant of the infamous Countess Báthory targeted as a valuable addition to the international vampire organization, The Brotherhood, who has made a cottage industry out of draining "blood cows" for sustenance. Cementing the film's Aussie horror credentials are the presence of actor David Hemmings (who had a notable career directing Down Under) and reliable composer Brian May, who was seemingly a contractual obligation on every '70s and early '80s genre title. The stylish scope lensing makes the film look considerably more expensive and ambitious than it really is, while director Rod Hardy (who was mostly relegated to Australian TV outside of this) makes the most of some of the more outré touches like a milk carton filled with blood and a memorable sanguinary shower sequence later reprised in **Death Ship** (1980) and the made-for-TV film, **This House Possessed** (1981). Despite its high-profile international rollout (including an American release from New Line), this would be the only Aussie vampire film for nearly a decade... but more on that later.

DRACULA, SOVEREIGN OF THE DAMNED

Japan, 1980
Directors: Akinori Nagaoka, Minoru Okazaki.
Screenplay: Tadaaki Yamazaki. Music: Seiji Yokoyama.
Cast: Kenji Utsumi (voice), Hiroko Suzuki (voice),
Kazuyuki Sogabe (voice), Yasuo Hisamatsu (voice),
Mami Koyama (voice), Ryo Ishihara (voice).

An animated showdown between Dracula and Satan already sounds like essential viewing, though it's unlikely anyone could have predicted what became of that high concept with this Japanese anime adaptation of Marvel's *Tomb of Dracula* comic book series. Begun in 1972, the American publication had just ceased in 1979 and upended the usual lore with Dracula (whose teeth can glow at will) veering between an arch-nemesis and ally to other superheroes in the canon. The characters and multiple storylines were condensed for the Japanese TV rendition from Toei Animation, originally titled **Yami no Teiō: Kyūketsuki Dorakyura**; here Dracula muscles into a Satanic cult and sires an offspring with the devil's betrothed, only to face resistance from a band of vampire hunters including a cross-sporting canine. The English-language version (which attempts to camouflage the Japanese origins entirely by crediting writing and direction to Robert Barron) suffers from a particularly clunky dub and poorly rendered computerized credits, both of which add to the already disjointed nature of the adaptation. However, the swooning romanticism of the approach makes for an unexpected change of pace all the way to the cosmic denouement and final tip of the hat to Vlad Tepes. A Marvel spin on Frankenstein's monster was also tackled by Toei in tandem with this film, **Kyōfu Densetsu Kaiki! Frankenstein** or **The Monster of Frankenstein** (1981).

DRACULA'S LAST RITES

USA, 1980
Director: Domonic Paris.
Producer: Kelly Van Horn. Screenplay: Ben Donnelly,
Domonic Paris. Music: Paul Jost, George Small.
Cinematography: Domonic Paris.
Cast: Patricia Lee Hammond, Gerald Fielding, Mimi Weddell,
Victor Jorge, Michael David Lally, Alfred Steinel.

The first (but by no means last) vampire effort from Cannon Films is a quirky, low-budget indie shot in New Jersey by filmmaker Dominic Paris, a future specialist in VHS-era clip reels and trailer compilations. The ingeniously named A. Lucard (Gerald Fielding) is a funeral home director who arranges accidents for passersby who end up not only on the morgue slab but in the blood-starved bellies of his town's vampire population. Enter Ted (Michael David Lally), who's decided his mother-in-law's funeral arrangements are going to be changed – after she's already been drained and is about to turn into a vampire if she doesn't get staked in time. Much budget-conscious pandemonium ensues.

Also known as simply **Last Rites**, this one has suffered from a terrible reputation over the years but does have quite a bit of charm if you love regional horror, not to mention a memorable design for its undead mother-in-law and a surprising, unsparing finale that breaks the mold just a little bit. In a sense this is also noteworthy as a precursor to the cult classic **Dead & Buried** (1981) with its small-town monstrous conspiracy and pivotal mortician character who is more influential than meets the eye.

MAMA DRACULA

Belgium/France, 1980
Director: Boris Szulzinger. Producer: Boris Szulzinger.
Screenplay: Pierre Sterckx, Boris Szulzinger, Marc-Henri Wajnberg.
Music: Roy Budd. Cinematography: Rufus Bohez, Willy Kurant.
Cast: Louise Fletcher, Maria Schneider, Marc-Henri Wajnberg,
Alexander Wajnberg, Jimmy Shuman, Jess Hahn.

A confounding film on many fronts, this Belgian horror comedy earns its place in the history books as the first lighthearted look at the blood-bathing antics of Countess Báthory. In this case the legendary murderess is portrayed by a very glammed-up, Hungarian-accented Louise Fletcher, who unleashes comedic pandemonium throughout her castle when she lures a synthetic blood researcher to help maintain her secret beauty formula. The Oscar-winning Fletcher was making many questionable career choices around this time, but the honour of most surprising cast member easily goes to the late Maria Schneider of **Last Tango in Paris** (1972) and **The Passenger** (1975) fame, who wasn't known

for her comic ability and made this back to back with the Klaus Kinski art film **Haine** (1980). Though this belated entry in the line of 1970s European vampire comedies earned a bit of enthusiastic coverage in the likes of *Famous Monsters* magazine, it wound up heading straight to TV and video in most countries. Director Boris Szulzinger, whose previous claim to fame was co-helming the naughty animated film **Tarzoon: Shame of the Jungle** (1975), loads the film up with elegant visuals that are difficult to appreciate in the substandard prints and video copies floating around. The oh-so-Eastern-European score is provided by none other than Roy Budd, best known now for **Get Carter** (1971).

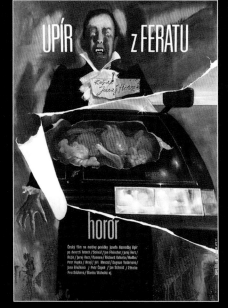

FERAT VAMPIRE

Czechoslovakia, 1982
Director: Juraj Herz. Screenplay: Jan Fleischer, Juraj Herz.
Music: Petr Hapka. Cinematography: Richard Valenta.
Cast: Jirí Menzel, Dagmar Veskrnová, Jana Brezková Petr Cepek,
Jan Schmid, Zdenka Procházková.

"Don't laugh, it might be circling around Prague now, and during every push on the accelerator pedal, your loved ones' blood is traveling through its internals!" Can an inanimate object be a vampire? Yes, it can, at least according to Czechoslovak director Juraj Herz who made this in the wake of his better-known masterpieces like **The Cremator** (1969), **Morgiana** (1972), and **Beauty and the Beast** (1978). The outrageous premise of **Ferat Vampire** (**Upír z Feratu**, a riff on the local title of 1922's **Nosferatu**) involves a new line of import Ferat automobiles whose red-scarfed company head (Zdenka Procházková) has come up with a cost-efficient innovation: human blood as car fuel. A mixture of satire, surrealism and full-blooded horror, Herz's film ran into temporary trouble in its native country due to its grotesque subject matter (and despite its obvious ribbing of consumerism). The fact that it's set up as an oddball detective story involving curious Dr. Marek (Jirí Menzel) and his former, speed-crazy ambulance driver Mima (Dagmar Havlová) makes the premise more palatable than one might expect; it's also surprising when the film makes brief detours into full-blown human vampirism as well, though it would be criminal to say when or how. A similar premise was later used in the far more obscure **Blood Car** (2007).

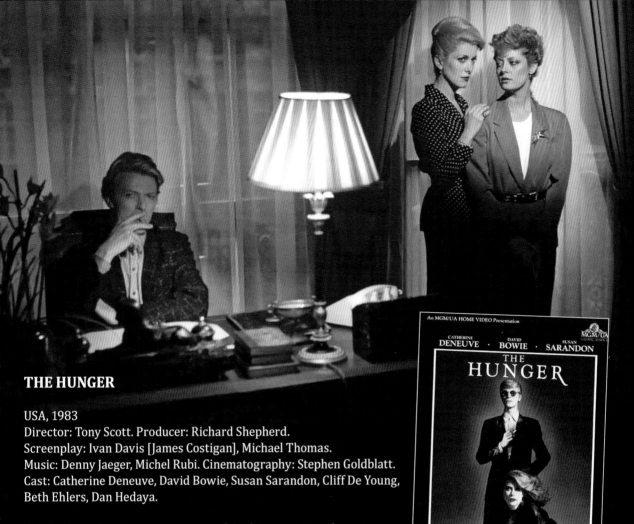

THE HUNGER

USA, 1983
Director: Tony Scott. Producer: Richard Shepherd.
Screenplay: Ivan Davis [James Costigan], Michael Thomas.
Music: Denny Jaeger, Michel Rubi. Cinematography: Stephen Goldblatt.
Cast: Catherine Deneuve, David Bowie, Susan Sarandon, Cliff De Young,
Beth Ehlers, Dan Hedaya.

The final word in cinematic vampire chic, this arresting adaptation
of Whitley Streiber's 1981 novel charts two significant relationships
in the life of wealthy, predatory Manhattan socialite Miriam Blaylock
(Catherine Deneuve), whose current companion, John (David Bowie,
born to play a vampire), suddenly begins aging at an accelerated rate
after centuries of sex and bloodshed. A scientific look at the nature
of vampirism is provided by gerontologist Sarah Roberts (Susan
Sarandon), who also falls under Miriam's spell but meets a different end. The downbeat resolution
of Streiber's novel is significantly changed here to ape the coda from **Daughters of Darkness** and Miriam's

background dating back to ancient Egypt is
only hinted at in quick flashes, but the spirit
remains the same with a fine modern gloss
provided by first-time feature director Tony
Scott, a pounding soundtrack that kicks off on
a thunderous note with Bauhaus' nightclub
rendition of "Bela Lugosi's Dead," and a much-
discussed lesbian love scene that made this
an enduring go-to title on video for years. The
film also introduced the ankh into popular
culture as a vampire symbol (via its use here
as a blood-drawing weapon rather than fangs),
and the film's cult success into the mid-1990s
inspired a British-Canadian TV series of the
same time that ran from 1997 to 2000.

FRIGHT NIGHT

USA, 1985
Director: Tom Holland. Producer: Herb Jaffe.
Screenplay: Tom Holland. Music: Brad Fiedel.
Cinematography: Jan Kiesser.
Cast: Chris Sarandon, William Ragsdale, Amanda Bearse,
Roddy McDowall, Stephen Geoffreys, Jonathan Stark.

Frustrated with Michael Winner's treatment of his
script for the lunatic thriller **Scream for Help** (1984),
screenwriter and former actor Tom Holland switched
to the director's chair for this clever, stylish ode to
Hammer and Universal classics with an '80s teen
twist. The story begins as another variation
on the boy who cried wolf as high schooler
Charlie Brewster (William Ragsdale)
is convinced that his new next door
neighbor Jerry Dandrige (Chris
Sarandon) is a vampire, much to
disbelief of his friends and the one
person he believes can help, horror
host and legendary vampire movie
actor Peter Vincent (Roddy McDowall).
Spectacular visual effects overseen
by the pioneering Richard Edlund and a
scene-stealing turn by Stephen Geoffreys as
the abrasive but multi-layered "Evil" Ed are among
the many highlights in one of the very few horror films
of the decade to win both near unanimous critical praise
and box office success. The film also amassed a major LGBT
following due to the presence of multiple out actors and plenty
of subtext involving Jerry's living arrangements and his alleyway
seduction of Ed, though Holland says this wasn't an intentional angle
at the time. McDowall and Ragsdale returned for the overachieving
but commercially jinxed sequel, **Fright Night Part 2** (1988), while
Holland sat that one out to do **Child's Play** (1988) instead. A well-
intentioned but only partially successful remake was released in
2011 (including a baffling change in Peter Vincent's profession
to an abrasive David Blaine-inspired stage magician played by
David Tennant), followed by a straight-to-video sequel, **Fright
Night 2: New Blood** (2013). A class act from start to finish,
this is ground zero for the vampire renaissance that ruled the
second half of the decade.

MR. VAMPIRE

Hong Kong, 1985
Director: Ricky Lau.
Producer: Sammo Hung.
Screenplay:
Szeto Cheuk-hon, Barry Wong.
Music: Anders Nelsson,
The Melody Bank.
Cinematography: Peter Ngor.
Cast: Ricky Hui, Moon Lee,
Chin Siu-ho, Lam Ching-ying,
Wong Siu-fung, Billy Lau.

The most beloved and important vampire film in Hong Kong history, **Mr. Vampire** created a global awareness of the *jiangshi* (or hopping vampire) and kicked off a franchise of four sequels and numerous unofficial imitations. With his distinctive eyebrows, authoritative presence and knack for physical comedy, actor Lam Ching-Ying found his niche here as Master Kau, a Taoist expert in paranormal spiritual matters whose assignment to perform a reburial for a wealthy family uncovers a vampiric secret that unleashes a springing menace on the region. Inspired by macabre folk tales from his childhood, producer and legendary comedy action star Sammo Hung shepherded this project through as a homegrown vampire saga with its own set of rules including the magical use of rice. The production famously stretched out for nearly half a year but proved to be worth the effort with its wild, knockabout vampire combat scenes, which put first-time director Ricky Lau on the map and ensured his place in the director's chair for the quartet of official sequels. (The franchise was also transformed into a theatrical production and video game, not surprisingly.) The film became one of the most popular discoveries for Western viewers during the Hong Kong renaissance of the late '80s and early '90s, with UK presenter Jonathan Ross playing a key role in evangelizing it to audiences alongside the works of Tsui Hark and John Woo.

ONCE BITTEN

USA, 1985
Director: Howard Storm.
Producers: Frank Hildebrand,
Dimitri Villard, Robert Wald.
Screenplay: David Hines, Jeffrey
Hause, Jonathan Roberts.
Music: John Du Prez.
Cinematography: Adam Greenberg.
Cast: Lauren Hutton, Jim Carrey,
Karen Kopins, Cleavon Little,
Thomas Ballatore, Skip Lackey.

The '80s teen sex comedy wave ushered in by the likes of **Porky's** (1981) and **Fast Times at Ridgemont High** (1982) had to get around to vampires eventually, though the end result is a questionable mixed bag of good-natured genre ribbing and queasy gay panic and virginity gags that were already antiquated when this hit theaters. A young, pre-fame Jim Carrey stars (in a role originally intended for Michael J. Fox) as the only teenaged male virgin around who can sustain the supernatural youth of a beautiful vampire countess (Lauren Hutton), with her multiple nibbles on the young man causing his personality to slowly change and wreak havoc on his love life. Many of the gags stay at a TV sketch comedy level including a particularly squirm-inducing locker room sequence and a finale that swipes its punchline (albeit in less bloody form) from **Blood for Dracula**, though Hutton and Carrey have enough gusto to marginally redeem the material. In an obligatory move for the time, the catchy soundtrack is arguably the best thing about the film including a lively title song by 3-Speed and a pair of English-language versions of tunes by the beloved Germany synthpop band Hubert Kah.

VAMPIRE HUNTER D

Japan, 1985
Director: Toyoo Ashida. Producers: Hiroshi Kato, Mitsuhisa Koeda,
Yukio Nagasaki. Screenplay: Yasushi Hirano. Music: Tetsuya
Komuro. Cinematography: Yukio Sugiyama, Kazushi Torigoe.
Cast: Kaneto Shiozawa (voice), Michie Tomizawa (voice),
Seizô Katô (voice), Satoko Kifuji (voice), Kazuyuki Sogabe (voice),
Motomu Kiyokawa (voice).

The popular multi-volume novels by *Wicked City* author Hideyuki
Kikuchi about a futuristic wandering vampire killer named D had
its first adaptation soon after the initial publication in 1983 with
this wildly popular anime feature, which belatedly became a cult
hit in its English-speaking incarnation in 1992. In 12090 A.D.,
a vampire apocalypse has led to the enslavement of the human
race by the bloodsucking Nobles including Count Magnus Lee,
who bites a young pigtailed girl named Doris. To prevent her full
conversion to vampirism she hires the wandering half-human
hunter D to kill Lee, a quest that crosses paths with several
colorful characters, glowing-eyed creatures large and small,
mutants and vampires. With his enormous wide-brimmed hat,
stoic nature, and frequently shadowed face, D quickly became an
iconic figure in the vampire canon with a persona reminiscent of
classic spaghetti westerns. With its dark fusion of horror, western
and sci-fi tropes as well as splashes of gore, **Vampire Hunter D**
paved the way for Western acceptance of adult-targeted animated
fare and sparked a number of subsequent versions including
manga, radio drama, and video game incarnations as well as a
worthy second feature, **Vampire Hunter D: Bloodlust** (2000).

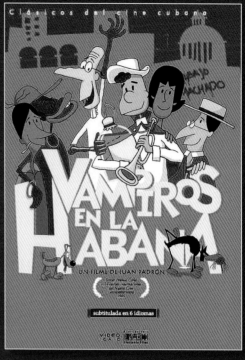

VAMPIRES IN HAVANA

Cuba, 1985
Director: Juan Padrón. Producer: Paco Prats.
Screenplay: Juan Padrón. Music: Rembert Egües.
Cinematography: Adalberto Hernández, Julio Simoneau.
Cast: Frank González (voice), Manuel Marín (voice),
Irela Bravo (voice), Carlos Gonzalez (voice),
Mirella Guillot (voice), Mirella Guillot (voice).

The world's first Cuban animated vampire feature (of only two!), **Vampires in Havana** (originally ¡Vampiros en La Habana!) offers a still-relevant social commentary mixed in with its rapid-fire gags involving international vampires going to war in 1930s Cuba. After the undead organized in 1870 and set up organizations in Chicago and Europe, Werner Amadeus, son of the deceased Count Dracula, has set up shop in Cuba to keep working on a formula that will allow vampires to walk in daylight. He succeeds with his nephew, Joseph Emmanuel, better known as trumpet player "Pepito" – who has no idea about his vampire heritage and becomes a target for vampires looking to exploit the valuable formula. Animated in a style best described as a cross between DePatie-Freleng, Ralph Bakshi and Bruno Bozzetto, this was

a significant hit for its animator director Juan Padrón and packs in a hefty number of jabs at dictatorships, cultural stereotypes, and the pitfalls of capitalism, all of which take a tumble during the giddy finale. However, it's always a comedy first with an onslaught of gags built around vampires scrambling to get their hands on a daylight formula (with an unforeseen side effect), decades before the same idea became a driving force on TV's **True Blood**. A belated sequel, **More Vampires in Havana!**, followed in 2003 with Padrón at the helm again.

VAMP

USA, 1986
Director: Richard Wenk. Producer: Donald P. Borchers.
Screenplay: Richard Wenk. Music: Jonathan Elias.
Cinematography: Elliot Davis.
Cast: Chris Makepeace, Sandy Baron, Robert Rusler,
Dedee Pfeiffer, Gedde Watanabe, Grace Jones.

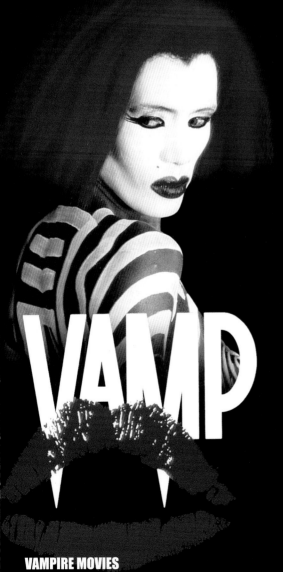

A night on the town in L.A. turns into a nightmare for three college students (Chris Makepeace, Robert Rusler and Gedde Watanabe) when a hazing order for strippers lands them in a gentlemen's club that doubles as a vampire nest. A stylish blend of black comedy and monster movie, this New World release banked heavily on the presence of singer and style icon Grace Jones just after her villainous role in **A View to a Kill** (1985); she does indeed make a strong impression, particularly her showstopping entrance wearing body art by the late Keith Haring, but the bulk of the film is more of an episodic journey through Makepeace's eyes through the city's off-the-wall underbelly a la the then-recent **After Hours** (1985). In addition to Rusler's winning performance as a wannabe frat boy turned bloodsucker, the film also benefits from a charismatic Dedee Pfeiffer as a sweet-natured club worker and an energetic electronic score by Jonathan Elias, something of a New World house composer at the time. Though largely overlooked at the time, the film has gone on to amass a small cult following and served as a calling card for first-time writer-director Richard Wenk, who would go on to write numerous high-profile Hollywood action films including **The Equalizer** (2014) and its 2018 sequel.

Starring
SILVIO
OLIVIERO,
HELEN PAPAS
and CLIFF STOKER

GRAVEYARD SHIFT

USA, 1987
Director: Jerry Ciccoritti. Producers: Robert Bergman, Michael Bockner, Jerry Ciccoritti. Screenplay: Jerry Ciccoritti. Music: Nicholas Pike. Cinematography: Robert Bergman.
Cast: Silvio Oliviero [Michael A. Miranda], Helen Papas, Cliff Stoker, Dorin Ferber, Dan Rose, John Haslett Cuff.

No relation to the 1990 Stephen King killer rat film of the same title, this urban night owl spin on modern vampire lore is even more influenced by the rise of music videos than its more famous '80s cinematic companions. The surprise success of this film on VHS (and DVD under the odd retitling of **Central Park Drifter**) after minimal theatrical play can be chalked up to its gritty setting (with the mean streets of Toronto posing as Manhattan) and slinky visuals containing just the right amount of eroticism.

Italian-Canadian actor Michael A. Miranda, billed as Silvio Oliviero, stars as cab driver Stephen Tsepes (get it?), whose overnight shift gives him the perfect opportunity to prey on vulnerable women – until he becomes involved with an ailing, married music video director. The fatalistic idea of lonely city dwellers with a death wish making ideal victims for a vampire is the most fascinating one at play here, and while the approach may be well in line with direct-to-video fare of the time, it's enough to make this one stick in the memory more than most of its peers. Despite major reported interference with the final cut by producers, director Jerry Ciccoritti (who went on to a lengthy, still-busy career in Canadian TV) brought back Miranda for a more meta take on the vampire idea with **The Understudy: Graveyard Shift II** (1988).

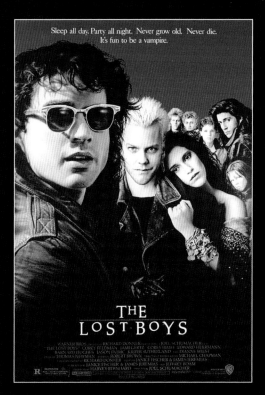

Sleep all day. Party all night. Never grow old. Never die.
It's fun to be a vampire.

THE
LOST·BOYS

THE LOST BOYS

USA, 1987
Director: Joel Schumacher. Producer: Harvey Bernhard.
Screenplay: Janice Fischer, James Jeremias, Jeffrey Boam.
Music: Thomas Newman.
Cinematography: Michael Chapman.
Cast: Jason Patric, Corey Haim, Dianne Wiest,
Barnard Hughes, Ed Herrmann, Kiefer Sutherland.

As the title implies, one of the most popular vampire films of the 1980s started life as a macabre twist on Peter Pan but evolved drastically on the way to the big screen to conform more closely to the popular Brat Pack trends of the era. Incredibly, that decision (along with a revolving door of directors including Richard Donner and Mary Lambert before final choice Joel Schumacher) didn't cause any harm to the tale of a single-parent family relocating to a seaside California town plagued by eternally young, au courant bloodsuckers. In addition to reintroducing the long-forgotten rule about inviting a vampire into your home, the film added many new elements to the cinematic canon including the droll Frog Brothers (Corey Feldman and Jamison Newlander), a pair of unforgettable adolescent Van Helsings in training, and a slew of Gothic-tinged rock songs like "Cry Little Sister," "Lost in the Shadows," and Echo and the Bunnymen's cover of The Doors' "People Are Strange" that still conjure up images of the title characters roaring out for blood on motorcycles. In keeping with the era and its director, the film introduces tinges of sexual ambiguity that have kept viewers sifting for subtext to this day (particularly the use of Jami Gertz's Star as female bait for a secretive enclave of leather-clad young men), but the film still works as pure spooky entertainment on a superficial level. Two direct-to-video sequels followed, **Lost Boys: The Tribe** (2008) and **Lost Boys: The Thirst** (2010), with Feldman reprising his role in both and Newlander only in the latter.

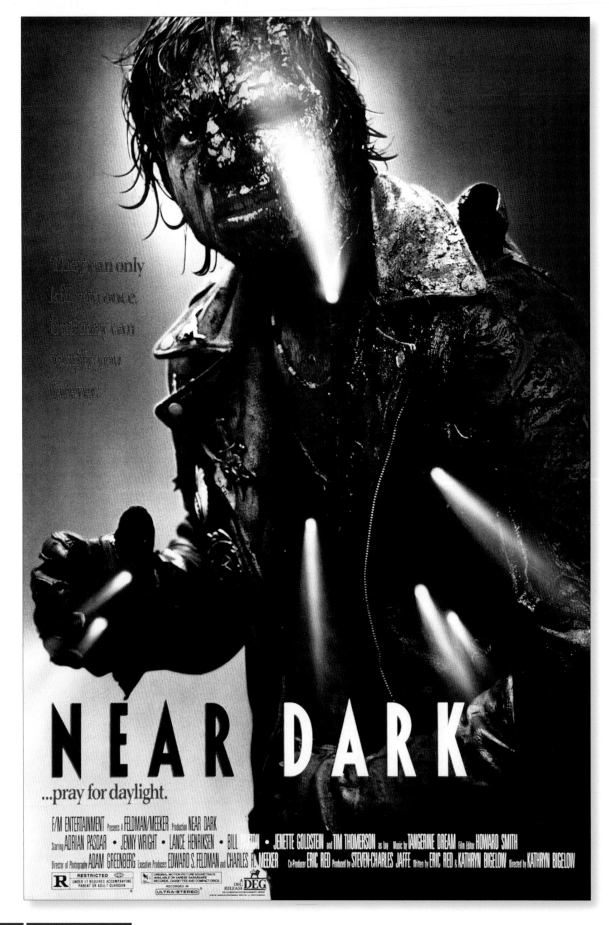

They can only
kill you once,
but they can
terrify you
forever.

NEAR DARK

...pray for daylight.

F/M ENTERTAINMENT Presents A FELDMAN/MEEKER Production NEAR DARK
Starring ADRIAN PASDAR • JENNY WRIGHT • LANCE HENRIKSEN • BILL PAXTON • JENETTE GOLDSTEIN and TIM THOMERSON as Loy   Music by TANGERINE DREAM   Film Editor HOWARD SMITH
Director of Photography ADAM GREENBERG   Executive Producers EDWARD S. FELDMAN and CHARLES R. MEEKER   Co-Producer ERIC RED   Produced by STEVEN-CHARLES JAFFE   Written by ERIC RED & KATHRYN BIGELOW   Directed by KATHRYN BIGELOW

NEAR DARK

USA, 1987
Director: Kathryn Bigelow. Producer: Steven-Charles Jaffe.
Screenplay: Kathryn Bigelow, Eric Red. Music: Tangerine Dream. Cinematography: Adam Greenberg.
Cast: Adrian Pasdar, Jenny Wright, Lance Henriksen, Bill Paxton, Jenette Goldstein, Tim Thomerson.

Horror fans were caught completely off guard by this powerhouse horror-action hybrid that transposed the idea of a nomadic vampire clan to the modern American Southwest. A future Oscar winner for **The Hurt Locker** (2008), Kathryn Bigelow teamed up with **The Hitcher** (1986) screenwriter Eric Red to write this script on spec together as part of a two-film agreement and decided to shake up the vampire rules, stripping out many of the tropes and finding new use for elements like blood transfusions. A fragile love story holds together the saga of farmer boy Caleb (Adrian Pasdar) who gets initiated by nocturnal waif Mae (Jenny Wright) into a roving band of vampires and **Aliens** (1986) veterans including Lance Henriksen, Jenette Goldstein, Joshua Miller, and a scene-stealing Bill Paxton who gets all of the best lines including "It's finger-lickin' good!" The legendary bar visit in the middle of the film has been rightly hailed as one of the most suspenseful (and quotable) sequences in vampire cinema, but the entire film is a textbook example of how to modernize the monsters on screen with kinetic shootouts and chase sequences to boot. A propulsive score by Tangerine Dream adds to the fun, and though the film's release was hampered by the collapse of distributor DeLaurentiis Entertainment Group, it quickly became an enduring cult classic on home video.

OUTBACK VAMPIRES

Australia, 1987
Director: Colin Eggleston. Producer: Jan Tyrrell.
Screenplay: Colin Eggleston, David Young. Music: Colin Bayley, Kevin Bayley, Murray Burns. Cinematography: Garry Wapshott.
Cast: Richard Morgan, Angela Kennedy, Brett Climo, John Doyle, Maggie Blinco, David Gibson.

Also circulated on home video as **The Wicked**, this very Australian made-for-TV lark was the penultimate film from idiosyncratic Colin Eggleston, who gave the world **Long Weekend** (1978) and the oddball slasher **Innocent Prey** (1989). Feeling very much like a Down Under variant on **The Old Dark House** (1932) reinterpreted by vaudeville performers, it's the story of rodeo-bound hitchhiker Lucy (Angela Kennedy) who hitches a ride in the dusty outback with Nick (Richard Morgan) and Bronco (Brett Climo). Of course, they immediately break down and end up with a family of vampires who are in cahoots with the locals to capture any passersby. With its quirky and flamboyant bloodsuckers ("Hi there, I'm George, I'm an Aries") and plentiful puns, this curio benefits from a cast of Aussie television thespians unknown to most overseas viewers and a deliberately absurd theatricality including the then-obligatory music video interlude. Most interesting is the focus on the hammy, self-interested human residents nearby, who wear garlic accoutrements on their jewelry and have no compunction about tossing innocents to the wolves to spare their own skins – on every occasion possible. Some surprising gender-bender twists get thrown in as well on the way to a bizarre climax with the (literally) biggest vampire in movie history.

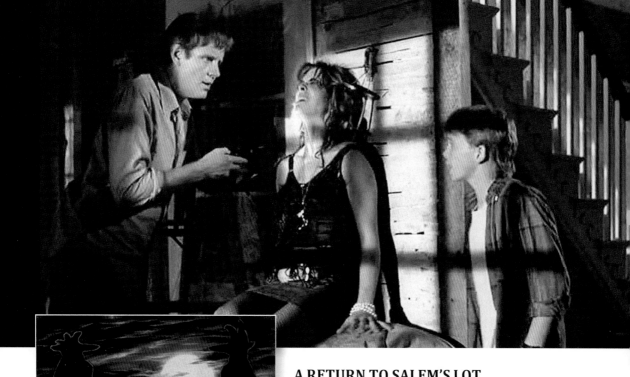

A RETURN TO SALEM'S LOT

USA, 1987
Director: Larry Cohen. Producer: Paul Kurta.
Screenplay: Larry Cohen, James Dixon.
Music: Michael Minard. Cinematography: Daniel Pearl.
Cast: Michael Moriarty, Ricky Addison Reed, Samuel
Fuller, Andrew Duggan, Evelyn Keyes, Jill Gatsby.

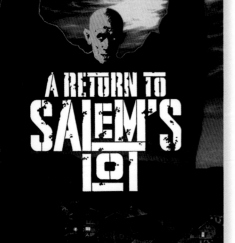

A strong contender for the strangest sequel in vampire cinema history, this belated follow-up to Tobe Hooper's **Salem's Lot** came from the same short-lived Warner Bros. deal with writer-director Larry Cohen that also produced his eccentric **It's Alive III: Island of the Alive** (1987). This film has nothing to do with King's own short story sequels, "Jerusalem's Lot" and "One for the Road;" instead it's Cohen in full-on horror satire mode complete with his most valuable leading man, Michael Moriarty, and a startling appearance by legendary filmmaker Samuel Fuller as Nazi hunter and vampire killer Dr. Van Meer. Vermont substitutes for King's beloved state of Maine here for the tale of anthropologist Moriarty being recruited to write a bible evangelizing the lifestyle of vampire town, whose residents have used the few remaining humans and even cows in their day-to-day subsistence. Completely breaking continuity with its titular source, the film also makes the vampires part of America's heritage since its founding. As usual Cohen peppers the film with fascinating ideas and colorful character moments, though as a horror film this pleased few – especially with a flat-out dishonest shot of Reggie Nalder's Barlow on all the promotional art.

400 years ago
she disappeared.
Now she's back—
on the prowl.

DRACULA'S WIDOW

She'll rip your heart out.

A D CONSTANTINE CONTE Production DRACULA'S WIDOW - SYLVIA KRISTEL - JOSEF SOMMER and LENNY VON DOHLEN Original Music by JAMES CAMPBELL
Production Designer ALEXANDRA KICZUK Editor TOM SIITER Director of Photography GIUSEPPE MACCARI Written by KATHRYN ANN THOMAS and CHRISTOPHER COPPOLA
R RESTRICTED Co-Producer STEPHEN TRAXLER Produced by D CONSTANTINE CONTE Directed by CHRISTOPHER COPPOLA

DRACULA'S WIDOW

USA, 1988
Director: Christopher Coppola.
Producer: Stephen Traxler.
Screenplay: Kathryn Ann Thomas,
Christopher Coppola.
Music: James B. Campbell.
Cinematography: Giuseppe Maccari.
Cast: Sylvia Kristel, Josef Sommer,
Lenny von Dohlen, Marc Coppola,
Stefan Schnabel, Rachel Jones.

Hollywood's Coppola family went vampire crazy starting in 1988 with brothers Christopher Coppola and Nicolas Cage involved into two very different projects about young men whose lives are turned upside down by an alluring, undead mystery woman. Christopher made his directorial debut with this Hollywood saga about Raymond, played by Lenny von Dohlen from **Electric Dreams** (1984), who runs a tacky wax museum in Hollywood and gets a shipment of rare artifacts from Romania. In the process he unleashes the scowling Vanessa, played by Sylvia "Emmanuelle" Kristel in a ridiculous black wig. Informed that her husband, Dracula, was dispatched ages ago by Van Helsing while she was in storage, she enlists Raymond in a bloody revenge scheme. Priceless footage of late '80s Hollywood Blvd. is the main attraction here along with some very gory practical effects, while the wax museum setting allows for some affectionate throwbacks to classic monster movies not unlike another horror film released the same year, Anthony Hickox's cult classic **Waxwork**, which features an extraordinarily bloody vampire segment as well. Coppola jazzes up the film with very hyperactive MTV-influenced editing and stylized gel lighting throughout, and he mixes things up a bit by throwing in a band of devil worshippers and having Kristel occasionally transform into a latex-heavy monster worthy of a heavy metal album cover.

ROBO VAMPIRE

Hong Kong, 1988
Director: Joe Livingstone [Godfrey Ho]. Producer:
Tomas Tang. Screenplay: William Palmer [Godfrey Ho].
Music: Ian Wilson. Cinematography: Anthony Mang.
Cast: Robin Mackay, Nian Watts, Harry Myles,
Joe Browne, Nick Norman, George Tripos.

A strong contender for the foggiest vampire film ever made, this melding of bullet-spraying jungle action film and hopping vampire monster romp is an endearingly cut-rate pastiche from the irrepressible and wildly prolific Godfrey Ho, who made about 3,000 films with 'ninja' in the title and two other vampire films back to back with this one, **Vampire Raiders: Ninja Queen** (1988) and **The Vampire Is Still Alive** (1989). The success of Paul Verhoeven's **RoboCop** (1987) spurred many quick imitations involving men turned into cyborg crime fighters, with duties in this case falling on an American drug buster killing during a firefight in the so-called Golden Triangle who comes back as a metal warrior tangled up with a Taoist priest and members of bouncing undead, including one in a monkey mask who fires incendiary devices out of his hands. Though sent straight to video in most territories at the time, this marks one of Ho's more ambitious films and was even shot in scope to give it a more epic feel than usual. Nowhere else can you see a drug enforcer-hating crime kingpin priest wrangling a squad of Hong Kong vampires pitted against a cybernetic resurrected lawman, and once you throw in peekaboo see-through nudity and blaring synth music, you're clearly in for something special.

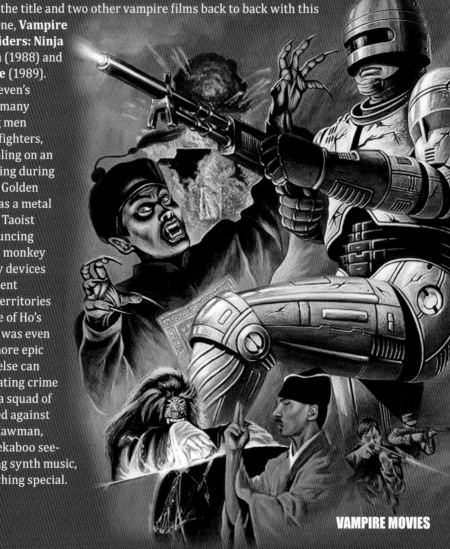

VAMPIRE IN VENICE

Italy, 1988
Directors: Augusto Caminito, Klaus Kinski [uncredited].
Producer: Augusto Caminito. Screenplay: Augusto Caminito.
Music: Luigi Ceccarelli, Vangelis. Cinematography: Tonino Nardi.
Cast: Klaus Kinski, Barbara De Rossi, Yorgo Voyagis, Anne Knecht,
Elvire Audray, Clara Colosimo.

Vampire sequels don't come much odder than this belated follow-up to Werner Herzog's **Nosferatu the Vampyre**, which brought back star Klaus Kinski but went through so many creative hands that it ended up bearing no narrative connection to its predecessor. Now with a full head of hair but still sporting his rat-style vampire fangs, Kinski is lurking within the alleys and canals of Venice while intrepid vampire hunter Professor Catalano (Christopher Plummer) leads a team including priest Donald Pleasence to track down the Transylvanian fiend now preying on the women of the Floating City. Originally released as **Nosferatu a Venezia** and circulated on video as **Prince of the Night**, the film went through multiple directors including Mario Caiano and Luigi Cozzi due to Kinski's infamous temperament on set, with the final credit going to screenwriter Augusto Caminito who had no prior feature film directing experience. By this point the Italian genre film industry was heading into a financial tailspin, and the film was barely shown in theatres outside of Italy, West Germany and Japan. However, its sumptuous Venetian photography, amped-up eroticism, and dizzying electronic score make it an unexpected curiosity for those dogged enough to hunt it down.

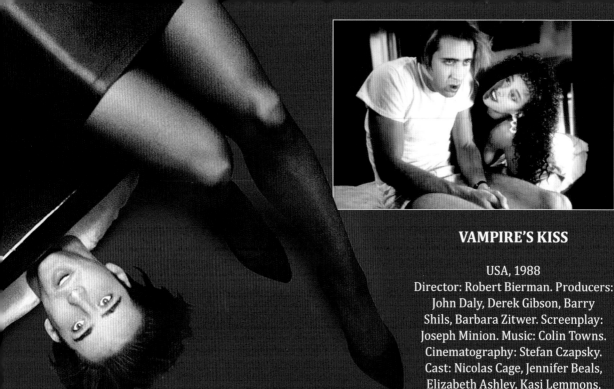

VAMPIRE'S KISS

USA, 1988
Director: Robert Bierman. Producers:
John Daly, Derek Gibson, Barry
Shils, Barbara Zitwer. Screenplay:
Joseph Minion. Music: Colin Towns.
Cinematography: Stefan Czapsky.
Cast: Nicolas Cage, Jennifer Beals,
Elizabeth Ashley, Kasi Lemmons,
Maria Conchita Alonso, Bob Lujan.

The wild-eyed, scenery-chewing performances of Nicolas Cage might seem commonplace now in the aftermath of **The Wicker Man** (2006) and **Color Out of Space** (2019), but he still hasn't topped the one that started it all. This cult classic was mostly greeted with confusion when its off-kilter mixture of horror and pitch-black, high-decibel comedy opened at the end of the Reagan era, bombing at the box office but garnering plenty of attention on cable TV. Stepping in after initial choice Dennis Quaid, Cage plays Peter Leow, a literary agent who's convinced he's transforming into a vampire after a one-night tryst with the enigmatic Rachel (Jennifer Beals). A frenetic critique of 1980s isolation and aggressive masculinity from the same wellspring as Bret Easton Ellis's *American Psycho*, this was the very unexpected follow-up film from screenwriter and native New Yorker Joseph Minion after his acclaimed debut with Martin Scorsese's **After Hours** (1985), which was barely hampered by a plagiarism accusation following its release. Today the film is most legendary for Cage's frothing rants at beleaguered secretary Maria Conchita Alonso and the show-stopping moment in which he tries to outdo Divine by chowing down a live cockroach on camera (which he washed down immediately afterwards with whiskey for a pair of takes). Even longtime horror fans can be jolted by the film, particularly during Cage's raving sequences in public (shot via long lenses with real, unaware passersby) and the jarring denouement that caps off a genuinely unforgettable urban nightmare comedy.

THE JITTERS

USA/Japan, 1989
Director: John Fasano. Producer: John Fasano.
Screenplay: Sonoko Kondo, Jeff McKay. Music: Tom Borton,
Daniel Linck. Cinematography: Paul Mitchnick.
Cast: Sal Viviano, Marilyn Tokuda, Randy Atmadja,
James Hong, Doug Silberstein, Frank Dietz.

Four years after the hopping vampire achieved its widest international cinematic popularity with
Mr. Vampire, this lesser known Toronto, Canada-shot horror comedy offers its own take on the springy
creatures in a very different context. In Chinatown, a roving gang breaks into an antique store owned
by Frank Lee (Randy Atmadja) and kills him in the process. His niece, Alice (Marilyn Tokuda), and her
boyfriend Michael (Sal Viviano) find their grieving process disturbed when Frank is revived from the dead
and ends up inflicting multiple hopping bloodsuckers on the community. This is the third and final feature

by late New York-born filmmaker John Fasano, who
had a brief cottage industry in heavy metal horror
with **Rock 'n' Roll Nightmare** (1987) and **Black Roses**
(1988); of course, there's still plenty of enormous
hair on display here to remind you who's behind the
camera. Here the proceedings are mostly played for
broad, budget-conscious laughs, though the impressive,
squishy latex effects and novelty of its culture clash
production make for a diverting time including an
amusing, scenery-chewing turn by James Hong, star of
this film's most obvious influence, **Big Trouble in Little
China** (1986). And yes, there is a theme song.

NISHI TRISHNA

India, 1989
Director: Parimal Bhattacharya.
Screenplay: Parimal Bhattacharya. Music: Ananda Mukhopadhyay.
Cast: Prasenjit Chatterjee, Moon Moon Sen, Shekhar Chatterjee,
Dhiman Chakraborty, Alpana Goswami, Seema Ghosh.

Though Hindi-language films may be the most famous segment of Indian
cinema, Bengali-language films hailing from the country's West Bengal
region have a significant and unique history of their own including the
output of Satyajit Ray. Affectionately referred to as Tollywood, they also had
to come up with their own vampire film at some point, and that day arrived in
1989 with this black-and-white variation on the old dark house chestnut infused

with some bloodsucker garnish. Complete with a wailing theme song called "Thirsty
Night" (a translation of the film's title), it's the tender story of a village terrorized by
a fanged fiend who sneaks into women's bedrooms at night and leaves them with
bloody throats. Four friends including a doctor and aspiring singer find their road trip
waylaid by car trouble and, upon arriving at a crumbling manor in the mountains,
have to contend with their mysterious host "Mr. John," his deaf-mute manservant,
eerie nocturnal songs of death, and the blood-slurping secrets of the property's crypt.
An entertaining throwback to the glory days of Gothic cinema, the film is memorable
for both its spiky-haired vampire and his primary adversary, a new twist on Van
Helsing as a savvy bespectacled woman who knows her way around a stake or two.

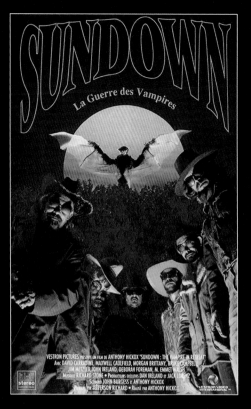

SUNDOWN: THE VAMPIRE IN RETREAT

USA, 1989
Director: Anthony Hickox. Producer: Jefferson Richard.
Screenplay: John Burgess, Anthony Hickox.
Music: Richard Stone. Cinematography: Levie Isaacks.
Cast: David Carradine, Morgan Brittany, Bruce Campbell,
Jim Metzler, Maxwell Caulfield, Deborah Foreman.

This very tongue-in-cheek spin on the tiny subgenre of
vampire westerns posits the notion of modern bloodsuckers
led by Count Mardulak (David Carradine) learning to abstain
from feeding and, stocked up on SPF 100 sunblock, planning
to comingle with humanity. Key to the plot is the problematic
development of artificial blood, an idea that would
become central to the wave of "good guy" vampire
films to come the following decade. Shot in Utah
and notable in the history books as one of
the last official productions for Vestron,
the film was directed and co-written by
Anthony Hickox as a follow up to his cult
favourite debut **Waxwork** and feels
designed to play as a midnight movie.
A mustachioed Bruce Campbell
has a field day as a Van Helsing
descendant who rides into town
during an escalating war involving
a rival cave-dwelling vampire
clan, while the rest of the cast is
filled out with unexpected faces
including a gloriously game M.
Emmet Walsh, Deborah Foreman
(as a particularly alluring vampire
in sunglasses), John Ireland, Dana
Ashbrook, and Maxwell Caulfield,
who gets one of the strangest stop-
motion vampire bat transformations
in film history. If possible, try to
hunt down this film in its full scope
aspect ratio to fully appreciate the wide
desert vistas, the rich variety of creature
effects on display, and the full range of
background movie posters including one for
Vestron's aborted **Ken Russell's Dracula**.

TO DIE FOR

USA, 1989
Director: Deran Sarafian.
Producer: Barin Kumar.
Screenplay: Leslie King.
Music: Cliff Eidelman.
Cinematography: Jacques Haitkin.
Cast: Brendan Hughes, Sydney Walsh,
Amanda Wyss, Scott Jacoby, Micah Grant, Duane Jones.

Home video turned out to be a major financial salvation for horror films in the late '80s, and few rode that wave more skillfully than this low-budget vampire love story that barely played in cinemas but became a massive hit on VHS. Taking a cue from the relatively recent attempts to connect Dracula to Romanian history, our vampire in this case is the immortal Vlad (Brendan Hughes) who cuts in on the relationship between L.A. realtor Kate (Sydney Walsh) and her boyfriend (Scott Jacoby) when he wants to buy a castle. However, his centuries-old rivalry with Tom (soap star Steve Bond) complicates matters along with the Kate's roommate, CiCi, played by Amanda Wyss of **A Nightmare on Elm Street** (1984) fame. Seemingly designed to play cable TV in perpetuity with its swooning soft jazz score and multiple romantic triangles, **To Die For** forged a career for director Deran Sarafian after his far lesser seen debut, **Alien Predators** (1986), leading to a long and still-continuing TV career. The screenplay by former actress Leslie King, who had appeared in several drive-in staples like **Gas Pump Girls** (1979), points the way to the female perspective that would become far more prominent in vampire fare very shortly; she would also write the semi-sequel, **Son of Darkness: To Die For II** (1991).

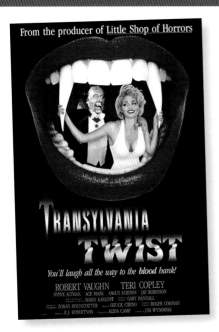

TRANSYLVANIA TWIST

USA, 1989
Director: Jim Wynorski. Producer: Alida Camp.
Screenplay: R.J. Robertson, Jim Wynorski.
Music: Chuck Cirino. Cinematography: Zoran Hochstätter.
Cast: Robert Vaughn, Teri Copley, Steve Altman, Ace Mask,
Angus Scrimm, Steve Franken.

Having proven his worth to Roger Corman on the strength of a rapid-fire quartet of films including **Chopping Mall** (1986) and **Not of This Earth** (1988), director and co-writer Jim Wynorski was given the freedom to run wild with this joke-laden homage to classic monster movies. A lifelong fan of **Abbott and Costello Meet Frankenstein** and TV's **The Man from U.N.C.L.E.**, Wynorski got to indulge in both by casting Robert Vaughn as Lord Byron Orlock, the head of a vampire clan in Transylvania who could pose an end to humanity. The opening Miracle Pictures logo and stampede of stock footage culled from prior Corman films make this a spiritual cousin of sorts to New World's **Hollywood Boulevard** (1986), here transposed to the world of Universal and Hammer vampire films with an MTV-friendly twist thanks to appealing sitcom vet Teri Copley as a pop star. (Her action movie musical homage is a keeper.) Corman was at the height of productivity with one movie per month being cranked out at his "lumber yard" in Venice Beach, though this one features unusually ambitious direction (especially for Wynorski) including original sets, plentiful dolly shots, and atmospheric lighting. Many of the vampire gags are truly funny as well, not to mention a game turn by Ace Mask as Van Helsing and welcome roles for Angus Scrimm and scream queens Monique Gabrielle and Brinke Stevens.

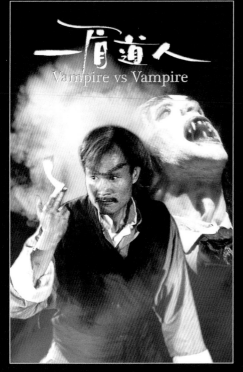

Vampire vs Vampire

VAMPIRE VS. VAMPIRE

Hong Kong, 1989
Director: Lam Ching-ying. Producer: Chua Lam.
Screenplay: Sam Chi-leung, Chan Kam-cheong, Sze Mei-yee.
Music: Anders Nelsson, The Melody Bank,
Alastair Monteith-Hodge, Tim Nugent.
Cinematography: Cho On-sun, Kwan Chi-kam.
Cast: Lam Ching-ying, Chin Siu-ho, David Lui, Sandra Ng,
Billy Lau, Maria Cordero.

A peculiar little detour in the hopping vampire canon, this fusion of Eastern and Western bloodsucker lore found its magnificently eyebrowed star Lam Ching-Ying of **Mr. Vampire** fame moving to the director's chair for the first of only two times. Here we have another unofficial one-off story about those pesky *jiangshi*, part of a brief cycle of his "Vampire Buster" standalones followed by **The Ultimate Vampire** (1991) and **The Musical Vampire** (1992). Echoing **The Legend of the 7 Golden Vampires**, here we have a hodgepodge of global monsters mingling with a traditional European vampire whose malefic influence (including a colony of bats) extends to the water supply of the One Eyebrow Priest's village. Things get spiced up with some ghostly ingredients and even a bit of possession, though the real scene stealer here is a comical young vampire boy sidekick likely inspired by the juvenile jumper in **Mr. Vampire II**. With its unusually high number of action scenes and visual effects thanks to the expanded bestiary, the film ran significantly over budget; however, Lam's decision to rescind his director's salary ensured goodwill in the local industry and he remained steadily busy with his legacy cemented via the popular TV series, **Vampire Expert**. Tragically Lam would pass away from liver cancer at the age of 44 in 1997, just as the third series was in preparation.

WOHI BHAYAANAK RAAT

India, 1989
Director: Vinod Talwar. Producers: S.K.Talwar, Vinod Talwar.
Screenplay: S. Tahir. Music: Surender Kohli.
Cinematography: Nishikant Telang.
Cast: Rohan Kapoor, Neeta Puri, Kiran Kumar,
Rakesh Bedi, Yunus Parvez, Asha Sharma.

India's storied tradition of recycling Hollywood product
for musical Bollywood productions has resulted in some
notoriously peculiar results over the years, though few have
involved vampires. One of the more notable rarities is this film
from Vinod Talwar, who had a brief run as the closest competitor to India's most famous genre specialists
of the era, the Ramsay Brothers. Openly riffing on **Fright Night** (particularly its extended discotheque
sequence), this was Talwar's second film after the gruesome **Raat Ke Andhere Mein** (1987), and he sticks
to the country's usual horror formula of a blood and thunder opening prologue (in this case involving a
pregnant woman and her ill-fated husband stumbling into a desolate mansion) before spending the next
hour or so on comic relief, romantic complications, and cheerful musical routines. Veteran actor Kiran
Kumar stars as our swarthy Jerry Dandrige stand-in who
can fire telekinetic animated lasers from his eyes and
becomes obsessed with the reincarnation of his long dead
true love (Neeta Puri) whose boyfriend (Rohan Kapoor)
isn't keen on losing her to the bloodsucking intruder. The
film makes some interesting tweaks to the lore including
having the vampire cast a reflection of his monstrous true
self (rather than none at all) and display an aversion to dogs,
which results in the film's most bizarre fight scene with a
stuffed Doberman getting hurled across a room.

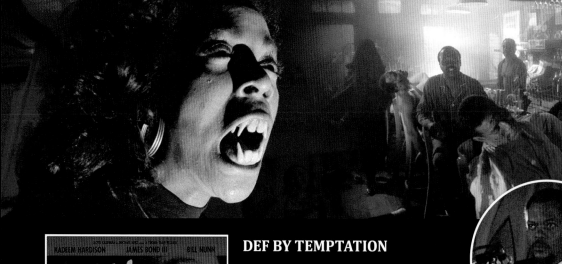

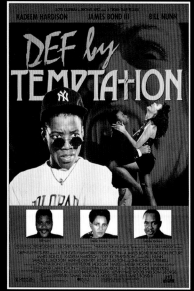

DEF BY TEMPTATION

USA, 1990
Director: James Bond III.
Producer: James Bond III.
Screenplay: James Bond III. Music: Paul
Laurence. Cinematography: Ernest R. Dickerson.
Cast: James Bond III, Kadeem Hardison, Bill Nunn, Samuel L. Jackson,
Minnie Gentry, Rony Clanton.

Easily one of the strongest theatrical releases from Lloyd Kaufman's
Troma Entertainment was this stylish offering from one-shot director
James Bond III, a former child actor and a then-recent member of
the Spike Lee players in **School Daze** (1988). Bond also stars as Joel,
a small-town seminary student whose introduction to city life has
him crossing paths with his childhood friend K (Kadeem Hardison of
TV's **A Different World**) and an alluring, gold-fingernailed predator
(Cynthia Bond) feeding on male pickups at Brooklyn dive bars. Far
weightier than the title and poster might have you believe, the film
presents a strong conflict between religious conviction and the
perils of temptation represented by the vampire villain who's infused
with succubus qualities for good measure. Bond also flips genre
conventions around by making men the primary victims, an approach
that extends to the nudity on display as well in a move that likely
affected the film's commercial prospects at the time but gives it an
unexpected edge now. Gifted cinematographer and fellow Spike Lee
collaborator Ernest Dickerson drenches the film in blinding colors
worthy of Mario Bava, while Samuel L. Jackson, Freddie Jackson and
Melba Moore pop up in juicy supporting roles.

DOCTOR VAMPIRE

Hong Kong, 1990
Director: Jamie Luk. Producer: Chua Lam.
Screenplay: Jamie Luk. Music: Alan Tsui.
Cinematography: Jim Yeung.
Cast: Bowie Lam, Ellen Chan, Sheila Chan,
David Wu, Lawrence Lau, Crystal Kwok.

A raucous change of pace from the usual Hong Kong vampire formula, this gore-spattered Golden Harvest comedy extends the net to include traditional Western bloodsucking when traveling surgeon Dr. Kueng (Bowie Lam just before his memorable turn in 1992's **Hard Boiled**) stops off at a castle in the Scottish Highlands only to find out it's a den for unscrupulous, undead prostitutes who roofie newcomers at the bar and steal more than their wallets. The Draculean owner demands the doc be recaptured because "His blood is like your Chinese ginseng," which leads to a mad chase as our hero finds a covert bite below the belt turning him into a vampire. Laser fights, vampiric target practice with syringes, stick fighting, and plenty of bawdy jokes about our hero's nibbled nether regions are among the highlights of one of the great unsung vampire party films. There's also a fair amount of sex appeal provided by the striking Ellen Chan as the bloodsucking courtesan tasked with luring our hero back into the fold. A onetime martial arts film staple in front of the camera in numerous Shaw Brothers productions throughout the 1970s, director Jamie Luk invests the film with so much verve it's no wonder he immediately followed this with the outrageous Category III classic, **Robotrix** (1991).

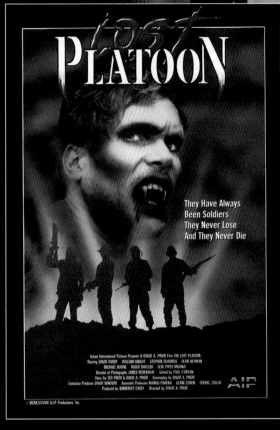

They Have Always
Been Soldiers
They Never Lose
And They Never Die

THE LOST PLATOON

USA, 1990
Director: David A. Prior. Producer: Kimberley Casey.
Screenplay: David A. Prior, Ted Prior.
Music: Tim James, Mark Mancina, Steve McClintock.
Cinematography: James Rosenthal.
Cast: William Frederick Knight, David Parry,
Stephen Quadros, Michael Wayne, Sean Heyman,
Lew Sleeman.

Replete with Sam Raimi-inspired swooshing camerawork and elaborate combat scenes, this military vampire oddity is one of the more impressive productions from Alabama-based exploitation factory David A. Prior. Along with his frequent co-writer and leading man brother Ted, he made his debut with the notorious shot-on-video stunner **Sledgehammer** (1983) and specialized in action and war films ready for the VHS and cable markets. One of six features the Priors made in 1990, **The Lost Platoon** was a relatively high-profile offering from bottom-rung exploitation label Action International Pictures (a.k.a. the other AIP) and benefits from a highly original premise: an undead platoon fighting in each major modern war, comprised of soldiers whose moment of death on the battlefield was averted by a vampire's bite. Now led by a Civil War-era combatant, they're ID'd by a World War II veteran in Nicaragua but have bigger fish to fry thanks to a nefarious rival vampire named Vladimir. After all, as they say, "We're soldiers, man. We fight the bad guys. Don't you know anything?" Dozens of rounds of ammunition get fired across the Alabama scenery standing in for South America and Europe, all accompanied by a synth score co-written by none other than future Grammy-winning Disney composer Mark Mancina. Not for all tastes, but it's a diverting, unique time killer – and don't miss the closing theme song.

MAGIC COP

Hong Kong, 1990
Director: Stephen Tung. Producer: Lam Ching-ying. Screenplay: Sam Chi-leung, Tsang Kan-cheung,
Cho On-sun, Kwan Chi-kan. Music: BMG Melody Bank. Cinematography: Raymond Lam.
Cast: Lam Ching-ying, Wilson Lam, Michael Miu, Wong Mei-wa, Michiko Nishiwaki, Wu Ma.

Taking a break from his slew of **Mr. Vampire** films (of which this was sometimes marketed as an unofficial
fifth entry), the magnetic Lam Ching-Ying has one of his meatiest roles in this modern-day supernatural
cop comedy that pelts the viewer with a nonstop barrage of stunts, jokes and monster mayhem. Here he
plays small town Uncle Feng, a police officer and experienced Taoist magic practitioner who goes to Hong
Kong on what seems like a drug smuggling hunt but instead encounters supernatural monkey business
caused by a necromancer (Michiko Nishwaki) and her growing menagerie of vampires and head-spiked
zombies. The villainess herself has vampire qualities (including some fun with the no-reflection rule and
an eye-catching black outfit) and makes for a formidable adversary including a punchy finale in which,
altered to her true monstrous form, she hunts our heroes through sound alone. Other highlights include an
impromptu magic ritual to hunt down a rogue bodybuilder perp, gravity-defying flying fireballs and other
assorted hocus pocus with magical incense, and as usual there's some lowbrow bodily function comedy.
Veteran stunt coordinator Stephen Tung Wei (a.k.a. Wei Tung) made his directorial debut here, followed by
only three more features including **Fox Hunter** (1995), **Hitman** (1998), and **Extreme Challenge** (2001).

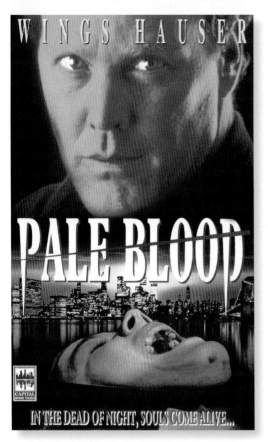

PALE BLOOD

USA, 1990
Directors: V.V. Dachin Hsu, Michael W. Leighton.
Producers: Omar Kaczmarczyk, Michael W. Leighton.
Screenplay: V.V. Dachin Hsu, Takashi Matsuoka.
Music: Jan A.P. Kaczmarek. Cinematography: Gerry Lively.
Cast: George Chakiris, Wings Hauser, Pamela Ludwig,
Diana Frank, Darcy DeMoss, Earl Garnes.

Any horror film that opens with the line "What you are about to see is one of the most dramatic pieces of art that has ever been created" at least gets points for chutzpah, a quality this one has in spades by pitting a vampire named Michael Fury played by George Chakiris, a long way from his Oscar-winning role in **West Side Story** (1961), against an unhinged serial predator known as "The Vampire Killer" (Wings Hauser). The gimmick here is Fury's intention to stop the imitator because he's causing bad publicity for the low-profile genuine members of the undead, so he enlists dogged investigator Lori (Pamela Ludwig) whose apartment is a riot of production designer in-jokes with vampire posters and tchotchkes filling every inch of available space. With its neon-heavy lighting and pop soundtrack, this is '80s designer horror all the way right from the first exsanguinated corpse discovered as part of a storefront display on Melrose Avenue. Despite its slick aesthetic, the film is hampered by its sleepy pacing and ended up being sent directly to VHS and laserdisc via the short-lived Columbia offshoot Triumph Home Video. That said, Hauser's typically intense performance and the vamp-crazy décor make it a cut above the straight to video norm even if writer-director V.V. Dachin Hsu didn't get much more out of it than landing a line producer gig on **Phat Beach** (1996).

RED BLOODED AMERICAN GIRL

Canada, 1990
Director: David Blyth. Producer: Nicolas Stiliadis.
Screenplay: Allan Moyle. Music: Jim Manzie.
Cinematography: Ludek Bogner.
Cast: Andrew Stevens, Heather Thomas, Christopher Plummer,
Kim Coates, Lydie Denier, Andrew Jackson.

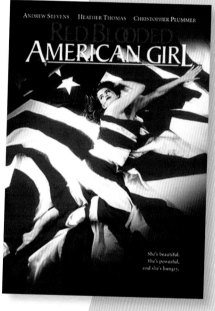

After getting ejected from the troubled production of **The Horror Show** (1989), New Zealand-born director David Blyth finally followed up his gory cult film **Death Warmed Up** (1984) with this strange, druggy, Toronto-shot vampire film with a medical twist reminiscent of David Cronenberg's **Rabid**. Barely released anywhere theatrically

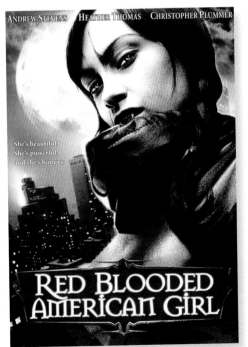

but omnipresent on home video, it's the tender story of Ecstasy developer Owen Augustus Urban III (Andrew Stevens on the cusp of his erotic thriller phase), who loses an arm-wrestling bout with Dr. John Alcore (Christopher Plummer) and gets roped into a cutting-edge enzyme biogenetics project. Since "blood is a profitable business," they're trying to come up with a lucrative form of synthetic blood under the banner of finding a cure for AIDS – but of course there's something more sinister at work when scientist Paula (**The Fall Guy**'s Heather Thomas) gets infected with tainted blood that turns her into a new form of vampire. The addiction and AIDS parallels run high here amidst the barrage of techno speak, synth music, and bare bodies, though all that pales next to the interpretive blood-drinking dance Thomas performs in blinding red pajamas on her kitchen countertop with a steak knife. Blyth followed this with an unrelated sequel, **Red Blooded American Girl II** (1997), which has no vampires – or any horror elements at all.

He's a vampire who hasn't scored in 400 years. Tonight's the night he keeps a date with fate.

ROCKULA

USA, 1990
Director: Luca Bercovici.
Producer: Jefery Levy.
Screenplay: Luca Bercovici, Jefery Levy,
Chris Ver Wiel. Music:
Hilary Bercovici, Osunlade.
Cinematography: John Schwartzman.
Cast: Dean Cameron, Toni Basil, Thomas
Dolby, Tawny Fere', Susan Tyrrell, Bo Diddley.

Made during the final gasps of Cannon Films, this exceptionally odd monster musical comedy was the second feature directed by busy actor Luca Bercovici, who had stepped behind the camera earlier as writer and helmer of the surprise hit **Ghoulies** (1987). Loved by horror genre fans as the splatter-loving Chainsaw from **Summer School** (1987), Dean Cameron stars as the centuries-old Ralph who still lives at home with his mother (Toni "Mickey" Basil) and keeps falling for the reincarnation of the same girl, Mona, who keeps getting killed arbitrarily with a hambone on Halloween every few decades. The bloodsucking aspect is almost completely sidelined with Ralph turned into an abstinent nice guy, though the surprise ending turns out to be incredibly ghoulish considering it essentially exposes a string of unnecessary serial killings. The grim nature of the back story is countered by a variety of quirky but highly memorable music numbers including the title song and the undeniably attention-grabbing 'Rapula (He's the DJ, I'm the Vampire)', both performed with gusto by Cameron. The music credentials are solidified by an extended acting and performance contribution by Bo Diddley, though perversely, Thomas Dolby also appears as Cameron's romantic rival – and never sings a single note since his one song intended for the film ended up being cut.

VAMPIRE MOVIES

CRAZY SAFARI

Hong Kong, 1991
Director: Billy Chan. Producers: Charles Heung, Barry Wong.
Screenplay: Barry Wong. Music: Lowell Lo.
Cinematography: Henry Chan, Wingle Chan.
Cast: N!xau, Lam Ching-ying, Sam Christopher Chan,
Peter Chan Lung, Stephen Chow, Ng Man-tat.

The worldwide success of Jamie Uys' slapstick comedy **The Gods Must Be Crazy** (1980) during its international release in 1984 was a pleasant surprise and made a brief star out of its leading man, charismatic Namibian farmer N!xau, who tries to deliver an errant Coke bottle from the sky back to the gods after it causes disruption in his tribe and the more brutal modern society nearby. As the most successful film in South African film history, it naturally spawned a sequel, **The Gods Must Be Crazy II** (1989). However, no one could have predicted what happened next when Hong Kong decided to mount three more unofficial sequels with N!xau starting with... a hopping vampire movie. In **Crazy Safari**, the body of a Chinese vampire is auctioned off (following an a/v presentation on bloodsuckers around the world) and won by its grandson (Sam Christopher Chow), who

teams up with the always reliable *jiangshi*-fighting priest Lam Ching-ying to transport it from England back to Hong Kong for a burial. Along the way a plane altercation sends the pair and the body plummeting to the African brush where the vampire becomes a useful new addition to N!xau's tribe. The formula for the South African sequences is essentially the same with wild goofball chase sequences, characters stuck in trees, and culture clash zaniness, but the vampire buddy angle catapults it to a level of cinematic strangeness all its own. Two more (non-vampire) sequels quickly followed, **Crazy Hong Kong** (1993) and **The Gods Must Be Funny in China** (1994).

MY SOUL IS SLASHED

Japan, 1991
Director: Shûsuke Kaneko.
Producers: Shohei Kota, Mistuo Sato,
Nobuaki Murooka. Screenplay: Shûsuke
Kaneko, Chigusa Shiota.
Music: Kow Otani.
Cinematography: Kôichi Kawakami.
Cast: Ken Ogata, Hideyo Amamoto,
Harumi Harada, Sumiyo Hasegawa,
Hikari Ishida, Narumi Yasuda.

Sharing its English title with a theme song by popular French
singer Mylène Farmer about love at the height of the HIV epidemic,
the world's only feel-good Japanese vampire AIDS-era comedy
(originally entitled **Kamitsukitai**) proved that Dracula lore was
far from exhausted. After the Count is vanquished in Romania, his
tainted, pulsating blood is transported to Japan where it ends up
being accidentally transfused into pharmaceutical salesman Ken
Ogata during a failed attempt to save him in the aftermath of a car
accident. The dead man's

wife and daughter end
up solving their family
problems under the
most unlikely of
circumstances when
his ashes and bones
turn into a crime-
fighting vampire
version of his
former self, with
shapeshifting
and flying
abilities
intact. Gothic
tropes like
thunder
storms,
howling wolves, vampire bats and spooky
music are amusingly employed in this tongue-
in-cheek curio with lines like "Papa, I don't
care if you're Dracula! You're a great person."
Despite the presence of screen great Ogata
and acknowledgement from a slew of Japanese
festivals and awards organizations, this film
never received an official English-subtitled release
and is inexplicably difficult to find now in any
format. However, Shûsuke Kaneko channeled it into
a successful genre career including all three of the
successful mid-1990s Gamera revivals and the cult
classic **Death Note** (2006).

SUBSPECIES

USA/Romania, 1991
Director: Ted Nicolaou. Producer: Ion Ionescu.
Screenplay: Jackson Barr, David Pabian.
Music: Richard Kosinski, Michael Portis, John Zereizke,
Stuart Brotman. Cinematography: Vlad Paunescu.
Cast: Angus Scrimm, Anders Hove, Irina Movila, Laura
Tate, Michelle McBride, Ivan Rado.

Shot for pocket change in Romania, this atmospheric
vampire saga marked the beginning of one of the prime
signature franchises for Charles Band's direct-to-video
company Full Moon Features. This film and its four
successors were all directed by Ted Nicolau, a Band
colleague dating back to their days at the defunct Empire
Pictures, and made a minor star out of actor Anders
Hove as the relentless, monstrous vampire Radu. Here he
uses his tiny stop-motion minions, the titular subspecies,
to aid his quest for the Bloodstone, a mystical and
powerful vampire family jewel comprised of the blood
of saints. That includes attempts to kill his more noble
brother and the rightful heir, Stefan (soap actor Michael
Watson), after dispatching their father (Angus Scrimm,
the Tall Man himself, in a bizarre white fright wig).
The production was a somewhat tense experience due
to Hove coping with his extensive makeup ordeal by
indulging in "a lot of drinking and temper tantrums"
according to Nicolau, though the two worked far more
harmoniously on the superior Murnau-inspired sequel,
Bloodstone: Subspecies II (1993) which paved the way
for the less flamboyant **Bloodlust: Subspecies 3** (1994),
Subspecies 4: Bloodstorm (1998), and the offshoot
Vampire Journals (1997).

BLOODLUST

Australia, 1992
Directors: Jon Hewitt, Richard Wolstencroft.
Producers: Jon Hewitt, Richard Wolstencroft.
Screenplay: Jon Hewitt, Richard Wolstencroft.
Music: Ross Hazeldine. Cinematography: Gary Ravenscroft.
Cast: Jane Stuart Wallace, Kelly Chapman, Robert James
O'Neill, Phil Motherwell, Paul Moder, James Young.

An easy winner for the worst American accents in any
vampire film, this scrappy shot-on-video Aussie production
took six weeks to film in Melbourne and managed to beat
out some of its better-known SOV vampire brethren to
the punch. The wafer-thin narrative involves low-class
vampires Tad (Robert James O'Neill), Lear (Jane Stuart
Wallace) and Frank (Kelly Chapman) being chased around
by a band of cross-waving fanatics while trying to figure
out a way to knock over a gambling den before they skip
town. Technically inept but very enthusiastic, this amateur
production features plenty of flashy editing and a loud
industrial soundtrack to remind you it's 1992. It also tries
to outdo Troma with pedophilia and necrophilia jokes,

gun fetishism, nudity,
vampire S&M and
humiliation, hillbilly cops (in Melbourne?), machine guns, missile
launchers, and a vampire crucifixion, resulting in a bad taste epic that
served as a calling card for newbie directors Jon Hewitt and Richard
Wolstencroft. This would be their only co-directing venture, though
they did pitch in later on each other's solo projects including **Pearls
Before Swine** (1999) and **X: Night of Vengeance** (2011) as they
remained prominent on the Melbourne genre scene for decades.

VAMPIRE MOVIES

BRAM STOKER'S DRACULA

USA, 1992
Director: Francis Ford Coppola. Producers: Francis Ford Coppola,
Fred Fuchs, Charles Mulvehill. Screenplay: James V. Hart.
Music: Wojciech Kilar. Cinematography: Michael Ballhaus.
Cast: Gary Oldman, Winona Ryder, Anthony Hopkins, Keanu Reeves,
Richard E. Grant, Cary Elwes.

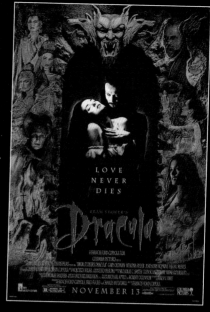

The splashiest big-budget American vampire film since the late
1970s touted itself as a faithful adaptation of the Stoker source
novel, though that promise is broken immediately with a stylized,
bloody prologue establishing Dracula (Gary Oldman) as the
immortal alias of Vlad the Impaler. Now pining for his lost suicidal
love in the modern incarnation of Mina (Winona Ryder), he embarks
on his familiar trek from Transylvania to London only to encounter
a squad of impromptu vampire hunters. The visual equivalent of
purple prose from start to finish, Francis Ford Coppola's lavish ode
to classic cinema from the silent era through Jean Cocteau managed to rack up three Academy Awards,
including a very well-deserved one for Eiko Ishioka's remarkable costumes, and remains a feast for the
senses with a barrage of colorful images and aggressive soundscapes. Oldman's romantic take on Dracula
retains the book's concept of reverse aging the villain after introducing him as an old man a la Jess Franco's
Count Dracula and puts him through numerous human and animal incarnations over the course of the
story, easily overshadowing many of the cast members apart from a scenery-chewing turn by Anthony
Hopkins as Van Helsing. The film marked a reconciliation for Ryder and Coppola after her abrupt departure
from **The Godfather Part III** (1990) when she brought him the script by James V. Hart, and amusingly
demonstrating how many liberties were taken with the source material, a tie-in novel keeping Stoker's
name in the title was even commissioned but penned by Fred Saberhagen. The film would become one

of the most frequently referenced and parodied films of its era,
including numerous nods on **The Simpsons**, and its inventive in-
camera visual effects (largely engineered by Roman Coppola) remain
refreshing in an era when CGI has become a dominant force.

BUFFY THE VAMPIRE SLAYER

USA, 1992
Director: Fran Rubel Kuzui. Producers: Kaz Kuzui, Howard Rosenman. Screenplay: Joss Whedon. Music: Carter Burwell. Cinematography: James Hayman.
Cast: Kristy Swanson, Donald Sutherland, Paul Reubens, Rutger Hauer, Luke Perry, Michele Abrams.

Far more famous now as the inspiration for the beloved 1997-2003 TV series than its own merits as a film, this vampire comedy marked the official screenwriting debut of that show's creator, Joss Whedon, who was motivated by his dissatisfaction with the result of this big-screen incarnation. Kristy Swanson stars as the high school cheerleader turned vampire slayer under the tutelage of Donald Sutherland, with the late Luke Perry providing teen audience value due to his popularity on TV's **Beverly Hills 90210**. Though tonally uneven, the film does add some value to vampire cinema primarily through the presence of Paul "Pee-wee Herman" Reubens, who steals the show right down to his improvised death scene, and the faultless casting of Rutger Hauer as the imposing vampire leader Lothos. The narrative also adheres closely to traditional vampire rules and played a key role in introducing them to a younger audience on a scale unseen since **The Lost Boys** (1987). Since its release the film has become regarded by Whedon and the show's fans as existing outside the official canon, though it remains essential as a dry run of sorts for what would become the most influential horror series of the 1990s and a game-changing entry in pop culture vampire lore.

VAMPIRE MOVIES

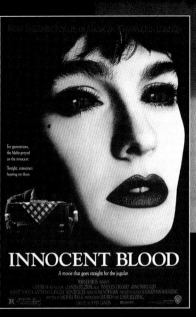

INNOCENT BLOOD

USA, 1992
Director: John Landis.
Producers: Leslie Belzberg, Lee Rich.
Screenplay: Michael Wolk.
Music: Ira Newborn. Cinematography: Mac Ahlberg.
Cast: Anne Parillaud, David Proval, Rocco Sisto, Chazz Palminteri,
Anthony LaPaglia, Robert Loggia.

In hot demand after her star turn in Luc Besson's **La Femme Nikita** (1990), Anne Parillaud made a bid for Hollywood stardom in this gory, comedic mixture of horror and gangster film from John Landis, returning to the genre-bending approach that defined **An American Werewolf in London** (1981). Here she plays Marie, a vampire who makes meals out of Pittsburgh mobsters but fails to finish off the ruthless Sal the Shark (Loggia). In keeping with the sympathetic treatment of its bloodsucking lead, the film also provides a romantic component courtesy of cop Anthony LaPaglia and echoes the nocturnal dreaminess of Landis' earlier **Into the Night** (1985) right down to its parade of guest star genre names (in this case including Tom Savini, Dario Argento, Sam Raimi, and Forrest J. Ackerman). A long-gestating project originally attached to director Jack Sholder, the film ended up with Landis after he left another aborted vampire project, *Red Sleep*, set in Las Vegas. The finished film encountered significant issues with the MPAA in the United States and was initially cut for both sex and violence, though it remained complete in most European countries and, despite disappointing box office returns, has since become a minor cult classic.

CRONOS

Mexico, 1993
Director: Guillermo del Toro.
Producers: Arthur Gorson, Bertha Navarro.
Screenplay: Guillermo del Toro.
Music: Javier Álvarez.
Cinematography: Guillermo Navarro.
Cast: Federico Luppi, Ron Perlman,
Claudio Brook, Margarita Isabel,
Tamara Shanath, Daniel Giménez Cacho.

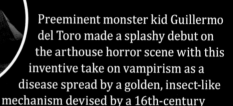

Preeminent monster kid Guillermo del Toro made a splashy debut on the arthouse horror scene with this inventive take on vampirism as a disease spread by a golden, insect-like mechanism devised by a 16th-century alchemist. Here the thirst for blood and eternal youth are bestowed upon aging antique dealer Jesus Gris (Federico Lupi), whose granddaughter is troubled by his transformation as mercenary forces close in to wrest the device from him. Boasting a grisly variation on **Blood for Dracula**'s floor-licking blood scene, the film is packed with intriguing fresh concepts like Lupi's reverse aging achieved through the molting of his skin, but it's the tender but tragic familial relationship at its heart that really sets the tone for the compassionate view of monsters and human outsiders that would defines del Toro's cinema though his Oscar-winning **The Shape of Water** (2017). He also adorns the film with nods to classic Mexican and European horror films, most notably with the villainous casting of **Alucarda** (1977)'s Claudio Brook. The luscious cinematography is provided by Guillermo Navarro, who would go on to shoot many subsequent del Toro films including the next two films in his loose Spanish-language supernatural trilogy, **The Devil's Backbone** (2001) and **Pan's Labyrinth** (2006).

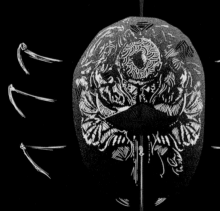

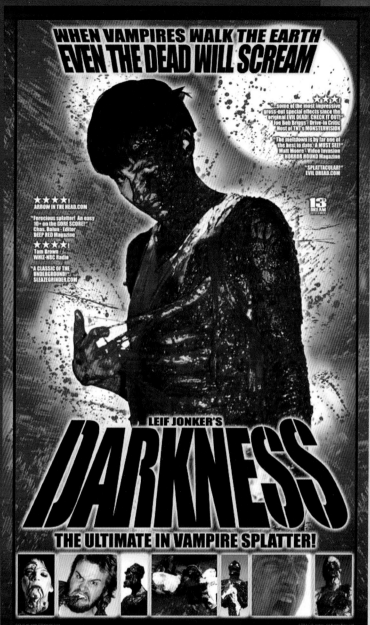

DARKNESS

USA, 1993
Director: Leif Jonker. Producer: Leif Jonker. Screenplay: Leif Jonker. Music: Michael Curtis, Billy Davis [Leif Jonker]. Cinematography: Franklin Hardesty [Leif Jonker]. Cast: Gary Miller, Michael Gisick, Randall Aviks, Cena Donham, Steve Brown, Lisa Franz.

Easily the wettest vampire film at the time of its release, this Wichita, Kansas amateur production shot mostly after hours arrived at the height of the horror fanzine wave when regional features still had a shot at finding a wide audience. Inspired by the calling card of Sami Raimi's **Within the Woods** (1978), the feature was originally mounted under the title **Vampires** but took two years to get rolling before a single camera in 1989 by the 19-year-old Leif Jonker for a mere $5,000 budget assembled piecemeal over time (and including one bounced check and a botched beer deal). Word of mouth quickly spread about this plasma-soaked wonder initially shot on Super 8 and edited with a pair of VCRs after the raw footage was shot with a camcorder off a screen mounted in a kitchen. Jonker (who also wore many other hats on the production including special effects) later did a more professional assembly from the original footage, so thank your lucky stars for the versions now available on home video. The plot about a small town under siege by a band of ruthless vampires after a brutal gas station attack is nothing new in and of itself, but the zeal of the execution makes all the difference with the mostly teenaged cast and crew ensuring the energy level never flags for a moment.

"Ambitious...visually striking"
-BLOCKBUSTER VIDEO MOVIE GUIDE

JUGULAR WINE
A VAMPIRE ODYSSEY

HENRY
ROLLINS

STAN
LEE

SHAUN
IRONS

LISA
MALKIEWICZ

A FILM BY BLAIR MURPHY

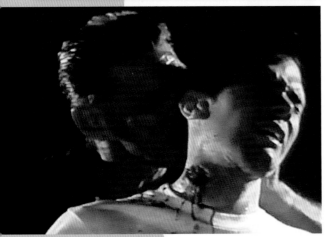

JUGULAR WINE: A VAMPIRE ODYSSEY

USA, 1993
Director: Blair Murphy. Producer: Blair Murphy.
Screenplay: Blair Murphy. Music: John Butler.
Cinematography: Baird Bryant.
Cast: Shaun Irons, Stan Lee, Frank Miller,
Meghan Bashaw, Grace Gongliewski, Gordon Capps.

Opening with a quote by Walt Whitman, this
narration-heavy dream poem feels like an art
project with vampire trappings and is most
startling now for its wild roster of celebrity
appearances including comic book legends Frank
Miller and a wildly overacting Stan Lee, who gets
to yell non sequiturs like "Why aren't you back
there with those Indians!" This passion project
for writer-director Blair Murphy was heavily
promoted on the horror fanzine circuit in the early
'90s and was one of the more readily available titles
from the indie Pagan Video label, though it really
didn't see the light of day outside the United States.
While sailing on the Bering Sea, anthropology
student James Grace (Shaun Irons) is enamored
with a female vampire only for her to be killed by
an undead hit squad. After some deft use of a flare
gun he makes it out alive but, upon returning to
Philadelphia, notes that "I'm not a vampire but I
don't feel right." From there it's a swirling haze
of vampire encounters including a trip to New
Orleans and an evening at a German Expressionist
nightclub called Caligari's Casket where they
project **Nosferatu** on the wall and a shirtless Henry
Rollins talks to himself in front of a **Planet of the
Vampires** (1965) poster. The slow pacing and
hallucinatory aesthetic may not be for all tastes,
but it's worth checking out on late at night when the
plot pieces don't all necessarily have to fit together.

LOVE BITES

LOVE BITES

USA, 1993
Director: Malcolm Marmorstein.
Producer: Wayne Marmorstein.
Screenplay: Malcolm Marmorstein.
Music: Mark Koval.
Cinematography: Stephen Lighthill.
Cast: Adam Ant, Kimberly Foster, Roger Rose,
Michelle Forbes, Philip Bruns, Judy Tenuta.

The early '90s saw no less than two Los Angeles vampire romantic comedies called **Love Bites** released within months of each other: a shot-on-video gay love story about a vampire hunter and his prey falling in love in West Hollywood, from USC veteran and monster movie buff Marvin Jones; and this oddball vehicle for English pop star Adam Ant, written and directed by longtime **Dark Shadows** scribe Malcolm Marmorstein in his final feature after the earlier Elliott Gould zombie comedy **Dead Men Don't Die** (1990). Here Ant plays Zachary Simms, a lovesick vampire who was deserted by his maker, Nerissa (Michelle Forbes), and ended up oversleeping for a century or so. Upon awakening in the present day, he ends up in a secret crypt within the home of Kendall (Kimberly Foster) whose persistent boyfriend, Dwight (Roger Rose), isn't happy about the new competition. Much of the film is spent on Zachary's attempts to become human again, including the consumption of regular food as well as his ascension up the corporate ladder with the yuppie lifestyle equated with a form of bloodsucking all its own. Lighthearted and crammed with that post-'80s hangover feeling that clung on for at least half a decade, it's a good-natured diversion that's perfect for friends who don't normally watch vampire movies. Ant never made it to movie star status given his penchant for picking quirky supporting character roles instead, but he makes for a benign bloodsucker with a heart of gold trying to make sense of a whole new world around him.

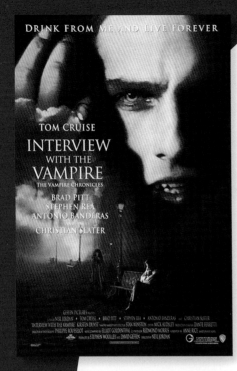

INTERVIEW WITH THE VAMPIRE

USA, 1994
Director: Neil Jordan. Producers: David Geffen, Stephen Woolley. Screenplay: Anne Rice. Music: Elliot Goldenthal. Cinematography: Philippe Rousselot.
Cast: Tom Cruise, Brad Pitt, Stephen Rea, Antonio Banderas, Christian Slater, Kirsten Dunst.

No prior vampire film inspired the protracted media frenzy that surrounded the making of this long-gestating Warner Bros. and Geffen Films adaptation of Anne Rice's classic 1976 novel, a first-person account by vampire Louis (Brad Pitt) of his conversion at the hands of Lestat (Tom Cruise) in Louisiana and their exploits over the centuries including the adoption of the prepubescent undead Claudia (Kirsten Dunst). Many screenwriters (including Rice herself) and casting choices came and went over the years, including a temporary gender switch for Louis, and Rice herself was critical at first of the seemingly bizarre, commercial-minded casting of Cruise. Against the odds, director (and uncredited writer) Neil Jordan pulled the enterprise off and delivered a visual feast aided considerably by Dante Ferretti's striking sets. The cutting-edge vampire effects are also executed with panache, particularly when placed against a classical backdrop like the Rollin-esque Théâtre des Vampires performance and the harrowing final fate of Claudia. The project marked an end to the ongoing collaboration between Jordan and composer George Fenton, whose romantic score was rejected in favor of one by Elliot Goldenthal—one month before the film's release at Geffen's behest. Though Rice came around to Cruise's charismatic interpretation and praised the final product (which adheres closely to the source apart from a tacked-on ending), the film was famously derided by none other than Oprah Winfrey for its extreme moral darkness.

NADJA

USA, 1994
Director: Michael Almereyda.
Producers: Amy Hobby, Mary Sweeney.
Screenplay: Michael Almereyda. Music: Simon Fisher-Turner. Cinematography: Jim Denault.
Cast: Elina Löwensohn, Peter Fonda, Suzy Amis, Galaxy Craze, Martin Donovan, Karl Geary.

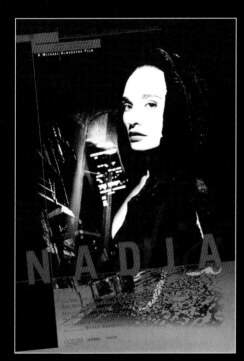

David Lynch presents and briefly appears in this prototypical mid-'90s indie with far more material from Bram Stoker than most viewers expected. Romanian-born Elina Löwensohn took on the title role just after a trio of roles for deadpan film darling Hal Hartley, whose laconic style was frequently compared to this film. Nadja, the daughter of Count Dracula, claims her father's ashes after he's dispatched by Van Helsing (a long-haired Peter Fonda), whose nephew Jim (fellow Hartley repertory player Martin Donovan) is engaged to one of Nadja's next conquests, Lucy (Galaxy Craze). Shot in grainy black-and-white film stock with some stylized sequences captured on the lo-res, short-lived Fisher-Price "Pixelvision" PXL-2000, the film sits at an uneasy juncture between horror film, music video and art film, with Löwensohn making for a visually arresting queen of darkness with her pale skin and black hooded garments. The film was a marked change of pace for young writer-director Michael Almereyda, a Kansas native who first drew attention with his quirky dysfunctional family comedy **Twister** (1989) whose star, Suzy Amis, appears in this film as the virtuous Cassandra. He was also one of the credited writers of Wim Wenders' **Until the End of the World** (1991) and would find his biggest arthouse success with the modern-day Ethan Hawke version of **Hamlet** (2000), though nothing else in his filmography bears any resemblance to his one contribution to vampire cinema.

THE ADDICTION

USA, 1995
Director: Abel Ferrara.
Producers: Denis Hann, Fernando
Sulichin. Screenplay: Nicholas St. John.
Music: Joe Delia.
Cinematography: Ken Kelsch.
Cast: Lili Taylor, Christopher Walken,
Annabella Sciorra, Edie Falco,
Paul Calderon, Fredro Starr.

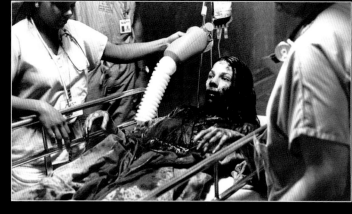

One of the great cinematic chroniclers of New York City, Abel Ferrara offered his own spin on vampirism with a distinctly urban flair in this black-and-white look at the transformation of philosophy grad student

Kathleen (Lili Taylor at the height of her anxious acting powers) after she's bitten while walking home one night. The parallels between blood drinking and drug addiction had long been noted since films like **Martin** with a particular resurgence at the height of the AIDS era, but the distinction here lies in the placement of the events entirely in Taylor's head complete with meditations about her changing existence and her place in a world that seems to be deteriorating or at least molting right in front of her eyes. That introspective approach is entirely in keeping with Ferrara's approach at the time with this film tucked in with his other post-studio arthouse projects, **Dangerous Game** (1993) and **The Funeral** (1995), while his cachet still enabled him to assemble a solid roster of East Coast thespian talent (mostly in one-scene roles) including Christopher Walken, Annabella Sciorra, and a pre-**The Sopranos** pairing of Edie Falco and Michael Imperioli (who was dating Taylor at the time).

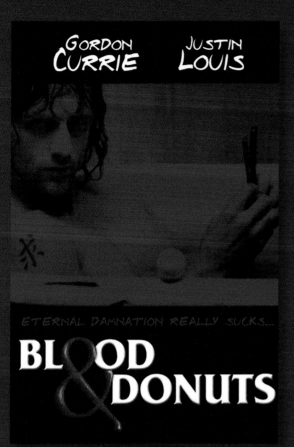

BLOOD & DONUTS

Canada, 1995
Director: Holly Dale. Producer: Steven Hoban.
Screenplay: Andrew Rai Berzins.
Music: Nash the Slash. Cinematography: Paul Sarossy.
Cast: Gordon Currie, Justin Louis [Louis Ferreira],
Helene Clarkson, Fiona Reid, Frank Moore,
David Cronenberg.

No other Canadian horror film is quite like this quirky character study from director Holly Dale, a documentarian who switched to narrative features for the first time here and went on to a long career in television. Awakened by an errant golf ball after a quarter-century hibernation, vampire Boya (Gordon Currie) emerges to find society in Toronto radically changed and falls in love with donut shop employee Molly (Helene Clarkson). He also becomes embroiled in the local underworld (led by David Cronenberg!) thanks to his association with cabbie Earl (Justin Louis). One of the more sweet-natured vampire films around, **Blood & Donuts** finds some new material to mine from its already shopworn concept of an abstinent vampire feeding on vermin thanks to Currie's appealing performance and a soundtrack filled with familiar tunes commenting on our protagonist's supernatural predicament. Amusing moments abound along with a few ghoulish flourishes as you'd expect, but the bulk of the running time is devoted to the relationships forged between Boya and his two new friends as he tries to suppress the natural urges within him. Awkward title aside, this remains a strong viewing choice for vampire viewing when you want a break from screaming and bloodshed.

DRACULA: DEAD AND LOVING IT

USA, 1995
Director: Mel Brooks. Producer: Mel Brooks.
Screenplay: Mel Brooks, Rudy De Luca, Steve Haberman.
Music: Hummie Mann. Cinematography: Michael D. O'Shea.
Cast: Leslie Nielsen, Peter MacNicol, Steven Weber,
Amy Yasbeck, Lysette Anthony, Harvey Korman.

Over two decades after spoofing Mary Shelley with the classic **Young Frankenstein** (1974), Mel Brooks finally tackled Bram Stoker with this scattershot farce that adheres to the source novel with surprising fidelity. Still in his broad Zucker Brothers comedy mode, Leslie Nielsen stars as the Count who travels to London and tangles with the usual array of characters including Brooks himself as Van Helsing and Peter MacNichol as a scene-stealing Renfield. Clearly inspired by the success of **Bram Stoker's Dracula** three years earlier right down to Nielsen's bun hairstyle at the beginning, the script by Brooks, Rudy De Luca and Steve Haberman is actually more accurate than Coppola's version and comes complete with nods to plenty of Universal and Hammer classics (including Brooks' wife, Anne Bancroft, as the gypsy "Madame Ouspenskaya"). Critics were mostly hostile to the film but it does have its moments, particularly a staking with firehose-levels of blood dousing Brooks and an exasperated Jonathan Harker played by Steven Weber.

Brooks would later return to vampire territory as the voice of patriarch Vlad in the animated **Hotel Transylvania 2** (2015) and **Hotel Transylvania 3: Summer Vacation** (2018).

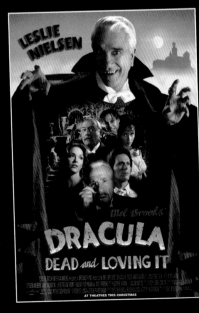

EMBRACE OF THE VAMPIRE

USA, 1995
Director: Anne Goursaud. Producers: Alan Mruvka, Marilyn Vance.
Screenplay: Halle Eaton, Nicole Coady, Rick Bitzelberger.
Music: Joseph Williams. Cinematography: Suki Medencevic.
Cast: Alyssa Milano, Martin Kemp, Harrison Pruett [Harold Pruett],
Jordan Ladd, Rachel True, Charlotte Lewis.

The direct-to-video erotic thriller craze of the 1990s was bound to intersect with vampires at some point, and no film did it more profitably than this glossy softcore yarn given a major push in video stores by New Line Cinema (in both rated and spicy unrated versions). The big selling point here was the presence of Alyssa Milano, formerly a child star on the sitcom **Who's the Boss?** and later a vocal political activist. Here she plays a wholesome college student named Charlotte whose daily life is upended by intense erotic dreams involving a nameless vampire played by Spandau Ballet member and **EastEnders** star Martin Kemp. They eventually meet face to face after he bestows her with an ankh, apparently after watching **The Hunger**, and beguiles her with lines like "I'm your destiny." Kemp's romanticized bloodsucker gets a limited number of attack scenes, though one neck-biting gag through a giant net is effectively executed. Longtime editor Anne Goursaud (who cut **Bram Stoker's Dracula**) made her feature directing debut here and reteamed with Milano immediately afterwards for another long-running rental classic, **Poison Ivy II** (1996). Announced on its title card as part of a nonexistent series called **The Nosferatu Diaries**, the film has since attained legendary status for Milano's nude scenes but also stands as one of the most popular vampire films of the '90s.

"Grabs You By The Throat" – PLAYBOY

"The most believable VAMPIRE flick I have ever seen."
– CHICAGO TRIBUNE

HABIT

USA, 1995
Director: Larry Fessenden. Producer: Dayton Taylor.
Screenplay: Larry Fessenden. Music: Geoffrey Kidde.
Cinematography: Frank G. DeMarco.
Cast: Larry Fessenden, Meredith Snaider, Aaron Beall,
Patricia Coleman, Heather Woodbury, Jesse Hartman.

The ideal companion piece to the same year's **The Addiction**, this grungy, meditative breakthrough second feature for director, actor and Glass Eye Pix founder Larry Fessenden is a self-described autobiographical 16mm production with a vampire twist inspired by Hitchcock, Polanski, Scorsese and Stoker. The project had originated as a 17-minute shot-on-video short in 1981 about a shaggy-haired Manhattan dweller who gets infected with an escalating thirst for blood that sends him on a self-destructive path. The candid depictions of sexuality and nudity in the film certainly didn't hurt its reputation on the indie scene at the time, though it also functions well as an addiction parable with strong fidelity to the classic vampire rules. The level of personal detail gives the dark descent an extra layer of verisimilitude, right down to the use of Fessenden's own father in a ghostly graveyard scene and the integration of the trademark real missing front tooth Fessenden lost in a 1985 mugging (and which has never been replaced). Unlike Ferrara's monochrome film around the same time, this one is shot in heavily saturated color with borderline expressionist use of red and green accenting the costumes and production design, particularly during the bloodletting sex scene in a medical supply room that surely qualifies as a cinematic first.

VAMPIRE IN BROOKLYN

USA, 1995
Director: Wes Craven.
Producers: Mark Lipsky, Eddie Murphy.
Screenplay: Charlie Murphy, Michael Lucker, Chris Parker.
Music: J. Peter Robinson.
Cinematography: Mark Irwin.
Cast: Eddie Murphy, Angela Bassett, Allen Payne,
Kadeem Hardison, John Witherspoon, Zakes Mokae.

Director Wes Craven enjoyed his biggest budget with this
major studio spin on the black vampire concept, with
studio Paramount supplying one of its biggest stars, Eddie Murphy. Fresh off her Oscar-nominated turn
as Tina Turner in **What's Love Got to Do with It** (1993), Angela Bassett also enjoyed a change of pace as a
strong and multi-faceted female lead in a story that originated with Murphy, his cousin Vernon Lynch Jr.,
and brother Charles Murphy, with the latter eventually writing the first draft of the screenplay. Murphy's
penchant for playing multiple characters continues here as
Caribbean bloodsucker Maximillian, along with the zealous
Preacher Pauly and low-life hitman Guido. Despite the
title, the film was shot almost entirely in L.A. and was
plagued by problems including a clash between the
studio and the creative team over the film's tone (with
the latter intending to make a more straightforward
horror film) and the death of stuntwoman Sonja
Davis following a failed building fall. The film
opened just in time for Halloween on October 27 to
a lukewarm reception, but its grisly use of vampire
tropes (including a memorable opening variation
on Stoker's vampire death ship) makes it a noble
attempt to try something a little bit different.

BORDELLO OF BLOOD

USA, 1996
Director: Gilbert Adler. Producer: Gilbert Adler.
Screenplay: Gilbert Adler. Music: Chris Boardman.
Cinematography: Tom Priestley Jr.
Cast: John Kassir (voice), Dennis Miller, Erika Eleniak,
Angie Everhart, Chris Sarandon, Corey Feldman.

Bowing in the summer of 1989 and running for seven years, the HBO television series **Tales from the Crypt** successfully translated the scandalous EC Comics of the 1950s to the small screen thanks to heavyweights behind the scenes including Joel Silver, Robert Zemeckis and Walter Hill. The inevitable move to the big screen proved to be trickier, with the short-form formula of grisly horror and black comedy difficult to translate to a 90-minute format. Released quickly after the first attempt, **Demon Knight** (1995), this second entry proved to be the brand's last gasp, opening two months after the series had ended. Stand-up comic Dennis Miller stars as a private eye whose latest assignment, searching for a missing Corey Feldman, lands him in a brothel inside a funeral home whose employees are voracious vampires in the service of their queen, Lilith (Angie Everhart). Dating back to 1973 as a jokey script written by USC students Zemeckis and Bob Gale, which explains a brief reference to it in Brian De Palma's **Blow Out** (1981), this film was greeted with an indifferent shrug upon its release; however, it has since become something of a fan favourite, largely due to elements like a plummy Chris Sarandon and the use of holy water-filled Super Soakers as weapons. However, the same year would see a much more successful take on a similar idea...

FROM DUSK TILL DAWN

USA, 1996
Director: Robert Rodriguez.
Producers: Gianni Nunnari, Meir Teper.
Screenplay: Quentin Tarantino. Music: Graeme
Revell. Cinematography: Guillermo Navarro.
Cast: George Clooney, Quentin Tarantino, Harvey
Keitel, Juliette Lewis, Salma Hayek, Cheech Marin.

The first paid screenplay written by Quentin Tarantino was
under consideration as the second film in the **Tales from the
Crypt** big-screen cycle, but instead it ended up at Miramax Films
who had just scored big with Tarantino's **Pulp Fiction** (1994). This time

the unorthodox narrative starts as a crime film about
a family abducted by the two criminal Gecko brothers,
Seth (George Clooney) and Richard (Tarantino), before
suddenly turning into a splatter-loaded vampire epic once
they arrive at a Mexican biker bar called the Titty Twister.
Though many of the monstrous surprises were given away
by the initial marketing, the film marked a significant
course change for director Robert Rodriguez after his first
two straightforward action films, **El Mariachi** (1992) and
Desperado (1995). A showstopping appearance by Salma
Hayek as the foot fetish-appeasing stripper, Satanico

Pandemonium is just one of the highlights along with roles
for an eye-popping host of cult favourites including Tom
Savini, Danny Trejo, Cheech Marin, Fred Williamson, and
John Saxon, as well as impressive effects from the busy
Howard Berger and Greg Nicotero with a wide variety of
vampire makeup creations. In addition to inspiring two
direct-to-video sequels and a TV series, the film cemented
an ongoing cinematic bond between Tarantino and
Rodriguez including their ambitious two-story anthology
film, **Grindhouse** (2007).

THE NIGHT FLIER

USA/Italy, 1997
Director: Mark Pavia. Producers: Mitchell Galin,
Richard P. Rubinstein. Screenplay: Mark Pavia, Jack O'Donnell.
Music: Brian Keane. Cinematography: David Connell.
Cast: Miguel Ferrer, Julie Entwisle, Dan Monahan,
Michael H. Moss, John Bennes, Beverly Skinner.

One of the finer neglected Stephen King adaptations, this clever modern vampire thriller originated years earlier when King and producer Richard Rubinstein received a zombie-themed short, **Drag**, directed by Mark Pavia. A horror fan who started off with an amateur two-minute version of **Dracula**, Pavia was selected to helm this feature version of King's short story most famously presented in the 1993 anthology **Nightmares & Dreamscapes** about a vampire who uses remote airspaces to find its prey while flying a small charter plane. Portrayed in the film by Miguel Ferrer, the foul-tempered tabloid reporter Richard Dees is a continuing King character first encountered in the novel *The Dead Zone*; also faithful to the source is the sinister Cessna Skymaster plane, which was found in Columbus, Ohio and rented for two months. Originally intended as a major theatrical release with an offer from Paramount, the independent production instead wound up bowing on HBO in 1997 with minimal theatrical play from New Line afterwards. However, it amassed a bit of a following at the time thanks to its novel premise and effectively grisly practical effects by the now legendary team at KNB EFX Group, who would go on to TV's **The Walking Dead** and multiple Quentin Tarantino projects.

TWO ORPHAN VAMPIRES

France, 1997
Director: Jean Rollin. Producer: Jean Rollin.
Screenplay: Jean Rollin. Music: Philippe d'Aram.
Cinematography: Norbert Marfaing-Sintes.
Cast: Alexandra Pic, Isabelle Teboul, Natalie Perrey,
Anne Duguël, Bernard Charnacé, Brigitte Lahaie.

After spending several years turning out a series of five novels about a pair of blind orphan bloodsuckers, Jean Rollin streamlined the material for the big screen for what would be his penultimate vampire film. His trademark sex and violence are dialed down almost to zero here for a more meditative look at the vampire condition as experienced by the young Louise (Alexandra Pic) and Henriette (Isabelle Teboul), who are blind by day at their religious orphanage but acquire a kind of color-blind sight at night when they go on the prowl for blood. Rollin's return to vampire material for the first time in over two decades finds him in a sweet and benevolent mood, with the casting of past muse Brigitte Lahaie adding to the sense of a creator looking back kindly on his past work (as would be the case with his final three films after this). The idea of the girls being viewed as psychosomatic cases by the institution's eye doctor also offers a different take than usual for Rollin, offering a subtext of an ongoing tension between a self-induced fantasy state and the cold nature of reality that also serves as a nice metaphor for the conditions of Rollin's entire output as a whole.

BLADE

USA, 1998
Director: Stephen Norrington. Producers: Robert Engelman,
Peter Frankfurt, Wesley Snipes. Screenplay: David S. Goyer.
Music: Mark Isham. Cinematography: Theo van de Sande.
Cast: Wesley Snipes, Stephen Dorff, Kris Kristofferson,
N'Bushe Wright, Donal Logue, Udo Kier.

The modern fusion of vampire and action cinema could not exist without this initial cinematic incarnation of the Marvel Comics character who was first introduced in 1973. An amalgam of prominent black leaders and celebrities at the time, the leather-clad, sunglasses-sporting Blade (portrayed by Wesley Snipes) is a vampire hunter who shares qualities with his prey thanks to the tragic fate of his mother. Fighting his own blood-drinking urges and aided by weapons engineer Abraham Whistler (Kris Kristofferson) and afflicted hematologist Dr. Karen Jenson (N'Bushe Wright), he faces off against megalomaniacal vampire Deacon Frost (Stephen Dorff) who plans to vanquish humanity once and for all. From its blood shower club opener featuring none other than Traci Lords, this New Line release (launched in the wake of a failed attempt at a Black Panther feature) was a bumpy production necessitating numerous reshoots including the entire climax, which originally featured a very unconvincing maelstrom of blood. However, the result proved to be a polished crowd pleaser and greatly expanded the possibilities for comic adaptations before the official Marvel post-Disney switchover. The first bona fide box office success for a Marvel property, the film spawned two sequels, Guillermo del Toro's **Blade II** (2002) and David S. Goyer's **Blade: Trinity** (2004), followed by a single-season TV series in 2006 and a revival feature in 2020 starring Mahershala Ali from the post-Disney Marvel. Another Marvel character was also adapted for the big screen the same year by Sony with **Morbius** (2020), featuring Jared Leto as the titular superhero spawned by side effects from his blood disease treatments.

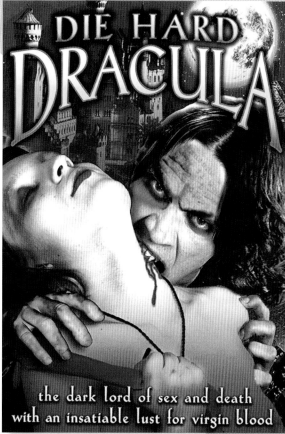

DIE HARD DRACULA

USA, 1998
Director: Peter Horak. Producer: Peter Horak.
Screenplay: Peter Horak. Music: Ivan Koutikov.
Cinematography: Mark Morris.
Cast: Bruce Glover, Denny Sachen, Kerry Dustin,
Ernest M. Garcia, Chaba Hrotko, Tom McGowan.

the dark lord of sex and death
with an insatiable lust for virgin blood

There may be worse shot-on-video vampire
films out there than this perplexing American
production shot in the Czech Republic, but none has gained quite the level of infamy or can boast such
a shameless title. However, this one doesn't involve a master of the undead mowing down bad guys in a
skyscraper; instead you get a computer-generated coffin flying over Europe to the
strains of 'The Ride of the Valkyries' before disgorging a chubby, gray-haired
Dracula who feasts on a young maiden. Bruce Glover, father of Crispin and
star of **Diamonds Are Forever** (1971), devours the scenery here (and
gets a credit for "acting coach & additional dialogue") as a modern-
day Van Helsing called in when visiting Californian Steven (Denny
Sachen) falls afoul of Dracula and encounters the spitting image of his
girlfriend who just died in a freak water-skiing accident. For reasons
never made entirely clear (though likely due to production scheduling
issues), Dracula is played by two different actors (Tom McGowan and
Chaba Hrotko); more amazingly, this was the sole directorial effort for
American stunt coordinator Peter Horak, who went on to more mundane
films like **The Nutty Professor** (1996) and **National Security** (2003).
Watch at your own risk, but you'll never forget it.

RAZOR BLADE SMILE

UK, 1998
Director: Jake West. Producers: Rob Mercer,
Jake West. Screenplay: Jake West.
Music: Richard Wells. Cinematography: Jim Solan.
Cast: Eileen Daly, Christopher Adamson, Jonathan Coote,
Kevin Howarth, David Warbeck, Heidi James.

Eileen Daly, the face of Redemption Films and its onetime
video hostess, scored her first lead role in this low-
budget precursor to the **Underworld** series, with all
the gun action and fetishy attire that implies. Though
lost a bit in the glut of 1998 vampire films, this was a
significant calling card for newcomer Jake West before
his gore-soaked **Evil Aliens** (2005) and dozens of horror
genre featurettes. A prototypical late '90s direct-to-
video effort just on the cusp of the CGI invasion, this
action-horror hybrid charts the adventures of vampire
assassin Lilith Silver (Daly), who was converted during
an 18th-century duel gone very wrong involving the
undead Sethane (Christopher Adamson). Her signature contract killings
(complete with bullet wounds to camouflage her bite marks a la **Innocent
Blood**) have attracted the attention of the police, just as she's uncovered a
secret conspiracy ruled by her old archrival. Both cast and crew are packed
with British names from the genre scene at the time, none more recognizable
than the great David Warbeck in his final role (shot just before his death in
1997). The ensuing decades of cheap
video productions have helped make
this film's microbudget DIY 16mm
aesthetic more appealing now in
retrospect, right down to its amusing
twist ending and quasi-007 opening
credits.

VAMPIRES

USA, 1998
Director: John Carpenter.
Producer: Sandy King. Screenplay: Don Jakoby.
Music: John Carpenter. Cinematography: Gary B. Kibbe.
Cast: James Woods, Daniel Baldwin, Sheryl Lee,
Thomas Ian Griffith, Maximilian Schell, Tim Guinee.

The closest thing to a western in the filmography of writer-director John Carpenter also happens to be his only vampire film, a loose, long-gestating adaptation of John Steakley's 1990 novel **Vampire$**. Set in New Mexico, the film hits the ground running with an ongoing showdown between a nest of vampires, a small band of hunters led by Jack Crow (James Woods) and Tony Montoya (Daniel Baldwin), and the Catholic Church, represented by a particularly ripe Maximilian Schell. Though hampered by severe last-minute budget cuts and the deeply unpleasant treatment of an infected prostitute played by **Twin Peaks'** Sheryl Lee, the film features some appealing twists on traditional lore such as using winches to drag the vampires out into daylight and depicting varying degrees of sympathy among the undead from savage, soulless predators to tortured infected ones living on borrowed time. However, the major selling point here is Woods in a rare leading man performance from the era; famously improvising many of his saltier moments, he creates a vampire hunter who truly feels weathered by his job. Though only moderately successful at the box office, the film proved popular enough on home video to spawn two sequels, **Vampires: Los Muertos** (2002) and **Vampires: The Turning** (2005).

THE WISDOM OF CROCODILES

UK, 1998
Director: Po-Chih Leong. Producers: Carolyn Choa,
David Lascelles. Screenplay: Paul Hoffman.
Music: Orlando Gough, John Lunn.
Cinematography: Oliver Curtis.
Cast: Jude Law, Elina Löwensohn, Timothy Spall,
Jack Davenport, Colin Salmon, Hitler Wong.

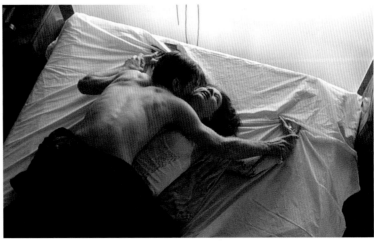

The arthouse vampire wave of the '90s came to a close with this ambitious mood piece starring a young Jude Law as Steven, a modern-day empathetic predator who not only absorbs his victims' blood but also their emotions which, in a Cronenbergian touch, his body materializes as glass-like fragments. His quest for female companionship crosses paths with the suicidal Anna, played by **Nadja**'s Elina Löwensohn, who may be the key to realizing his destiny after he saves her from throwing herself in front of a train. After a small U.K. theatrical run, Miramax snapped up this film intending to ride the wave of interest in Law, who was at the beginning of a Hollywood push to leading man status at the time. However, it was sent virtually straight to video under the bland title **Immortality** instead. British-born director Po-Chih Leong takes a subdued approach here that disappointed those looking for a traditional horror film but has an odd resonance thanks to Law's nuanced performance. Screenwriter and onetime BBFC censor Paul Hoffman had spent thirteen years hammering the material into a more peculiar and political novel, which was ultimately completed and published two years after this film with the vampirism angle coexisting with a study in modern terrorism and economic upheaval.

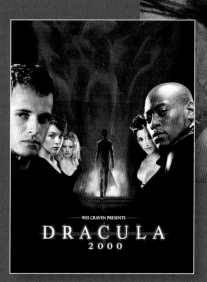

DRACULA 2000

USA, 2000
Director: Patrick Lussier.
Producers: W.K. Border, Joel Soisson. Screenplay: Joel Soisson.
Music: Marco Beltrami. Cinematography: Peter Pau.
Cast: Gerard Butler, Christopher Plummer, Jonny Lee Miller, Justine Waddell, Colleen Ann Fitzpatrick [Vitamin C], Jennifer Esposito.

Miramax's Dimension Films brought Bram Stoker's famous creation to the new millennium for Christmas of 2000 with this flawed but stylish modern-day sequel of sorts to the classic novel. The film was helmed by Patrick Lussier, Wes Craven's most recent film editor who had cut **Scream** (1996) and its first two sequels. Right down to its "Wes Craven Presents" banner, late '90s widescreen gloss, and roaring Marco Beltrami score, this was a clear bid to recapture the magic that launched the **Scream** series but didn't receive quite as warm a welcome. Here a very young Gerard Butler appears as Dracula, revived from his imposed eternal sleep in modern day New Orleans after a **Son of Dracula**-inspired plunge into a swamp. Creating new vampires upon his arrival, he faces off against a team of vampire hunters including Matthew Van Helsing (Christopher Plummer) and his protégé, Simon (Jonny Lee Miller). If that sounds like a thinly disguised redo of **Dracula A.D. 1972**, well, essentially it is. Lussier went on to direct two sequels, **Dracula II: Ascension** (2003) and **Dracula III: Legacy** (2005), though he still stuck around as an editor long enough to have far less luck with werewolves by earning a cinematic purple heart bringing **Cursed** (2005) to completion.

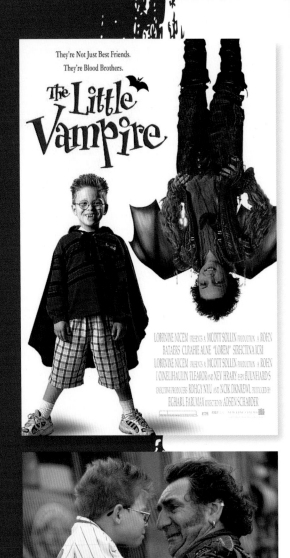

THE LITTLE VAMPIRE

Germany/Netherlands/USA, 2000
Director: Uli Edel. Producer: Richard Claus. Screenplay:
Karey Kirkpatrick, Larry Wilson. Music: Nigel Clarke,
Michael Csányi-Wills. Cinematography: Bernd Heinl.
Cast: Jonathan Lipnicki, Richard E. Grant, Jim Carter,
Alice Krige, Pamela Gidley, Tommy Hinkley, Rollo Weeks.

Far stranger and more intriguing than its generic kiddie
promotional art would have you believe, this stylish and
charming supernatural fantasy is the most high-profile
adaptation of the long-running German book series,
Der kleine Vampir, which was started by author Angela
Sommer-Bodenburg in 1979 and went on to spawn
sixteen volumes and two TV series. When his father
moves the family from California to Scotland to work
on a golf course project, young Tony, played by Jonathan
Lipnicki during his post-**Jerry Maguire** (1996) fame,
finds himself bullied and isolated. His fortunes change
when a bat gets into his home and turns into Rudolph
(Rollo Weeks), a pint-sized vampire
whose family's fate is tied to a
prophecy involving a comet and a
nearby vampire hunter who wants
them dead. German director Uli
Edel, who broke through on the
international scene with **Christiane
F.** (1981), was coming off of a strange
stint in Hollywood ranging from
Last Exit to Brooklyn (1989) to
Body of Evidence (1992) when he
tackled this multinational attempt
to tap into the young adult fantasy
film market just before the Harry
Potter movie onslaught. Not to be
overlooked is the fact that this earns
its place in the history books as the
first film with vampire cows.

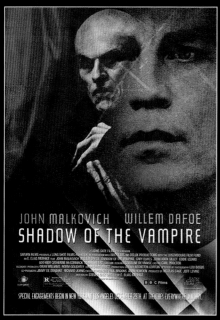

SHADOW OF THE VAMPIRE

UK/Luxembourg/USA, 2000
Director: E. Elias Merhige. Producers: Nicolas Cage, Jeff Levine.
Screenplay: Steven Katz. Music: Dan Jones.
Cinematography: Lou Bogue.
Cast: John Malkovich, Willem Dafoe, Udo Kier, Cary Elwes,
Catherine McCormack, Eddie Izzard.

A decade after shaking up the American underground scene with his disturbing **Begotten** (1990), New York filmmaker E. Elias Merhige joined the indie arthouse wave with this fictional, speculative look at the making of **Nosferatu** with F.W Murnau (John Malkovich) opportunistically using a real vampire, Max Schreck (Willem Dafoe), to play the terrifying, claw-handed Count Orlok. Simultaneously a black comedy, an acidic look at the high cost of one's artistic vision, and a grisly horror film in its own right, this would become the second vampire film to earn acknowledgement from the Oscars (a Supporting Actor nomination for Dafoe's performance) following **Bram Stoker's Dracula**, both featuring Cary Elwes in their casts. Merhige wrings both comedy and queasy tension out of his painstaking recreations of the production of Murnau's film, here rendered in delicate earth tones that reflect the tinting common to silent films of the era while amusing film buffs with an idea of what it might have been like to be on the set circa 1921. That approach also belies the surprising violence and cruelty of the final act, which presents a spin on the fate of the cinematic Orlok with a wry commentary about the sacrifices made for art. The idea of integrating Murnau into a fanciful horror story was later revisited in the TV series **American Horror Story: Hotel**.

THE BREED

USA, 2001
Director: Michael Oblowitz.
Producers: Jim Burke, Kelli Konop, Brad Krevoy, Adam Richman.
Screenplay: Christos N. Gage, Ruth Fletcher. Music: Roy Hay.
Cinematography: Chris Squires.
Cast: Adrian Paul, Bokeem Woodbine, Bai Ling, Péter Halász,
James Booth, Lo Ming.

Dystopian vampire epics have been a dime a dozen for the past couple of decades, but a different tactic can be found in this cross between a futuristic buddy cop movie and plague thriller. When his partner is murdered "in the near future," police detective Stephen Grant (Bokeem Woodbine) is paired up with Aaron Gray (Adrian Paul), a covert vampire who's part of a movement to help them assimilate into society at large. Also on the force is the cheekily named Lucy Westenra (Hollywood club staple Bai Ling), who becomes a romantic interest for Grant, but there are bigger fish to fry when a full-on vampire uprising is brewing-- and humanity has its own less than ethical response being prepared. Complete with early '00s style to burn (take that as you will) and more Stoker nods like a gung-ho, anti-vampire agent named Seward, this isn't a film to take completely seriously even if it does want to say something about population suppression – something driven home by shooting in real former Jewish ghettos on location in Hungary. The Eastern European locales prove to be a big asset all around in the end, giving the film a kind of netherworld atmosphere that pairs up nicely with the heavily noir-influenced aesthetic.

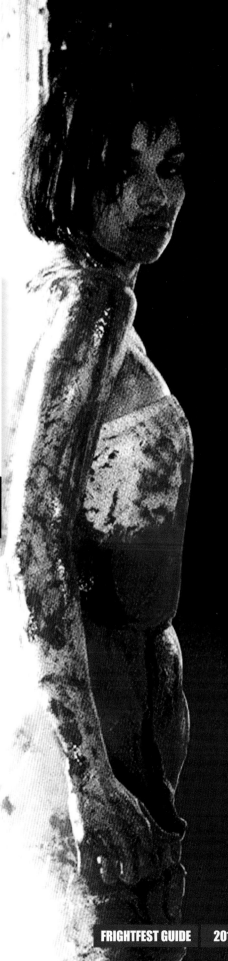

TROUBLE EVERY DAY

France/Germany/Japan, 2001
Director: Claire Denis.
Producers: Philippe Liégeois,
Georges Benayoun, Jean-Michel
Rey. Screenplay: Claire Denis,
Jean-Pol Fargeau.
Music: Tindersticks.
Cinematography: Agnès Godard.
Cast: Vincent Gallo, Tricia Vessey,
Béatrice Dalle, Alex Descas,
Caille Nicolas Duvauchelle,
Florence Loiret.

The most misunderstood film by acclaimed French writer-director Claire Denis had a rocky reception from viewers expecting the artistic sociological approach of her more famous films like **Beau travail** (1999). Closer in spirit to **Ganja & Hess** than your standard vampire film, this is the dreamy saga of a newly married couple (Vincent Gallo and Tricia Vessey) traveling from America to Paris to track down one of his medical colleagues, who now keeps his wife, Coré (Béatrice Dalle), locked away due to her proclivity for tearing into men with her teeth during intercourse. Casting the live wire Dalle as a vampire was a no brainer given her incendiary portrayal of madness in **Betty Blue** (1986), though this film now also forms a neat trilogy along with her terrifying role as the baby-coveting madwoman in Julien Maury and Alexandre Bustillo's **Inside** (2007). In retrospect this film (which takes its title from the Frank Zappa song of the same name) has been categorized as an installment in the ongoing New French Extremity movement that began in the early 1990s due to its bloody, intense feeding sequences. However, its contemplative treatment of the connection between vampirism, disease, and sex makes it challenging fare that can still lure in unexpecting viewers open to its skewed approach to the horror genre.

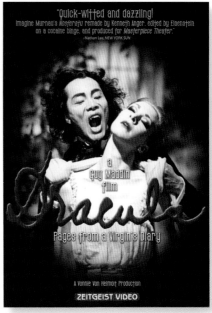

"Quick-witted and dazzling! Imagine Murnau's *Nosferatu* remade by Kenneth Anger, edited by Eisenstein on a cocaine binge, and produced for *Masterpiece Theater*."
-Nathan Lee, NEW YORK SUN

a Guy Maddin film
Dracula
Pages from a Virgin's Diary
A Vonnie Von Helmolt Production
ZEITGEIST VIDEO

DRACULA: PAGES FROM A VIRGIN'S DIARY

Canada, 2002
Director: Guy Maddin. Producer: Vonnie von Helmolt.
Screenplay: Mark Godden. Cinematography: Paul Suderman.
Cast: Zhang Wei-Qiang, Tara Birtwhistle, David Moroni,
CindyMarie Small, Johnny A. Wright, Stephane Leonard.

Best known for his audacious experiments in cinematic antiquity like **Tales from the Gimli Hospital** (1988) and **Careful** (1992), Winnipeg-based filmmaker and artist Guy Maddin made a marked change in direction with this vivid Canadian Broadcasting Corporation production originally intended only for TV broadcast but sent to the big screen in limited release after a warm reception.

Using his trademark yellow intertitles and throwback cinematic techniques echoing classic silent cinema, Maddin adapts the ballet *Dracula* by Texas native Mark Godden, whose training with the Royal Winnipeg Ballet ensured the troupe's participation in this film. The ballet was originally staged as a 1997 tribute to the centennial celebration of Bram Stoker's novel, though it has since been revived as recently as 2018. The narrative sticks closely to the originally story picking up with the London arrival of Dracula, here performed by Zhang Wei-Qiang in an effective twist on the novel's theme of British society reacting to the intrusion of an aristocratic foreigner. In classic William Castle style, the black-and-white film briefly bursts with bright red blood at key moments, and there's no denying the gleeful novelty of seeing familiar characters like Quincy Morris, Van Helsing and Lucy Westenra doing pirouettes in front of the camera.

DRACULA'S FIANCÉE

France, 2002
Director: Jean Rollin. Producer: Jacques Orth.
Screenplay: Jean Rollin. Music: Philippe d'Aram.
Cinematography: Norbert Marfaing-Sintes.
Cast: Cyrille Iste [Cyrille Gaudin], Sandrine Thoquet, Jacques Régis [Jacques Orth], Brigitte Lahaie,
Thomas Smith, Thomas Desfossé.

Originally released as **La fiancée de Dracula**, Jean Rollin's final vampire film offers a checklist of visual tropes and poetic themes running rampant through his prior films. Here the action is focused around a convent where Dracula (Thomas Desfossé) holds sway over the beautiful Isabelle (Cyrille Iste) and plans to make her his next betrothed, against the best efforts of a pair of vampire hunters. Rollin lucky charm Brigitte Lahaie, overcast beachscapes, an enchanted clock, sexy nuns, shipwrecks, nocturnal graveyard encounters, and random surreal elements like a cannibal ogress keep this firmly in Rollin territory from the outset, here downplaying the horrific to focus instead of a wistful romanticism common to the filmmaker's later work. That extends to the vampires themselves, who were tragic but cold-blooded creatures of the night for the most part in his early work but take on a wholly sympathetic cast here. Perhaps even more than the prior **Two Orphan Vampires**, this tale is heavily indebted to classic serials and pulp comics with a menagerie of oddball characters and brief but gruesome violent shocks like improvised heart surgery via claw hammer. Extra points for what may be the only time a vampire film has cast its Van Helsing character with an adult film director, Jacques Orth, billed here as Jacques Régis.

QUEEN OF THE DAMNED

USA/Australia, 2002
Director: Michael Rymer.
Producer: Jorge Saralegui.
Screenplay: Scott Abbott, Michael Petroni.
Music: Jonathan Davis, Richard Gibbs.
Cinematography: Ian Baker.
Cast: Stuart Townsend, Marguerite Moreau, Aaliyah, Vincent Perez, Paul McGann, Lena Olin.

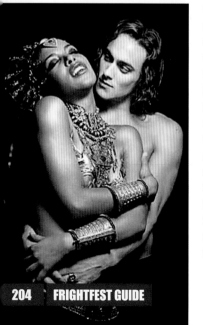

Anne Rice's belated literary sequels to her breakthrough debut novel, 1976's *Interview with the Vampire*, expanded the scope of her imaginary world considerably starting with *The Vampire Lestat* in 1985 and *The Queen of the Damned* in 1988. Despite the considerable success of the film version of **Interview with the Vampire** (1994), an entirely different creative team was assembled for this follow-up feature that uses the stripped-down plot of the third book (concerning the origins of vampirism) liberally sprinkled with bits of the second one. The end result shows every sign of its tortuous origins, rushed into production to retain the rights to the series and ignoring Rice's offer to adapt the books herself. Singer and actress Aaliyah, who tragically died in a plane crash just after shooting her role, is the star attraction here as Akasha, the first vampire, who is awakened from her centuries-long sleep by a rock performance featuring Lestat (Stuart Townsend). Now openly flaunting the nature of existence, Lestat has earned the ire of his fellow undead and finds himself falling under the sway of the queen's influence as they confront the antagonized Ancient Vampires. The Australian-shot production marked a dead end on the big screen for Rice's ongoing saga, but it did eventually rise from the dead as a 2022 TV series from AMC.

THE ERA OF VAMPIRES

Hong Kong, 2003
Director: Wellson Chin. Producer: Tsui Hark.
Screenplay: Tsui Hark. Music: J.M. Logan.
Cinematography: Joe Chan, Sunny Tsang, Herman Yau.
Cast: Danny Chan, Michael Chow, Ken Chang, Lam Suet,
Yu Rongguang, Anya.

Widely released in a heavily edited version as **Tsui Hark's Vampire Hunters**, this fantasy-action spectacle offered audiences a more Westernized take on the subject than usual since it's a loose spin on the Hammer Films and Shaw Brothers venture, **The Legend of the 7 Golden Vampires**. Once again we have a fleet of resurrected Hong Kong vampires (who feed in a novel method of blood respiration) facing off against a quartet of hunters, here dropped into a story about spectacularly unfortunate wedding planning and reworked with far more elaborate, *wuxia*-style martial arts skills. That approach isn't surprising given that this film was heavily promoted with the name of writer-producer Tsui Hark, one of the leading lights in the Hong Kong cinematic breakthrough wave of the 1980s with his Film Workshop productions like **A Chinese Ghost Story** (1987) and **Zu: Warriors from the Magic Mountain** (1983). Technically this film was an attempt to revive the hopping vampire subgenre that had largely fallen out of fashion, albeit handled here with far less comedy and a stronger emphasis on combat sequences. Though not as successful as hoped, the film did manage to kickstart a minor *jiangshi* revival including Dante Lam and Donnie Yen's **The Twins Effect** (2003) and Juno Mak's **Rigor Mortis** (2013).

STRANGE THINGS HAPPEN AT SUNDOWN

USA, 2003
Director: Marc Fratto. Producer: Brandi
Metaxas. Screenplay: Marc Fratto.
Music: Marc Fratto, Frank Garfi.
Cinematography: Marc Fratto.
Cast: J. Scott Green, Masha Sapron, Jocasta
Bryan, Joseph DeVito, Joshua Nelson,
Shannon Moore.

So steeped in Italian-American tropes you'd
expect the plentiful fake blood to be made
from marinara sauce, this foul-mouthed,
indulgent, rambling, bullet-riddled cheapie
plays like a supernatural homage to **The Boondock
Saints** (1999). Whether that's an enticement or a warning
will be up to you, but there's undeniable novelty in
seeing a scrappy, epic-length crime film with characters
like Nicky the Tooth and Jimmy Fangs. Shot on video
around Brooklyn, this marked the debut for Queens-born
director and co-writer Marc Fratto, a veteran of local TV
news productions, whose script is peppered with lines
like "Don't talk to her 'cuz we're gonna be eating her
tomorrow." The episodic storyline follows the bloody,
quippy havoc that erupts when a young couple on the way
to Quebec with $100,000 in stolen vampire mob money
end up crossing paths with their pursuers, leading to a
massive body count and some of the loudest domestic
squabbling ever recorded. The sprawling running time
allows for curious tangents involving details about
vampire regeneration (especially when it comes to
gunshots), religious debates, and a smoky, hallucinatory
climax that feels like Gaspar Noé on a dime store budget.
Today the film is of particular interest for its pulsating
electronic soundtrack (composed by Fratto and Frank
Garfi), which anticipates the synthwave craze that would
become a major part of horror and action scores within
the following decade.

UNDERWORLD

USA/UK/Germany/Hungary, 2003
Director: Len Wiseman. Producers: Gary Lucchesi, Tom
Rosenberg, Richard S. Wright. Screenplay: Danny McBride.
Music: Paul Haslinger. Cinematography: Tony Pierce-Roberts.
Cast: Kate Beckinsale, Scott Speedman, Michael Sheen,
Shane Brolly, Bill Nighy, Erwin Leder.

The European vampire film stormed into the new millennium
with this action-horror hybrid about a centuries-long battle
waged against werewolves ("lycans"), a plot device that
would be reused numerous times in later years (and itself a
carryover from several novels, video games and comic books).
Onetime indie arthouse favourite Kate Beckinsale made her
bid for blockbuster superstardom here as Selene, a Death
Dealer (a.k.a. undead assassin) whose quest to exterminate
any remaining lycanthropes in sight is dramatically sidelined
when she meets Michael (Scott Speedman), a valuable human
who is fatefully bitten and becomes a test to her loyalties. The film marked an auspicious feature debut
for onetime propman Len Wiseman, who married Beckinsale a year after this film's release. Much ink was
spilled at the time since she had previously been with actor Michael Sheen, who delivers the film's most
spirited performance as lycan leader Lucian. The worldwide success of the film ensured no less than four
live-action sequels to date-- **Underworld: Evolution** (2006), **Underworld: Rise of the Lycans** (2009),
Underworld: Awakening (2012) and **Underworld: Blood Wars** (2016)—as well as a handful of imitators
like **Ultraviolet** (2006). This seemed likely to be the dominating vampire franchise for the entire decade,
but that would change dramatically just five years later...

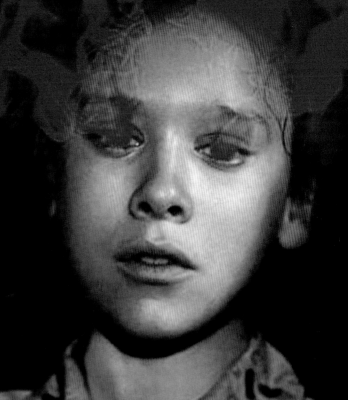

NIGHT WATCH

Russia, 2004
Director: Timur Bekmambetov. Producers: Konstantin Ernst, Anatoliy Maksimov. Screenplay: Timur Bekmambetov, Laeta Kalogridis. Music: Yuri Poteyenko. Cinematography: Sergei Trofimov.
Cast: Konstantin Khabensky, Vladimir Menshov, Valeri Zolotukhin, Mariya Poroshina, Galina Tyunina, Yuriy Kutsenko.

One of the first internationally successful variants of literary-based vampirism in the current millennium came with this derivation from the work of novelist Sergei Lukyanenko. Complete with a convoluted mythos and elaborate CGI, the film and its less popular sequel, **Day Watch** (2006), concern an ongoing battle between the forces of Light and Dark as conducted by the Others, supernaturally endowed humans with enhanced abilities and lifespans. Caught in the middle is supernatural cop Anton (Konstantin Khabensky), whose personal struggles intersect with an ancient prophecy. With its frenetic action sequences, emphasis on chic digital landscapes, and flashy manipulated English subtitles, the films arrived at the dawn of the modern, genre-bending vampire film represented more traditionally by **Underworld**. Not to be outdone, director Timur Bekmambetov made the leap to Hollywood where he tackled more traditional bloodsuckers with **Abraham Lincoln: Vampire Hunter** (2012), part of a brief fad for literary and historical mashup narratives inaugurated by Seth Grahame-Smith's 2009 novel, *Pride and Prejudice and Zombies*. Grahame-Smith wrote the source novel and adapted it into a screenplay for Bekmambetov's film (followed by a 2015 sequel novel, *The Last American Vampire*), portraying the presidency of Abraham Lincoln as a parallel history with the fight against American vampirism flourishing in the South.

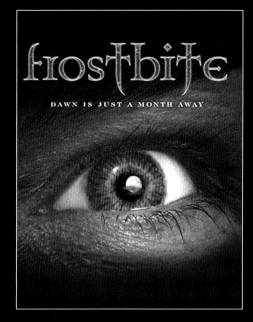

FROSTBITE

Sweden, 2006
Director: Anders Banke.
Producers: Göran Lindström, Magnus Paulsson.
Screenplay: Daniel Ojanlatva, Pidde Andersson.
Music: Anthony Lledo. Cinematography: Chris Maris.
Cast: Petra Nielsen, Carl-Åke Eriksson, Grete Havnesköld,
Emma Åberg, Jonas Lawes, Niklas Grönberg.

The first (but certainly not last) bona fide Swedish vampire
film is this cheeky, humorous horror outing from first-time
feature director Anders Banke, which parallels the comic
30 Days of Night by locating its story in the permanent
nightfall of the northern region's midwinter season.
Originally conceived as a more sprawling anthology with
multiple storylines, the effects-laden production took
eight years to reach the screen (under its original domestic
title, **Frostbiten**) and draws in some borderline sci-fi
elements with its tale of pills made from concentrated
vampire blood upending a small town just after the arrival
of scientist Annika (Petra Nielsen) and her daughter, Saga
(Grete Havnesköld). The premise itself is essentially a
modern riff on ideas that have been around since the 1970s,
but this outing distinguishes itself with touches like an
atmospheric World War II-set prologue and a more layered villain then usual whose plot has evolved from
attempts to cure vampirism entirely. Though barely distributed in its native country and brushed off
for its supposedly insufficient artistic merit, the film was circulated throughout the rest of Scandinavia
by Paramount and marked a resurgence in international vampire cinema that would soon become a
maelstrom by the decade's end.

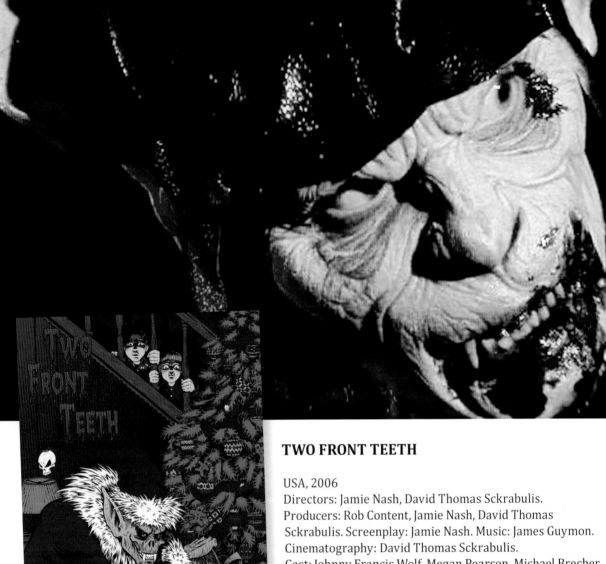

TWO FRONT TEETH

USA, 2006
Directors: Jamie Nash, David Thomas Sckrabulis.
Producers: Rob Content, Jamie Nash, David Thomas
Sckrabulis. Screenplay: Jamie Nash. Music: James Guymon.
Cinematography: David Thomas Sckrabulis.
Cast: Johnny Francis Wolf, Megan Pearson, Michael Brecher,
Joseph L. Johnson, Eric Messner, Lisa Oberg.

"We hate Christmas... and we wanted to destroy Christmas
in every way." That's the mission statement offered by co-
director Jamie Nash for this raucous DIY yuletide horror
cheapie which earns points for introducing the character
"Clausferatu" and the questionable use of live firearms
on set, surely a first in vampire

cinema. On Christmas Eve, conspiracy journalist Gabe Snow (Johnny Francis Wolf)
has determined that a recent plane crash is part of the ongoing handiwork of a
monstrous force coming out of the North Pole with a glowing-nosed bloodsucker
calling the shots and the fate of his very fragile marriage to Noel (Megan Pearson)
at, er, stake. Boasting seasonal gags galore like a severed head mounted on a toy
train (under a Christmas tree, of course), a vampire hunter nun squad called the
Silent Knights, and a gaggle of malicious helper elves with razor-sharp vampire
fangs, this Baltimore-shot ode to 1980s films ranging from **The Evil Dead** (1981)
to **Blood Simple** (1984) boasts some inventive creature designs involving pointy
ears and black leather, not to mention a barrage of saturated red and green lighting.
However, the make or break point for most viewers will be the knockabout, gory
martial arts showdown between the main vampire and a beloved holiday figure
that should earn this a place in a few horror fans' regular holiday viewing rotation.

30 DAYS OF NIGHT

USA, 2007
Director: David Slade. Producers: Sam Raimi, Rob Tapert.
Screenplay: Steve Niles, Stuart Beattie, Brian Nelson. Music:
Brian Reitzell. Cinematography: Jo Willems.
Cast: Josh Hartnett, Melissa George, Danny Huston, Ben
Foster, Mark Boone Junior, Mark Rendall.

In 2002 the striking three-part horror comic *30 Days of Night*
turned heads among horror fans with its vivid depiction
of vampires descending upon the town of Barrow, Alaska,
whose month-long dark spell provides a perfect feeding
ground. Creator Steve Niles had also pitched the idea as a
film during the creative process but didn't see that
idea come to fruition for five years when it was
shepherded through by Columbia and Ghost
House. Niles himself wrote the early drafts
of the script (later given polishes by
Stuart Beattie and Brian Nelson)
about Sheriff Eben Oleson (Josh
Hartnett, not quite the Inuit
character of the source
material) and his wife,
Stella (Melissa George), contending with the threat swallowing up their
town under the leadership of vampire leader Marlow (Danny Huston).
Marked by a scene-stealing early performance by Ben Foster as the
unnamed (and undead) harbinger of death, the film was a highlight
among an unusually busy genre year alongside 2007 fare like **The
Mist, [REC], Paranormal Activity** and **The Orphanage**, setting the
stage for a new wave of American vampire cinema and inspiring a
direct-to-video sequel,
**30 Days of Night:
Dark Days** (2010),
two limited
series in 2007
called **Dust
to Dust**
and **Blood
Trails,** and
a slew of
spin-off
stories.

LET THE RIGHT ONE IN

Sweden, 2008
Director: Tomas Alfredson. Producers: Carl Molinder, John Nordling.
Screenplay: John Ajvide Lindqvist. Music: Johan Söderqvist. Cinematography: Hoyte Van Hoytema.
Cast: Kåre Hedebrant, Lina Leandersson, Per Ragnar, Henrik Dahl, Karin Bergquist, Peter Carlberg.

The vampire film truly entered the new millennium with **Låt den rätte komma in** or **Let the Right One In,** adapted by John Ajvide Lindqvist from his own, significantly more graphic novel (which would be legally unfilmable in its entirety). Set in a snowy Swedish town during the 1980s, the story revolves around young bullied Oskar (Kåre Hedebrant) entering the world of his mysterious new neighbor, eternally young child vampire Eli (Lina Leandersson), whose human familiar procures blood from local residents. Both emotionally moving and chilling, the film offers a fresh take on the trope of a vampire-human romance here spun into a relationship that thrives on ambiguity and the manipulation of viewer sympathies; it's only as the end credits roll that we fully absorb the full gruesome consequences of what has occurred and what remains to come. Aided by special effects trickery and sparing vocal manipulation, Eli is one of the screen's most complex and compelling undead characters whose vulnerability always feels like a mask that could slip at any moment to reveal the much older predator underneath. A respectable American remake from director Matt Reeves, **Let Me In** (2010), soon followed from the newly reformed Hammer Films and largely follows its source apart from the location changed to New Mexico and a standout new single-shot car sequence set to "Don't Fear the Reaper" that justifies the film's existence all by itself.

TWILIGHT

USA, 2008
Director: Catherine Hardwicke.
Producers: Wyck Godfrey, Greg Mooradian,
Mark Morgan. Screenplay: Melissa Rosenberg.
Music: Carter Burwell.
Cinematography: Elliot Davis.
Cast: Kristen Stewart, Robert Pattinson,
Peter Facinelli, Jackson Rathbone,
Ashley Greene, Kellan Lutz.

The young adult book craze that began in
earnest with Harry Potter hit its vampire
phase with Stephenie Meyer's 2005 novel,
Twilight, which took three years to reach the
screen after phasing away from development
at Paramount's MTV Films. Newly arrived
to Washington State, teenager Bella Swan
(Kristen Stewart) begins a tortured romance
with a 109-year-old vampire, Edward Cullen
(Robert Pattinson), who still looks like an
adolescent and subsists with his undead
family on animal blood. Catherine Hardwicke,
director of the indie success **Thirteen**
(2003), helmed this first entry which was
shot in Oregon and became a major surprise
success for Summit Entertainment. In keeping
with the novel, these cinematic Cullens
have no fangs, sport golden eyes, and move
with striking, inhuman grace achieved by
bringing in a dance choreographer to coach
the actors. After considerable press coverage
and scrutiny of both the director and stars,
Hardwicke was replaced on future entries
of what became dubbed **The Twilight Saga**
including **New Moon** (2009), **Eclipse** (2010),
and Breaking Dawn – Part 1 (2011) and
Part 2 (2012). The later films introduced a
werewolf clan and an increasingly surreal
direction for the central love story, but this
first installment is a straightforward tale of
high school angst with a supernatural twist.

DAYBREAKERS

Australia/USA, 2009
Director: The Spierig Brothers [Michael and Peter Spierig].
Producers: Chris Brown, Bryan Furst, Sean Furst.
Screenplay: The Spierig Brothers [Michael and Peter Spierig].
Music: Christopher Gordon. Cinematography: Ben Nott.
Cast: Ethan Hawke, Willem Dafoe, Claudia Karvan, Michael Dorman, Sam Neill, Vince Colosimo.

Applying conceptual sci-fi to vampire stories can produce fascinating results, as seen in this ambitious depiction of a world in which the undead hold sway over most of society with only a small remaining portion of humans left in the dwindling food supply. Worst of all, starving vampires regress into savage, monstrous beasts, a fate doomed to befall everyone if hematologist and conscientious vampire Edward Dalton (Ethan Hawke) can't come up with a solution. As much a warning about the dangers of unchecked corporate greed as the perils of recklessly depleting the world's life-sustaining resources, this stylish tale features a welcome return to the subgenre for Willem Dafoe after **Shadow of the Vampire** and boasts striking use of color manipulation during the film's digital intermediate post-production process with an unearthly green and grey aesthetic mirroring the radically altered nature of civilization itself. Shot in the Brisbane and Gold Coast areas of Australia, the film marked a belated follow-up to the novel zombie film **Undead** (2003) by identical twin directing brothers Peter and Michael Spierig, who had cut their cinematic teeth on TV commercials. The film was particularly memorable at the time for its outrageous blood-spraying lobby climax, one of the goriest sequences in a major studio monster film at the time.

THIRST

South Korea/USA, 2009
Director: Park Chan-wook.
Producers: Park Chan-wook,
Ahn Soo-hyun. Screenplay: Park Chan-wook,
Jeong Seo-kyeong. Music: Jo Yeong-wook.
Cinematography: Chung Chung-hoon.
Cast: Song Kang-ho, Kim Ok-bin,
Kim Hae-sook, Shin Ha-kyun, Park In-hwan,
Song Young-chang.

The only vampire film openly inspired by the works of Émile Zola (specifically *Thérèse Raquin*), this tortured romance charts the extremely dark path of Catholic priest Sang-hyun (Song Kang-ho) when an experimental disease treatment procedure gives him a thirst for blood and aversion to sunlight. His infatuation with the married Tae-ju (Kim Ok-bin) sends them both into a bloody spiral that claims the lives of those around them, despite his best efforts to avoid killing as much as possible. Echoes of **Ganja & Hess** and Universal's **Son of Dracula** can be found in the story but the end result is very much in keeping with the work of director Chan-wook Park, who was in the international spotlight thanks to his recent 'Vengeance Trilogy' of

Sympathy for Mr. Vengeance (2002), **Oldboy** (2003) and **Lady Vengeance** (2005). Though the conflicted abstaining vampire concept had been largely driven into the ground by this point, Park and company find a new angle by mixing in elements of religion, hero worship (with our protagonist hailed as a savior due to his miraculous "recovery"), and questions about free will between the two characters who ultimately end up as undead predators. A longer cut was also prepared for the film's initial exhibition at Cannes but is only available (as of this writing) in an English-subtitled version from South Korea.

STAKE LAND

USA, 2010
Director: Jim Mickle. Producers: Derek Curl, Larry
Fessenden, Adam Folk, Brent Kunkle, Peter Phok.
Screenplay: Nick Damici, Jim Mickle. Music: Jeff Grace.
Cinematography: Ryan Samul.
Cast: Nick Damici, Connor Paolo, Michael Cerveris, Sean
Nelson, Kelly McGillis, Danielle Harris.

Following an impressive debut with **Mulberry Street** (2006), one of the stronger entries in the once
ubiquitous After Dark Horrorfest series, director and co-writer Jim Mickle upped the ante with this sleeper
indie surprise about a young man named Martin (Connor Paolo) who teams up with weathered vampire
hunter Mister (Nick Damici) to traverse a decimated United States en route to safety in Canada. Taking a
cue from Richard Matheson's *I Am Legend*, this blood-soaked coming of age story uses stakes as a means of
execution for its fanged monsters but blurs the line between vampires and zombies to such a degree that
this has earned frequent comparisons to the likes of **The
Walking Dead** and **Zombieland** (2009). Terence Malickian
narration, spirited action sequences (including some
ambitious car gags), and a fan-friendly cast (including Kelly
McGillis, Glass Eye Pix honcho and mascot Larry Fessenden,
and Danielle Harris) are among the more distinctive touches,
but the real heart of the film grungy, convincing depiction
of a vampire-ravaged landscape (actually Douglassville,
Pennsylvania) clearly evoking the devastation of predatory
economic practices on small towns around the country. As
visual metaphors go, it still holds up. A belated sequel, **Stake
Land II** (a.k.a. **The Stakelander**), followed in 2016.

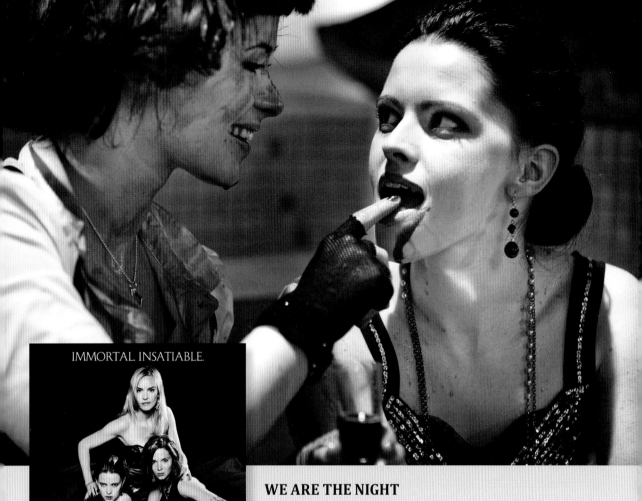

WE ARE THE NIGHT

Germany, 2010
Director: Dennis Gansel. Producer: Christian Becker.
Screenplay: Jan Berger, Dennis Gansel. Music: Heiko Maile.
Cinematography: Torsten Breuer.
Cast: Karoline Herfurth, Nina Hoss, Jennifer Ulrich,
Anna Fischer, Max Riemelt, Arved Birnbaum.

Turning the tried and true lesbian vampire formula on its head, this unexpectedly resonant Berlin-set character study that plays out like an MTV-friendly take on same-sex difficult romances like **Desert Hearts** (1985) or **High Art** (1998)… but with fangs, and in German. The awkward pickpocket Lena (Caroline Herfurth) thinks she's found her calling when she's initiated into a rowdy female vampire pack led by the imposing Louise (Nina Hoss), who also has a tricky past with fellow companion Charlotte (Jennifer Ulrich). **We Are the Night** (**Wir sind die Nacht**) was a passion project for director Dennis Gansel in the wake of his breakthrough success with **The Wave** (2008), also featuring Ulrich. Though superficially similar to the shiny nocturnal feel of other international vampire films (a style that continues today), it provides a story with women as the center of power and the driving forces of the narrative – even when it involves stolen cars, dead pimps, and cops in hot pursuit. The ambiguous ending may frustrate some (it was one of three filmed, not surprisingly), but it feels like the right choice for a film that feels like a bold step away from the norm at the height of **Twilight** fever.

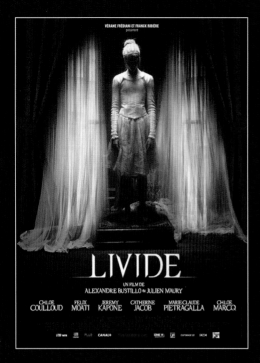

LIVIDE

France, 2011
Directors: Alexandre Bustillo, Julien Maury.
Producers: Vérane Frédiani, Franck Ribière.
Screenplay: Alexandre Bustillo, Julien Maury.
Music: Raphaël Gesqua. Cinematography: Laurent Barès.
Cast: Chloé Coulloud, Félix Moati, Jérémy Kapone,
Catherine Jacob, Béatrice Dalle, Chloé Marcq.

After multiple aborted projects, the French filmmaking duo of Julien Maury and Alexandre Bustillo finally followed up their accomplished and deeply disturbing debut feature, **Inside** (2007), with this stylish homage to classic European horror cinema. Though poorly received in its native country and given far less distribution than its predecessor, this is an ambitious mélange of horror tropes including a **Suspiria** (1977)-inspired elderly ballet instructor languishing in an old estate in Brittany. Newly arrived upon the scene is nursing trainee Lucie (Chloé Coulloud) who conspires with two others to scour the house for a rumored hidden treasure, only to be trapped in a hallucinatory nightmare involving a taxidermy bestiary, murderous ballerinas, and a vampiric family secret. Americanized dialogue references (including the Ku Klux Klan), the Halloween setting, and blatant homages to films like **Halloween III: Season of the Witch** (complete with the "Silver Shamrock" song) indicate the original intention to cross over to a wider audience, and in fact this was originally intended to be shot in English in the UK at one point. The approach here is still quite bloody and grotesque in brief spurts but a far cry from the extreme horror approach common to French fare at the time; instead the film tosses in any number of poetic horror elements, some of which land better than others for an end result that continues to provoke sharply divided reactions.

MIDNIGHT SON

USA, 2011
Director: Scott Leberecht. Producer: Matt Compton.
Screenplay: Scott Leberecht. Music: Kays Al-Atrakchi, Geoff Levin.
Cinematography: Lyn Moncrief.
Cast: Zak Kilberg, Maya Parish, Jo D. Jonz, Larry Cedar,
Arlen Escarpeta, Tracey Walter.

Pale, gaunt but striking security guard Jacob (Zak Kilberg) works
the night shift because of a skin condition that causes severe
welts via exposure to sunlight, and he's overcome by cravings
when he spies so much as a stained Band-Aid. In his off hours he
watches films like **Fright Night** and starts up a tentative romance
with bartender Mary (Maya Parish), but homicides in the area
and two bloody encounters very close to home force him to make
some major life changes. At first this seems like a digitally shot
update on **Martin**, but the "is he or isn't he?" angle is resolved
far more decisively and earlier here with the story veering in
a far different (and ultimately romantic) direction. Though
modest and technically rough around the edges, the film (which
originally premiered on the now defunct genre channel FEARnet)
finds strong resonance in its two leads' plight and closes on an
effectively macabre note. In turn it led the charge for a wave of
low-budget vampire films primarily geared for the home
market including such titles as **Blood for Irina**
(2012), **Rufus** (2012), and the strongest of
the pack, **The Transfiguration**
(2016).

PRIEST

USA, 2011
Director: Scott Stewart.
Producers: Michael De Luca,
Joshua Donen, Mitchell Peck.
Screenplay: Cory Goodman.
Music: Christopher Young.
Cinematography: Don Burgess.
Cast: Paul Bettany, Karl Urban,
Cam Gigandet, Maggie Q, Lily Collins,
Brad Dourif.

Action movie fans eager for vampire thrills at the same time found a solution with this American adaptation of the Korean comic series by Hyung Min-woo. In a rare heroic starring vehicle, Paul Bettany (replacing onetime Dracula actor Gerard Butler) plays the jaded vampire fighter Priest in a grim postapocalyptic world where he's enlisted to combat the forces of darkness. Designed by Screen Gems as a possible inheritor to its **Underworld** series, this interpretation presents vampires as a separate species of non-human origin; instead of turning victims into their own, they simply make any Homo sapiens at hand into their underlings instead. The film marked a reunion for Bettany and director Scott Stewart after the religious-themed horror film **Legion** (2010), and it was given a big summer rollout in hopes for a new blockbuster and franchise starter (complete with then-trendy 3-D conversion). A former visual effects artist, Stewart imbues the film with a great deal of stylistic flair to portray a world where the human vs. vampire battle has raged for so long no one can even seem to remember how it all started in the first place. If the end result misses the mark compared to its source material, at least it was a noble shot.

BYZANTIUM

UK/Ireland/USA, 2012
Director: Neil Jordan.
Producers: Sam Englebardt, William
D. Johnson, Elizabeth Karlsen, Alan
Moloney, Stephen Woolley. Screenplay:
Moira Buffini. Music: Javier Navarrete.
Cinematography: Sean Bobbitt.
Cast: Saoirse Ronan, Gemma Arterton,
Sam Riley, Jonny Lee Miller, Daniel Mays,
Caleb Landry Jones.

After giving mainstream vampire cinema a makeover with
Interview with the Vampire in 1994 and abstaining from the
horror genre after the poorly received **In Dreams** (1999), director
Neil Jordan returned to familiar terrain with this evocative time-
skipping mood piece for the art house crowd. Soarsie Ronan and
Gemma Arterton offer exceptional performances as two mysterious
women, ostensibly mother and daughter, who have holed up at the
crumbling Byzantium Hotel in a coastal town. Through flashbacks
their story unfolds as they become vampires via a mystical island
with a dark secret, and now they're on the run from forces that
would like to see them destroyed. Furthermore they have to grapple
with the presences of two very different men who will put their own
moral codes to the test. Adapted by screenwriter Moira Buffini from
her play *A Vampire Story* (complete with a brief nod to "Carmilla"),
this beautifully shot portrait of two very unusual women making
their way through a minefield bear its creator's unmistakable stamp
and sports a welcome romantic streak that doesn't fully coalesce
until the effective finale. Both Ronan and Arterton deliver excellent
performances, while the mood feels very much like what might
happen if Jean Rollin had taken off to make a film in Ireland.

DRACULA 3D

Italy/Spain, 2012
Director: Dario Argento.
Producers: Enrique Cerezo,
Roberto Di Girolamo, Giovanni Paolucci.
Screenplay: Dario Argento, Enrique Cerezo,
Stefano Piani, Antonio Tentori.
Music: Claudio Simonetti.
Cinematography: Luciano Tovoli.
Cast: Thomas Kretschmann, Marta Gastini, Asia Argento,
Unax Ugalde, Miriam Giovanelli, Rutger Hauer.

Capitulating to the same public polling that led to his eccentric **The Phantom of the Opera** (1998), director Dario Argento dipped his toes in the literary horror pool again with this flamboyant, often baffling 3-D adaptation of the Bram Stoker novel – with far more liberties taken than usual. Given a splashy welcome at Cannes and an instant online meme thanks to its outrageous giant praying mantis attack, the film bears few of Argento's cinematic fingerprints outside of a standout scene with Dracula, played by Thomas Kretschmann, exacting bloody punishment on a tavern full of villagers. Most of the characters from the novel have been jettisoned, though you do get Rutger Hauer's subdued take on Van Helsing and an unabashed Asia Argento as Lucy among the remainders. Though nearly unbearable in 2-D, the film has its occasional quirky pleasures including a strong focus on Dracula's ability to shapeshift into animals (via highly awkward CGI owls, flies, and wolves, among others) and fairy tale-style provincial Italian locations versus the usual London scenery. The weirdest element may be wildly inappropriate theremin-heavy score by Claudio Simonetti, whose band also supplies the metal theme song, "Kiss Me Dracula." A year later, Kretschmann would return to similar material cast as Van Helsing in the short-lived 2013 TV series **Dracula** opposite Jonathan Rhys Meyers.

KISS OF THE DAMNED

USA, 2012
Director: Xan Cassavetes. Producers: Jen Gatien, Alex Orlovsky.
Screenplay: Xan Cassavetes. Music: Steven Hufsteter.
Cinematography: Tobias Datum.
Cast: Joséphine de La Baume, Roxane Mesquida, Milo Ventimiglia, Caitlin Keats, Anna Mouglalis, Anna Mouglalis.

Vampirism has often been used to explore the darker side of family dynamics, and that's definitely the focus in this debut directorial feature from Xan Cassavetes, daughter of John Cassavetes and Gena Rowlands. Pulling inspiration from both '70s exploitation vampire films and art cinema (plus a fine soundtrack by Steven Hufsteter with a needle drop from **The Shiver of the Vampires**), the film holds particular interest now for the presence of a young Milo Ventimiglia, fresh off of TV's **Heroes**, in his indie horror phrase here as Paolo, a screenwriter turned into a creature of the night by the alluring Djuna (Joséphine de La Baume) after he romantically pursues her at a remote Connecticut home. Their newfound bliss, which is reliant on feeding from animals as human consumption is forbidden by vampire superiors, is disrupted by the arrival of Djuna's uncontrollable younger sister, Mimi (Roxane Mesquida), whose predatory habits could put them all in danger. The talented Riley Keough also turns up here in a smaller role as a potential sacrificial offering, and while the deliberate pacing hasn't proven to be to all tastes, fans of retro Euro-styled homages with a solid dramatic core at the center should find it appetizing enough.

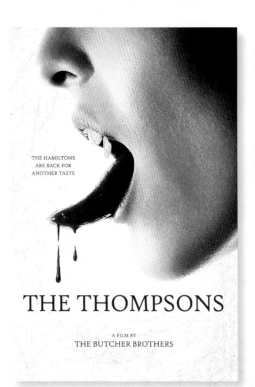

THE HAMILTONS
ARE BACK FOR
ANOTHER TASTE

THE THOMPSONS

A FILM BY
THE BUTCHER BROTHERS

THE THOMPSONS

USA/UK, 2012
Director: The Butcher Brothers [Mitchell Altieri and Phil Flores]. Producers: Eben Kostbar, Joseph McKelheer, Travis Stevens, Robert Weston. Screenplay: The Butcher Brothers [Mitchell Altieri and Phil Flores], Cory Knauf. Music: Kevin Kerrigan. Cinematography: Matthew Cooke, David Rom. Cast: Cory Knauf, Samuel Child, Mackenzie Firgens, Joseph McKelheer, Ryan Hartwig, Elizabeth Henstridge.

It's impossible to talk about this film without spoiling the one that preceded it, so consider yourself warned. The Butcher Brothers, a.k.a. American directors American film directors Mitchell Altieri and Phil Flores, scored one of the biggest hits of the annual After Dark Horrorfest, which featured a series of selected independent horror films for theatrical and home video festival-style viewing, with **The Hamiltons** (2006). The film concerned the titular family of presumed serial killers who are ultimately revealed to be natural-born vampires, living a nomadic life in front of one member's video camera. Adapted into a play in 2011, it eventually received a sequel the following year taking its title from the family's new name. Largely shot around Kent, this continuing adventure finds the family's winning chemistry to be its strongest asset as they search England for the Stuarts, an ancient family from which they may have been descended. Of course, it isn't long before the search starts to take a very Shakespearean turn. Since the cat's out of the bag from the outset, this one shakes up the formula by telling its story in a nonlinear fashion to keep viewers on their toes, delivering a satisfying sequel that can also stand on its own perfectly well.

AFFLICTED

Canada, 2013
Directors: Derek Lee, Clif Prowse.
Producers: Chris Ferguson,
Zach Lipovsky. Screenplay: Derek Lee,
Clif Prowse. Music: Edo Van Breemen.
Cinematography: Norm Li.
Cast: Derek Lee, Clif Prowse, Michael Gill,
Baya Rehaz, Benjamin Zeitoun, Zach Gray.

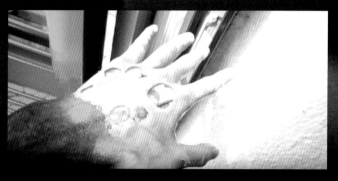

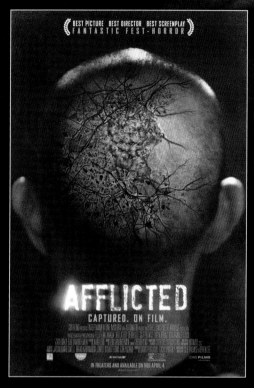

The found footage horror craze spawned by the release of **The Blair Witch Project** (1999) created a whole new realm to explore ghosts and zombies, but the vampire was left behind for most of its duration until a sudden burst of them starting with this Canadian indie shot for peanuts over the course of a trip across Europe. The fact that real-life friends Derek Lee and Clif Prowse serve as the directors, writers and stars of the film gives it a creepypasta vibe at times with the blood disorder elements impinging on what feels like a real document of a buddy vacation. (Not surprisingly, the project was originally intended to be a web series.) Suffering from a fatal cerebral condition, Derek is being treated by Clif to a carefree, libidinous trip that takes a nasty turn when Derek's first conquest leaves him wounded, sensitive to sunlight, and unable to consume normal food. Featuring a surprising plot twist halfway through and an ambitious number of gruesome visual effects, **Afflicted** avoids a shopworn approach to its story and aesthetic thanks to a convincing depiction of the erratic nature of young male impulses and a gradual, convincing etching of Derek's transition into something inhuman. And don't turn it off when the end credits start to roll.

ONLY LOVERS LEFT ALIVE

UK/Germany, 2013
Director: Jim Jarmusch. Producers:
Reinhard Brundig, Jeremy Thomas.
Screenplay: Jim Jarmusch. Music: Jozef van
Wissem. Cinematography: Yorick Le Saux.
Cast: Tilda Swinton, Tom Hiddleston,
Anton Yelchin, Mia Wasikowska,
Jeffrey Wright, Slimane Dazi.

Perhaps no other actor on earth is more suited to play a
vampire than Tilda Swinton, the creative muse who first
made her mark in the experimental films of Derek Jarman
and has since delivered a wide range of chameleonic
performances. A textbook example of an art vampire film
that never even mentions the monstrous condition by name
(and doesn't really qualify as a horror film at all), this Jim
Jarmusch character study provides a snapshot of the on-
and-off, centuries-long romance between Swinton's Eve and
Tom Hiddleston's world-weary musician Adam. A barrage
of musical, literary and cinematic references populates
the script, which is kicked into gear with the intrusion
of Eve's little sister, Ava (Mia Wasikowska), though the
most poignant aspect comes from ill-fated music rarities
procurer Ian played by Anton Yelchin, who would die
three years later under tragic circumstances. Featuring a
soundtrack dominated by Jarmusch's own band, SQÜRL, the
film also sports a prominent nod to an opera about Nikola
Tesla planned by the director concurrently with this film.
Encouraged by the warm critical response to his first foray
into overt supernatural territory, Jarmusch went back to the
same well with a deadpan zombie comedy, **The Dead Don't
Die** (2019), to a far more muted reception.

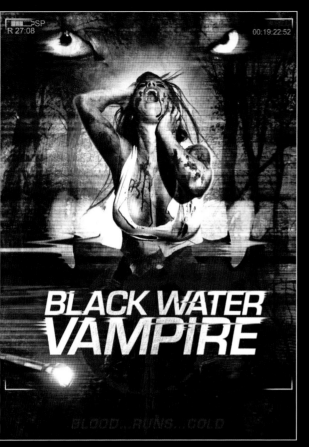

THE BLACK WATER VAMPIRE

USA, 2014
Director: Evan Tramel. Producers: Jesse Baget, Andrea Monier. Screenplay: Evan Tramel.
Music: Richard Figone.
Cast: Danielle Lozeau, Andrea Monier, Anthony Fanelli, Robin Steffen, Bill Oberst Jr., Brandon deSpain.

By far the most indebted to **The Blair Witch Project** of the tiny clutch of found footage vampire films is this low-budget production about a gang of young aspiring documentarians heading out through the region of Black Water where the exsanguinated bodies of young women have been turning up in sparse but regular intervals for decades. Unlike its more famous cinematic inspiration, this film makes no bones about revealing its monster in the final act (via an impressive creature design) and features a twist ending reminiscent of **Young Dracula**, oddly enough. In what amounts to a glorified guest spot, the standout name in the production is genre workhorse Bill Obserst Jr. as the accused perpetrator of the most recent slaying, though of course the audience already knows better. The most effective aspect of the film is its atmospheric lensing around Big Bear, California, a popular skiing and nature getaway location turned here into an ominous landscape of backwoods terror. Perhaps the most uncanny aspect of this film's production is the fact that its first-time director, Evan Tramel, radically shifted gears to focus exclusively on a prolific career turning out scores of micro-budget, computer-animated films for the children's market.

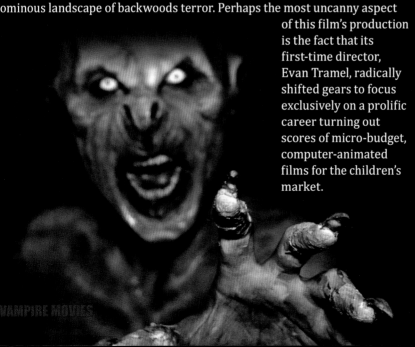

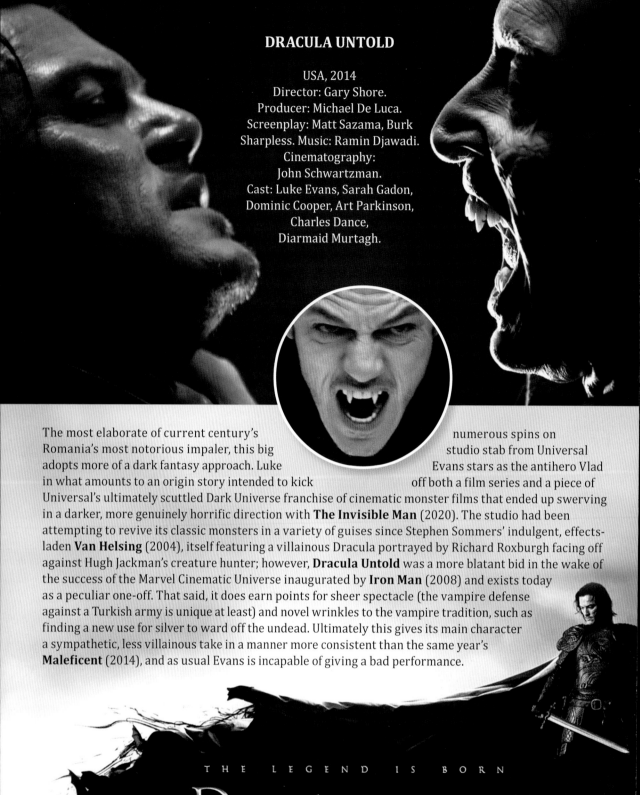

DRACULA UNTOLD

USA, 2014
Director: Gary Shore.
Producer: Michael De Luca.
Screenplay: Matt Sazama, Burk
Sharpless. Music: Ramin Djawadi.
Cinematography:
John Schwartzman.
Cast: Luke Evans, Sarah Gadon,
Dominic Cooper, Art Parkinson,
Charles Dance,
Diarmaid Murtagh.

The most elaborate of current century's numerous spins on Romania's most notorious impaler, this big studio stab from Universal adopts more of a dark fantasy approach. Luke Evans stars as the antihero Vlad in what amounts to an origin story intended to kick off both a film series and a piece of Universal's ultimately scuttled Dark Universe franchise of cinematic monster films that ended up swerving in a darker, more genuinely horrific direction with **The Invisible Man** (2020). The studio had been attempting to revive its classic monsters in a variety of guises since Stephen Sommers' indulgent, effects-laden **Van Helsing** (2004), itself featuring a villainous Dracula portrayed by Richard Roxburgh facing off against Hugh Jackman's creature hunter; however, **Dracula Untold** was a more blatant bid in the wake of the success of the Marvel Cinematic Universe inaugurated by **Iron Man** (2008) and exists today as a peculiar one-off. That said, it does earn points for sheer spectacle (the vampire defense against a Turkish army is unique at least) and novel wrinkles to the vampire tradition, such as finding a new use for silver to ward off the undead. Ultimately this gives its main character a sympathetic, less villainous take in a manner more consistent than the same year's **Maleficent** (2014), and as usual Evans is incapable of giving a bad performance.

THE LEGEND IS BORN

DRACULA
UNTOLD

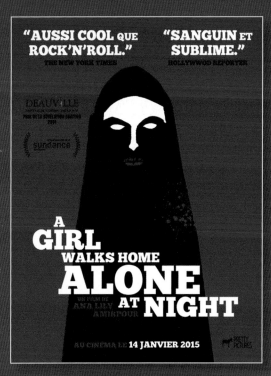

"AUSSI COOL QUE ROCK'N'ROLL."
THE NEW YORK TIMES

"SANGUIN ET SUBLIME."
HOLLYWOOD REPORTER

DEAUVILLE

sundance

A GIRL WALKS HOME ALONE AT NIGHT

UN FILM DE ANA LILY AMIRPOUR

AU CINÉMA LE **14 JANVIER 2015**

A GIRL WALKS HOME ALONE AT NIGHT

USA, 2014
Director: Ana Lily Amirpour. Producers: Justin Begnaud, Sina Sayyah. Screenplay: Ana Lily Amirpour.
Music: Bei Ru. Cinematography: Lyle Vincent.
Cast: Sheila Vand, Arash Marandi, Marshall Manesh, Mozhan Marnò, Dominic Rains, Rome Shadanloo.

The first (and, to date, only) Iranian-American vampire film was shot around Bakersfield, California thanks to a crowdfunding campaign by writer-director and onetime singer-bassist Ana Lily Amanpour to expand her 2011 short film of the same title into a Persian-language feature. Performance artist Sheila Vand cuts a memorable figure as the nameless girl of the title, an isolated, thoughtful, chador-wearing vampire in a town called Bad City seemingly devoid of law enforcement (as one might expect). Expressive physical acting and lustrous monochrome photography become the primary tools to show how her occasionally murderous routine crosses with a young man named Arash (Arash Mirandi) and his drug-addicted father, Hossein (Marshall Manesh) as they navigate through the criminal underworld. The marketing tagline, "The First Iranian Vampire Western," sets up hipster expectations that the film itself somewhat sidesteps, with Amanpour (an open admirer of directors like David Lynch and Quentin Tarantino) opting for a more poetic, dreamlike approach rather than the standard genre mash-up one might expect. A bit of Dracula roleplay, an ambiguous but tentatively atmospheric closing grace note, and a seductive two-shot sequence set to White Lies' "Death" are among the memorable moments in this evocative descendant of the black-and-white vampire character studies of the early '90s.

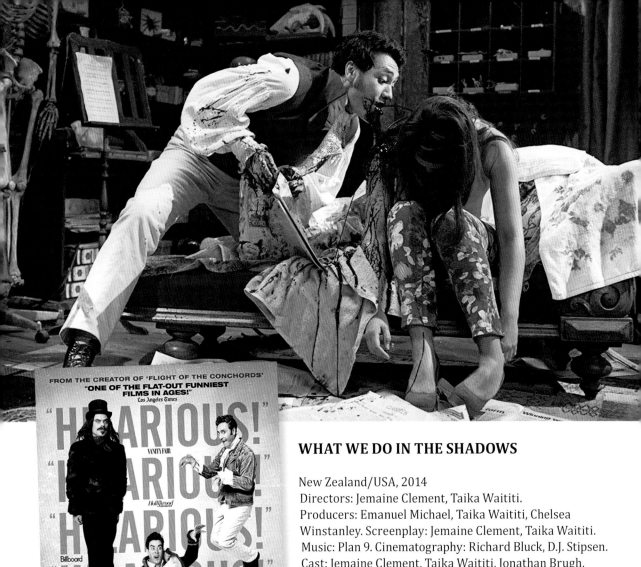

WHAT WE DO IN THE SHADOWS

New Zealand/USA, 2014
Directors: Jemaine Clement, Taika Waititi.
Producers: Emanuel Michael, Taika Waititi, Chelsea
Winstanley. Screenplay: Jemaine Clement, Taika Waititi.
Music: Plan 9. Cinematography: Richard Bluck, D.J. Stipsen.
Cast: Jemaine Clement, Taika Waititi, Jonathan Brugh,
Cori Gonzalez-Macuer, Stu Rutherford, Ben Fransham.

The interview-studded mockumentary format
popularized by the BBC Two series **The Office** (and
its offshoots like the Americanized series of the same
name and **Modern Family**) bore unexpected fruit for
vampire fans with this razor-sharp comedy about four
(and eventually more) members of the undead living as
flat mates in Wellington, New Zealand. Squabbles over
domestic chores share time with the bloody feeding
process and their interactions with the outside world
as they prepare for the upcoming Unholy Masquerade
and carry on an ongoing feud with a local pack of werewolves. Future **Thor: Ragnarok** (2017) helmer
and **Jojo Rabbit** (2019) Oscar winner Taika Waititi and **Flight of the Conchords'** Jemaine Clement
wrote, directed and starred in this largely improvised and sweet-natured depiction of vampire life in
the current millennium, first developed as a 2005 semi-prequel short film and later transformed into an
equally ingenious spin-off TV series of its own in 2019. The most relentlessly quotable mockumentary film
since **This Is Spinal Tap** (1984), **What We Do in the Shadows** also adheres very closely to traditional
vampire rules (often to uproarious effect), sketches in its characters' centuries-long histories with great
aplomb, and even delivers some shocking bouts of bloodletting and genuine moments of horror such as the
Nosferatu-inspired Petyr's harrowing fate in the basement.

GUARDIANS OF THE NIGHT

Russia, 2016
Director: Emilis Velyvis.
Producers: Ruben Dishdishyan,
Vadim Goryainov, Leonid Yarmolnik.
Screenplay: Oleg Malovichko.
Cinematography: Aleksey Kupriyanov.
Cast: Ivan Yankovskiy, Leonid Yarmolnik,
Lyubov Aksyonova, Sabina Akhmedova,
Mikhail Evlanov, Ekaterina Volkova.

An attempt to concoct a Russian answer
to the **Underworld** series resulted in
this ambitious, effects-laden vampire
fantasy shot in Moscow with an eye on the
lucrative international success enjoyed by
Timur Bekmambetov's vampire-adjacent
Night Watch and **Day Watch**, particularly
given that Bekmambetov made it to
Hollywood. Unfortunately, times had
changed and this film barely received

any attention outside of Continental Europe, a fate that also befell Sergey Ginzburg's **Ghouls** (2017). The
more elaborate **Guardians of the Night** (also shown as **Night Guards**) tosses plenty of action and fantasy
into the mix to depict on ongoing battle on the streets of Moscow (shot on location) led by the gun-toting
Gamayun, played by Leonid Yarmolnik from **Hard to Be a God** (2013). Following the now typical young
adult template, the mayhem is intruded upon by a teenager who stumbles into an apartment firefight
involving plentiful latex makeup and slow motion, leading to a string of loud, bullet-heavy encounters
in subway cars and parking garages. How much enjoyment comes out of this depends on a tolerance for
heavy CGI, but there's no denying the novelty value of the only film to date with a large-scale vampire
chase scene involving a squealing warthog.

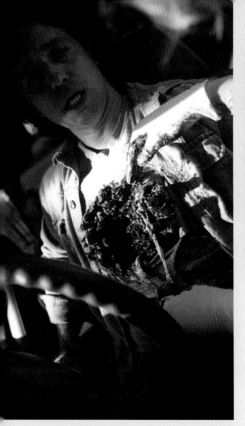

LIVING AMONG US

USA, 2018
Director: Brian A. Metcalf. Producers: Brian A. Metcalf,
Thomas Ian Nicholas. Screenplay: Brian A. Metcalf.
Cinematography: Brian A. Metcalf, Evan Okada.
Cast: Thomas Ian Nicholas, William Sadler, Esmé Bianco, Jordan
Hinson [Jordan Danger], Andrew Keegan, John Heard.

Taking a page from the documentary format of **What We Do in the Shadows**, this Los Angeles variant veers far more in the horror direction and ultimately justifies its existence by echoing real docs about the attempted assimilation of predatory fringe groups like **Welcome to Leith** (2015). Here the concept involves the revelation that vampires are not only real but exist within the fabric of society in makeshift family units, arguing that they're just like anyone else except that they subsist on blood contributed through the generosity of humans. A fair amount

of droll comedy can still be found in the early going as parental figures Andrew (John Hard) and Elleanor (**Game of Thrones'** Esmé Bianco) invite a documentary crew into their home to prove how wrong the superstitions about their kind really are. The production within the film allows for some potent commentary about the format with one of the younger vampires jockeying for screen time and stardom even as the blood flies with abandon across the screen, while the injection of occasional talk show clips features some wry commentary on social media and public relations tactics. Though minor in the grand scheme of vampire cinema, the film has since become notable as the one of final films by Heard, who passed away in 2017 before its release, and offers a zealous performance by the reliable William Sadler as Samuel, the esteemed vampire spokesman and guest of honour.

Hard work never killed anyone.
Until now.

BOYS FROM COUNTY HELL

BOYS FROM COUNTY HELL

Ireland/UK, 2020
Director: Chris Baugh. Producers: Yvonne Donohoe,
Brendan Mullin. Screenplay: Chris Baugh. Music: Steve Lynch.
Cinematography: Ryan Kernaghan.
Cast: Jack Rowan, Nigel O'Neill, Louisa Harland, Michael Hough,
John Lynch, Fra Fee.

In the pastoral Irish village of Six Mile Hill, the locals have a conflicted relationship with the fame of Bram Stoker who used their real local bloodsucking boogeyman, Abhartach, as fodder to write his classic novel. Recovering from witnessing the traumatic death of his best friend whose blood was mysteriously leeched down into the earth, Eugene (Jack Rowan) is entrusted with a construction job by his father (Nigel O'Neill) before bolting out of town to Australia. Already suspicious from the discovery of a human skull at the site of his dead mother's ancestral home, he soon unearths a long-hidden evil that leaves him, his dad, and a ragtag band of friends fighting for their lives. A blend of foul-mouthed verbal comedy (including a fine turn by **Derry Girls'** Louisa Harland) and reverence for vampire lore, the film gets a lot of mileage out of Stoker (right down to naming the local pub after him) including an amusing sequence with our vampire hunters trying to decode fact from fiction in the original **Dracula**. However, the film's biggest contribution is its concept of a primal vampire force capable of remotely drawing blood from its victims' orifices to its underground lair, essentially making this the vampire equivalent of Stephen King's **It** with a very Irish spin.

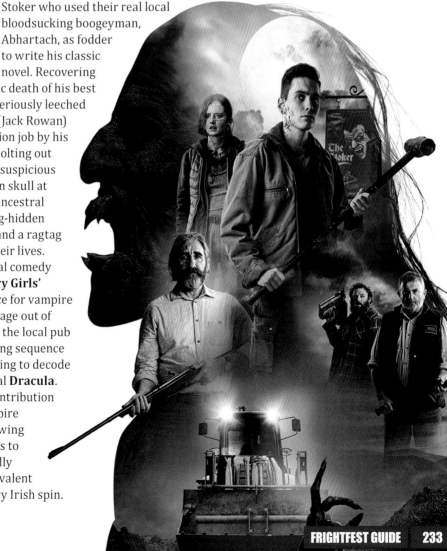

BLACK AS NIGHT

USA, 2021
Director: Maritte Lee Go. Producer: John H. Brister.
Screenplay: Sherman Payne. Music: Jacques Brautbar.
Cinematography: Cybel Martin.
Cast: Asjha Cooper, Fabrizio Guido, Mason Beauchamp,
Abbie Gayle, Craig Tate, Keith David.

It was inevitable that the ongoing 'Welcome to the Blumhouse'
series of streaming horror films would get around to
vampires after its start in 2020, and that quickly came to
pass with this coming-of-age story of bloodsucker hunting set in New Orleans. Director Maritte Lee Go and
writer Sherman Payne draw on the recent Black Lives Matter movement, soapy teen dramas, the lingering
aftermath of Hurricane Katrina, and the focus on Black-themed horror films for this tale of creatures of
the night feeding on the city's homeless denizens – essentially a supernatural take on **Hard Target** (1993).
Enter Shawna (Asjha Cooper), a high schooler who recruits her peers to hunt down the nocturnal forces
whose feeding is hitting too close to home.

Social commentary has always been a strong
undercurrent of vampire narratives, and here
it's wide out in the open with imagery of public
housing and dramatic class contrast mixing with
the traditional tropes of fangs, garlic, and wooden
stakes. Framing it as a "how I spent my summer"
narrative from Shawna separates the film from
its peers with high school elements like the rich
snob and the secret crush juxtaposed with its
particularly vicious and animalistic monsters and
what amounts to an extended but scene-stealing
cameo from the great Keith David.

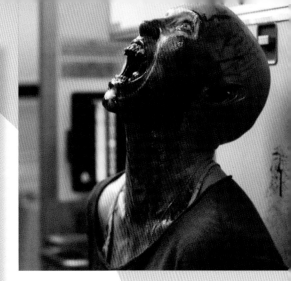

BLOOD RED SKY

Germany/UK, 2021
Director: Peter Thorwarth. Producers: Christian Becker, Benjamin Munz. Screenplay: Stefan Holtz, Peter Thorwarth. Music: Dascha Dauenhauer. Cinematography: Yoshi Heimrath. Cast: Peri Baumeister, Carl Anton Koch, Alexander Scheer, Kais Setti, Roland Møller, Dominic Purcell.

With horror movies delivering snakes, zombies, and exorcisms on commercial plane flights, it was just a matter of time before vampires got their turn. That day arrived with this German-language production sporting a unique wrinkle, making its main bloodsucker a sympathetic maternal figure fighting for the well-being of her son. Scrambling with her son Elias (Carl Koch) to get to the U.S. for medical treatment, Nadja (Perl Baumeister) finds herself in a tough spot when hijackers including the co-pilot overtake her flight with plans to frame an Arabic passenger. After multiple gunshots leave her for dead, Nadja's secret is revealed: she's a reluctant vampire turned against her will, and when her contagion gets loose throughout the plane, she has to fight not only for her son but the dwindling number of living passengers as well. Shot in Prague during the first full year of the Covid pandemic, the film was picked up by Netflix for global distribution and thankfully proves to be an anomaly among the streaming company's lackluster track record for horror originals. Crafty plotting and a committed performance from Baumeister keep it compelling throughout, and while the final stretch slackens into absurdity with the fates of its villains, the overall result is more resonant than expected.

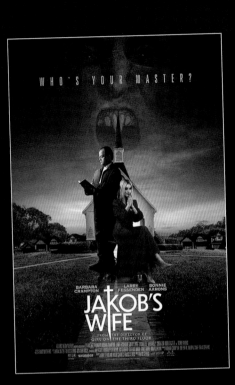

JAKOB'S WIFE

USA, 2021
Director: Travis Stevens. Producers: Barbara Crampton,
Bob Portal, Inderpal Singh, Travis Stevens.
Screenplay: Mark Steensland, Kathy Charles, Travis Stevens.
Music: Tara Busch. Cinematography: David Matthews.
Cast: Barbara Crampton, Larry Fessenden, Bonnie Aarons,
Nyisha Bell, Sarah Lind, Mark Kelly.

Religion has been a strong element in vampire cinema since the
beginning, but modern Christianity has been largely sidelined for
much of the current millennium. One exception is this mordant
look at a marriage gone haywire between conservative minister
Jakob Fedder (indie filmmaking legend Larry Fessenden) and
his frustrated wife, Anne (horror veteran Barbara Crampton in
one of her strongest showcases). After she's infected during a
nocturnal attack, Anne finds the freedom to rebel against her
husband even if it means putting the entire neighborhood at
risk. Relying on its two strong central performances and a bevy
of practical bloodletting effects, the film is ultimately a sly portrait of the pitfalls of an uncommunicative
coupling ("I feel more alive than I have in years") in which partners can become more psychologically
shackled than they realize. The use of the traditional vampire "Master" takes on a new meaning as well,
its glinting-eyed androgyny subbing her as a metaphor for adultery the little (and not so little) everyday
secrets spouses can keep from each other. Also canny is the decision to set the film in a gray and forbidding
version of suburbia rather than the typical bright and colorful version standard in satirical films, here
mirroring Anne's own malnourished life suddenly injected with lifeblood in every sense.

NIGHT TEETH

USA, 2021
Director: Adam Randall. Producers: Vincent Gatewood, Charlie Morrison, Ben Pugh. Screenplay: Brent Dillon. Music: Drum & Lace, Ian Hultquist. Cinematography: Eben Bolter. Cast: Jorge Lendeborg Jr., Debby Ryan, Lucy Fry, Raúl Castillo, Alfie Allen, Marlene Forte.

A dramatic about-face from his sleeper gem thriller **I See You** (2019), director Adam Randall's synthwave-laced nighttime prowl follows the adventures of young Benny (Jorge Lendeborg Jr.) agrees to step in for his brother's driving gig. Much to his surprise, his pair of well-to-do passengers, Blaire (Debby Ryan) and Zoe (Lucy Fry), turn out to be part of the local vampire population who have been existing profitably with the approval of law enforcement as long as they only feed on willing humans and don't kill. Finding himself in the middle of a plan to break the century-old truce, Benny spends the night trying to outwit the undead and stay alive till dawn. Sort of a fanged variation on **Collateral** (2004), **Night Teeth** is stylized almost to the point of distraction with its scope framing packed with chic, glittering surfaces as far as the eye can see. That said, the approach does make sense as a cinematic equivalent to L.A.'s real surface-deep nightlife scene, and the story manages to steer smoothly between its story of two devoted brothers caught in a life-threatening situation and an oddball love story that pays off a bit differently from the usual modern vampire CGI battles.

INDEX OF FILM TITLES

Page references in **bold** refer exclusively to illustrations.

7 Brothers Meet Dracula, The see *Legend of the 7 Golden Vampires, The*
12 Hour Shift 5
28 Days Later 25, 64
30 Days of Night 209, 211
30 Days of Night: Blood Trails (TV mini-series) 211
30 Days of Night: Dark Days 211
30 Days of Night: Dust to Dust (TV mini-series) 211
1982: One Amazing Summer! 6
Aaron's Blood 38
Abbott and Costello Meet Frankenstein 16, 46, 159
Abby 96
Abraham Lincoln: Vampire Hunter 208
Addams Family (TV series), *The* 33
Addiction, The 182, 186
Afflicted 225
After Hours 147, 156
After Midnight 6
Alien Predators 159
Aliens 151
Alone in the Dark 6
Alucarda 122, 176
amante del vampiro, L' see *Vampire and the Ballerina, The*
American Beauty 35
American Horror Story: Hotel (TV series) 35, 199
American Werewolf in London, An 175
...And God Created Woman 56
Andy Warhol's Dracula see *Blood for Dracula*
Angel (TV series) 34
Angels Gone 20
Antichrist 97
Apostle of Dracula 38
Apple, The 6
Are You Afraid of the Dark? (TV series) 6
ataúd del vampiro, El see *Vampire's Coffin, The*
Avengers (TV series), *The* 92, 115
Bad Dreams 6
Bare-Breasted Countess, The see *Female Vampire*
Barry McKenzie Holds His Own 137
Bathory: Countess of Blood 20, 38
Batman vs. Dracula , The 11
Bay of Blood 89
Beast in Heat, The 24
Beast Must Die, The 109
Beast of Blood 68
Beau travail 201
Beauty and the Beast 140
Begotten 199
Being Human (TV series) 36
belle captive, La 26, 27
Ben-Hur 93
Betty Blue 201
Beverly Hills 90210 (TV series) 174
Beyond the Door 6
Beyond the Valley of the Dolls 95
Big Sleep, The 48
Big Trouble in Little China 157
Bigger Than Life 51
Billy the Kid and the Green Baize Vampire 30
Billy the Kid Versus Dracula 5, 66
Bite of Love, A 25
Bitten: Victoria's Shadow 38
Black As Night 234
Black Pit of Dr. M, The 56

Black Roses 157
Black Sabbath 22, 24, 61, 101
Black Sunday 10, 21, 59, 61
Black Vampire see *Ganja & Hess*
Black Water Vampire, The 227
Blackenstein 96
Blacula 96
Blade 192
Blade II 192
Blade: Trinity 192
Blair Witch Project, The 225, 227
Blood 76
Blood & Donuts 183
Blood + Roses 38
Blood and Roses 5, 24, 31, 56
Blood Bath 67
Blood Car 140
Blood Castle see *Legend of Blood Castle, The*
Blood Couple see *Ganja & Hess*
Blood Cure 38
Blood Drinkers, The 5, 63, 68
Blood Feast 73
Blood for Dracula 114
Blood for Irina 219
Blood Is My Heritage see *Blood of Dracula*
Blood Kisses 38
Blood of Dracula 50
Blood of the Vampire 53
Blood of the Vampires see *Curse of the Vampires*
Blood of the Virgins 5, 70
Blood on Satan's Claw, The 92, 115
Blood Queen, The 38
Blood Red Sky 235
Blood Simple 210
Blood Spattered Bride, The 97
Blood Ties 33, 34
Blood Ties (TV series) 37
Bloodlust 5, 172
Bloodlust: Subspecies 3 171
BloodRayne 38
BloodRayne: Deliverance 38
BloodRayne: The Third Reich 38
Bloodstone: Subspecies II 171
Bloodsucking Bastards 4
Blow Out 188
Body Beneath, The 76
Body of Evidence 198
Bonnie & Clyde vs. Dracula 11
Boondock Saints, The 206
Bordello of Blood 188
Boys from County Hell 233
Brainiac, The 52
Bram Stoker's Dracula 19, 173, 184, 185, 199
Breaking Dawn - Part 1 213
Breaking Dawn - Part 2 213
Breed, The 200
Bride's Initiation, The 32
Brides of Dracula, The 57, 116
Bucket of Blood, A 67
Buffy the Vampire Slayer 34, 174
Buffy the Vampire Slayer (TV series) 34, 174
Butcher Baker Nightmare Maker 6
Byzantium 4, 8, 221
Cabinet of Dr. Caligari, The 15
cage aux folles, La 124
Caged Virgins see *Requiem for a Vampire*
Caligula 6
Cannibal Apocalypse 6
Captain Kronos: Vampire Hunter 4, 115
Card Player, The 6
Careful 202
Carrie 136

Castle of Doom see *Vampyr*
Castlevania (TV series) 37
Cat People 8
Cave of the Living Dead 24
Central Park Drifter see *Graveyard Shift*
Ceremonia sangrienta see *Legend of Blood Castle, The*
Chapelwaite (TV series) 136
Chi o Sū Bara see *Evil of Dracula*
Child's Play 6, 142
Chinese Ghost Story, A 25, 205
Chopping Mall 159
Christiane F. 198
Chuck Steel: Night of the Trampires 4
Church, The 6
Cirque du Freak: The Vampire's Assistant 38
City of the Living Dead 6
Clueless 38
Coach 128
Collateral 237
Color Out of Space 156
Condemned to Live 8
Conquest 6
Count Dracula 16, 77, 94, 173
Count Dracula and His Vampire Bride see *Satanic Rites of Dracula, The*
Count Dracula's Great Love 105
Count Yorga, Vampire 78, 96, 110
Countess Dracula 4, 29, 87, 92
Countess Dracula's Orgy of Blood 8
Countess, The 20
Crawling Eye, The 53
Crazy Hong Kong 169
Crazy Safari 169
Creature Features (TV show) 127
Cremator, The 140
cripta e l'incubo, La see *Terror in the Crypt*
Cronos 176
Crypt of the Living Dead see *Young Hannah, Queen of the Vampires*
Curious Dr. Humpp, The 70
Curse of Frankenstein, The 16, 54
Curse of Nostradamus, The 52
Curse of the Undead 17
Curse of the Vampires 68
Cursed 197
Da Sweet Blood of Jesus 109
Daddy, Father Frost Is Dead 101
Dance of the Damned 33
Dance of the Vampires see *Fearless Vampire Killers, The*
Dangerous Game 6
Dark Prince: The True Story of Dracula 19
Dark Shadows (TV series) 33, 79, 88, 102, 179
Darkness 177
Daughter of Darkness 34
Daughter of Dracula 98
Daughters of Darkness 10, 24, 88, 141
Dawn of the Dead 126
Day Watch 208, 231
Daybreakers 214
Dead & Buried 138
Dead Don't Die, The 226
Dead Men Don't Die 179
Dear Dracula 30
Death Note 170
Death Ship 137
Death Warmed Up 167
Def By Temptation 162
Deliler 19

Delirium 64
Demon Knight 188
Demoniacs, The 103
Demons 5: The Devil's Veil 22
Demon's Brew, The see *Bride's Initiation, The*
Derry Girls (TV series) 233
Desert Hearts 217
Desperado 189
Devil Dog: The Hound of Hell 128
Devil Doll 6
Devil Rides Out, The 74
Devil's Backbone, The 176
Devil's Daffodil, The 24
Devil's Nightmare, The 113
Devil's Plaything, The 106
Diamonds Are Forever 112, 193
Die Hard Dracula 193
Different World (TV series), *A* 162
dinastía de Dracula, La 122
Discovery of Witches (TV series), *A* 37
Doctor Dracula 129
Doctor Sleep 26
Doctor Vampire 163
Does Dracula Really Suck? see *Guess What Happened to Count Dracula?*
Dolce Vita, La 23
Don't Answer the Phone! 6
Double Possession see *Ganja & Hess*
Dr. Black, Mr. Hyde 96
Dr. Jekyll & Sister Hyde 115
Dr. Terror's House of Horrors **28**, 29
Dracula (1931) 4, 9, 14, 15, 41, 50, 131, 133, 233
Drácula (1931, Spanish) 9, 42
Dracula (1958) 16, 53, 54, 57, 67
Dracula (1973) 17
Dracula (1977) 125
Dracula (1979) 18, 131
Dracula (The Dirty Old Man) 31
Dracula (TV mini-series) 36, 37
Dracula (TV series) 222
Dracula 3D 10, 222
Dracula 2000 37, 197
Dracula A.D. 1972 99, 112, 197
Dracula and Son 16, 23, 124
Dracula and the Boys see *Guess What Happened to Count Dracula?*
Dracula Blows His Cool 19
Dracula Exotica 130
Dracula Has Risen from the Grave 74, 83, 93
Dracula II: Ascension 197
Dracula III: Legacy 10, 197
Dracula in Pakistan see *Living Corpse, The*
Dracula père et fils see *Dracula and Son*
Dracula Prince of Darkness 4, 6, 69
Dracula Saga, The 107, 113
Dracula Sucks 11, 32, 130
Dracula the Impaler 19
Dracula Untold 19, 228
Dracula, Prisoner of Frankenstein 98
Dracula, Sovereign of the Damned 138
Dracula: Dead and Loving It 184
Dracula: Pages from a Virgin's Diary 4, 202
Dracula: The Series (TV series) 34
Dracula: The True Story 19
Dracula's Fiancée 203

Dracula's Daughter 15, 45
Dracula's Death see *Drakula halála*
Dracula's Dog see *Zoltan, Hound of Dracula*
Dracula's Last Rites 138
Dracula's Widow 153
Drag 190
Drakula halála 14
Drakula İstanbul'da 5, 16, 50
Dream No Evil 100
EastEnders (TV series) 185
Eclipse 213
Ed Wood 9
Electric Dreams 153
Elvira Madigan 93
Emanuelle in America 6
Embrace of the Vampire 32, 185
Emmanuelle vs. Dracula 11
Empire Strikes Back, The 48
Encounters of the Spooky Kind 25
Equalizer, The 147
Era of Vampires, The 205
Erotic Rites of Frankenstein, The 98
Eroticist, The 123
Erotikill see *Female Vampire*
Evil Aliens 194
Evil Dead, The 210
Evil of Dracula 116
Evil of Frankenstein, The 74
Evil Spirit 22
eXistenZ 6
Expulsion of the Devil 120
extraño amor de los vampiros, El see *Strange Love of the Vampires, The*
Extreme Challenge 165
F Troop (TV series) 29
Fall Guy (TV series), *The* 167
Family Ties (TV series) 33
Fanged Up 4
Fangs of the Living Dead see *Malenka*
Fantastic Disappearing Man, The see *Return of Dracula, The*
Fascination 132
Fast Times at Ridgemont High 144
Fear Itself (TV series) 35, 101
Fearless Vampire Killers, The 71, 93
Feast of Flesh 70
Female Butcher, The see *Legend of Blood Castle, The*
Female Vampire 108, 113
Femme Nikita, La 175
Ferat Vampire 28, 140
fiancée de Dracula, La see *Dracula's Fiancée*
Flesh for Frankenstein 114
Flight of the Conchords (TV series) 230
Fluch der grünen Augen, Der see *Cave of the Living Dead*
Fool There Was, A 15
Forbidden Kingdom 22
Forbidden World 6
Forever Knight (TV series) 37
Four of the Apocalypse 123
Fox Hunter 165
Frankenstein 14, 41
Frankenstein and the Monster from Hell 115
Frankenstein Meets the Wolf Man 15, 46
Freaks 44
Fright Night 142, 161, 219
Fright Night 2: New Blood 142
Fright Night Part 2 142
From Dusk Till Dawn 189
Frostbite 209
Funeral, The 182

Game of Thrones (TV series) 232
Ganja & Hess 109, 201
Garden of the Dead 100
Gas Pump Girls 159
Gayracula 32
Gebissen wird nur nachts see Vampire Happening, The
Genuine 15
Get Carter 139
Get Smart (TV series) 124
Ghoulies 168
Ghouls 231
Girl Walks Home Alone at Night, A 229
Gladiator 6
Glass Cell, The 80
Godfather Part III, The 173
Gods Must Be Crazy, The 169
Gods Must Be Crazy II, The 169
Gods Must Be Funny in China, The 169
Gogol (film series)
Goke, Body Snatcher from Hell 25
Golden Voyage of Sinbad, The 115
Goosebumps (TV series) 34
Graf Dracula in Oberbayern see Dracula Blows His Cool
grande trouille, La see Tender Dracula
Grave of the Vampire 6, 100, 128
Graveyard Shift 148
Grindhouse 189
Guardians of the Night 231
Guess What Happened to Count Dracula? 31
Habit 186
Haine 139
Halloween 134
Halloween III: Season of the Witch 218
Hamiltons, The 224
Hamlet 181
Hands of the Ripper 87
Hard Boiled 163
Hard Target 234
Hard to Be a God 231
Haunting, The 6
Heartstopper 33
Hello Dracula 25
Hemlock Grove (TV series) 36
Hercules in the Haunted World 59
Hercules vs. the Vampires see Hercules in the Haunted World
Heroes (TV series) 223
Higanjima: Escape from Vampire Island 4
High Art 217
Hitcher, The 151
Hitman 165
Hollywood Boulevard 159
Horrible Sexy Vampire, The 31
Horror Express 112
Horror of Dracula see Dracula (1958)
Horror Show, The 167
Hotel Transylvania 30
Hotel Transylvania 2 30, 184
Hotel Transylvania 3: Summer Vacation 30, 184
House of Dark Shadows 79
House of Dracula 15, 16, 47
House of Frankenstein 15, 47
House on the Edge of the Park 121
House That Dripped Blood, The 29
House with Laughing Windows, The 6
Humongous 6
Hunchback of the Morgue 105
Hunger, The 141, 185
Hunted 38
Hunting Party, The 6
Hurt Locker, The 151
I Am Legend 64

I Bought a Vampire Motorcycle 28
I Dismember Mama 97
I See You 237
I Was a Teenage Frankenstein 50
I Was a Teenage Werewolf 50
I, Desire 34
Immoral Tales 20
Immortality see Wisdom of Crocodiles, The
In Dreams 6, 221
In Search of Dracula 18
Innocent Blood 175
Innocent Prey 151
Inside 201, 218
Intercourse with the Vampire 11
Interview with the Vampire 180, 204, 221
Into the Night 175
Invisible Man, The 228
Iron Man 228
Iron Rose, The 103
Isle of the Dead 8
It (TV mini-series) 233
It Was a Colossal Teenage Movie Machine: The American International Pictures Story 6
It's Alive III: Island of the Alive 151
Jack the Ripper 53
Jakob's Wife 5, 236
Jerry Maguire 198
Jesse James Meets Frankenstein's Daughter 66
Jesus Christ Vampire Hunter 37
Jitters, The 157
Jojo Rabbit 230
Joke, The 84
Jonathan 80
Jugular Wine: A Vampire Odyssey 178
Kamitsukitai see My Soul Is Slashed
Karmina 33
Keep, The 26, 66
Kindred: The Embraced 34
King Cohen 6
Kingdom of the Vampire 33
Kiss of Evil see Kiss of the Vampire, The
Kiss of the Damned 223
Kiss of the Vampire 38
Kiss of the Vampire, The 6, 62
Kojak (TV series) 112
Kolchak: The Night Stalker (TV series) 102
Kyôfu Densetsu Kaiki! Frankenstein see Monster of Frankenstein, The
Lady Dracula 93
Lady Vampire, The 85
Lady Vanishes, The 62
Lady Vengeance 215
Lady with Red Boots, The 120
Lair (TV series), The 37
Lair of the White Worm, The 27
Lake of Dracula 89, 116
Last Exit to Brooklyn 198
Last Man on Earth, The 64, 65
Last Rites see Dracula's Last Rites
Last Sect, The 38
Last Tango in Paris 139
Låt den rätte komma in see Let the Right One In
Laure 121
Legacies (TV series) 35
Legend of Blood Castle, The 20
Legend of the 7 Golden Vampires, The 10, 117, 160, 205
Legion 220
Lemora: A Child's Tale of the Supernatural 110
Leonor 120
Leptirica 5, 111
Lesbian Vampire Killers 4, 37
Let Me In 212

Let the Right One In 4, 10, 212
Let the Wrong One In 4
Let's Scare Jessica to Death 10, 28, 122
Lèvres de sang see Lips of Blood
lèvres rouge, Les see Daughters of Darkness
Lifeforce 25, 26
Lips of Blood 121
Little Girl Who Lives Down the Lane, The 6
Little Vampire, The 198
Livide 218
Living Among Us 232
Living Coffin, The 56
Living Corpse, The 72
London After Midnight 8, 14, 44
Long Goodbye, The 48
Long Weekend 151
Lost Boys, The 149, 174
Lost Boys: The Thirst 149
Lost Boys: The Tribe 149
Lost Platoon, The 164
Love at First Bite 10, 18, 23, 133
Love Bites 179
Love Witch, The 5
Lovers: A True Story 97
Loves of Count Iorga, The see Count Yorga, Vampire
Loves of Irina, The see Female Vampire
Lucifer's Women 129
Lust at First Bite see Dracula Sucks
Lust for a Vampire 90
M 19
Mad Doctor of Blood Island 6
Magic Christian, The 16, 17, 124
Magic Cop 165
Maleficent 228
Malenka 23
Malibu Beach 128
Mama Dracula 5, 139
Man from U.N.C.L.E. (TV series), The 159
Manhattan Undying 38
manoir du diable, Le 15
Mansion of Madness, The 122
Manson 32
Mariachi, El 189
Mark of the Devil 24
Mark of the Vampire 8, 14, 44
Martin 11, 21, 126
Mary, Mary, Bloody Mary 122
maschera del demonio, La see Black Sunday
Mask of Satan, The see Black Sunday
Masters of Horror (TV series) 35
Mephisto Waltz, The 6
Messiah of Evil 113, 122
Midnight Hour, The 34
Midnight Mass (TV mini-series) 38
Midnight Son 219
Midnight Vampire 25
Mighty Peking Man 93
Mighty Quinn, The 19
Mill of the Stone Women 101
Mist, The 211
Mistress of the Devil see Leonor
Modern Family (TV series) 230
Modern Vampires 33
Monster Club, The 29
Monster of Frankenstein, The 138
Monster Squad, The 30
Monster That Challenged the World, The 51
Monty Python and the Holy Grail 114
Moonlight (TV series) 37
Morbius 192
More Vampires in Havana! 146
Morgiana 140
Mosquito der Schänder 21
mostro dell'opera, Il see Vampire of the Opera
Mother Riley Meets the Vampire 16

Mr. Vampire 25, 143, 160, 165
Mr. Vampire II 160
Muffy the Vampire Layer 11
Mulberry Street 216
Mummy, The 17
mundo de los vampiros, El see World of the Vampires, The
Munsters (TV series), The 33
Muppet Show (TV series), The 30
Musical Vampire, The 160
My Father Die 5
My Grandpa Is a Vampire 33
My Soul Is Slashed 170
Mystery Science Theater 3000 (TV series) 60
Nächte des Grauens 15
Nadja 181, 196
Near Dark 150, 151
Neon Demon, The 28
Never Take Sweets from a Stranger 74
New Moon 213
Nick Knight 37
Night Flier, The 190
Night Gallery (TV series) 28, 33, 55
Night Guards see Guardians of the Night
Night Hunter 33
Night of Dark Shadows 79
Night of Horror see Nächte des Grauens, A
Night of the Devils 61, 101
Night of the Living Dead 109
Night of the Vampire, The see Vampire Doll, The
Night of the Walking Dead see Strange Love of the Vampires
Night Stalker, The 34, 102
Night Strangler, The 102
Night Teeth 237
Night Watch 208, 231
Nightmare Before Christmas, The 30
Nightmare in Blood 127
Nightmare on Elm Street, A 159
Nightwing 19
Nishi Trishna 157
Nocturna 19, 134
Noroi no Yakata Chi o Sū Me see Lake of Dracula
NOS4A2 (TV series) 37
Nosferatu 9, 14, 34, 40, 50, 140, 178, 199
Nosferatu a Venezia see Vampire in Venice
Nosferatu the Vampyre 9, 18, 134, 135, 155
Not Against Flesh see Vampyr
Not of This Earth 159
novia ensangrentada, La see Blood Spattered Bride, The
Nude Vampire, The 81
Nutty Professor, The 193
Office (TV series), The 230
Old Dark House, The 151
Old Dracula see Vampira
Oldboy 215
Omega Man, The 64
Once Bitten 19
Only Lovers Left Alive 226
Onna kyûketsuki see Lady Vampire, The
Opera 6
Operation Titian 67
Originals (TV series), The 35
Orphanage, The 211
Outback Vampires 151
Pale Blood 166
Pan's Labyrinth 176
Papa, umer Ded Moroz see Daddy, Father Frost Is Dead
Paranoiac 74
Paranormal Activity 211
pasión turca, La 97
Passenger, The 139
Passion of Joan of Arc, The 43
Pearls Before Swine 172

Penny Dreadful (TV series) 36
Phantom of the Opera, The 222
Phase IV 92
Phat Beach 166
Placer sangriento see Feast of Flesh
Planet of the Vampires 22, 178
Playgirls and the Vampire, The 24
Poison Ivy II 185
Poltergeist 26
Porky's 144
Portrait in Terror 67
Preacher (TV series) 36
Priest 220
Prince of the Night see Vampire in Venice
Project Vampire 33
Pulp Fiction 189
Pyushchye krovi see Vampire (1991), The
Queen of the Damned 21, 204
quinto jinete (TV series), El 101
Raat Ke Andhere Mein 161
Rabid 25, 167
Raging Moon , The 11
Rape of the Vampire, The 75, 81
Raven, The 46
Razor Blade Smile 194
[REC] 211
Red Blooded American Girl 167
Red Blooded American Girl II 167
Red Scorpion 6
Reflecting Skin, The 27
Reincarnation of Isabel, The 64
Relic 5
Renfield the Undead 38
Reptile, The 27
Requiem for a Vampire 103
Return of Count Yorga, The 78
Return of Dracula, The 16, 55
Return of the Vampire, The 16, 46
Return to Salem's Lot, A 136, 152
Revamped 38
Revenge of the Vampire see Black Sunday
Rigor Mortis 205
Robo Vampire 154
RoboCop 154
Robotrix 163
Rock 'n' Roll Nightmare 157
Rockula 168
Rosemary's Baby 71, 107
Rufus 219
Sadistic Baron Von Klaus, The 98
saga de los Drácula, La see Dracula Saga, The
Saint (TV series), The 53
Salem's Lot 9, 130, 136, 152
Samson vs. the Vampire Women see Santo vs. the Vampire Women
Sanctuary (TV series) 37
Sangre de virgenes see Blood of the Virgins
Santo vs. the Vampire Women 5, 60
Satanic Rites of Dracula, The 112
Saturday Night Fever 131, 134
Scars of Dracula 82, 86
School Daze 162
Scooby-Doo! and the Legend of the Vampire 30
Scooby-Doo! Music of the Vampire 30
Scream 34, 197
Scream Blacula Scream 96
Scream for Help 142
Semya vurdalakov see Vampire Family, The
Sentinel, The 6
Sesame Street (TV series) 18
Sex and the Single Vampire 31
Sexual-Terror der entfesselten Vampire see Shiver of the

Vampires, The
Shack Out on 101 17
Shadow of a Doubt 55
Shadow of the Vampire 9, 127, 199, 214
Shadowland 38
Shaft 96
Shape of Water, The 176
Shatter 117
She Killed in Ecstasy 94
She-Butterfly, The see Leptirica
Sherlock (TV series) 36
Shiver of the Vampires, The 91, 103, 223
Shredder 6
Silent Partner, The 6
Silent Scream 6
Simpsons (TV series), The 173
Sin You Sinners 106
Siren, The 5
Slaughter of the Vampires 24
Sledgehammer 164
Sleepless 6
Sleepwalkers 26
Some Kind of Hate 5
Son of Darkness: To Die For II 159
Son of Dracula (1943) 15, 47, 197
Son of Dracula (1974) 17
Sopranos (TV series), The 100
Spermula 27
Stake Land 216
Stake Land II 216
Stakelander, The see Stake Land II
Stan Helsing 38
Step Down to Terror 55
Strain (TV series), The 37
Strange Love of the Vampires 31
Strange Things Happen at Night see Shiver of the Vampires, The
Strange Things Happen at Sundown 206
Student Nurses, The 95
Stunt Rock 6
Subspecies 171
Subspecies 4: Bloodstorm 171
Suce-moi vampire see Lips of Blood
Suckula (1973) 32
Suckula (1974) 32
Sugar Hill 96
Summer School 168
Sundown: The Vampire in Retreat 158
Super Fly 96
Supernatural (American TV series) 34

Supernatural (British TV series) 36
Suspiria (1977) 120, 218
Suspiria (2018) 64
Sweet Sweetback's Baadasssss Song 96
Sympathy for Mr. Vengeance 215
Symptoms 119
Tale of a Vampire 33
Tales from the Crypt 29, 93
Tales from the Crypt (TV series) 34, 188, 189
Tales from the Gimli Hospital 202
Tales from the Hood 2 30
Taoism Drunkard 25
Tarzoon: Shame of the Jungle 139
Taste of Blood, A 73
Taste the Blood of Dracula 83, 87
Tempi duri per i vampiri see Uncle Was a Vampire
Tender Dracula 118
Tenderness of the Wolves 19
Teorema 32
Terror in the Crypt 23
Terror Is a Man 63
Texas Chain Saw Massacre, The 136
Thirst (1979) 137
Thirst (2009) 5, 215
Thirteen 213
This House Possessed 137
This Is Spinal Tap 230
This Is Us 36
Thompsons, The 224
Thor: Ragnarok 230
Thriller (TV series) 6, 61
Ticks 6
Tingler, The 55
To Die For 159
To Sleep with a Vampire 33
Tombs of the Blind Dead 23
Tommy 92
Totmacher, Der 20
Track of the Vampire see Blood Bath
Transfiguration, The 4, 11, 219
Transylvania 6-5000 30
Transylvania Twist 23, 159
tre volti della paura, I see Black Sabbath
Trog 93
Trouble Every Day 201
True Blood (TV series) 35, 146
Tsui Hark's Vampire Hunters see Era of Vampires, The

Twice-Told Tales 64
Twilight 213
Twilight Saga (film series), The 37, 213, 217
Twin Peaks (TV series) 195
Twins Effect, The 205
Twins of Evil 4, 11, 92
Twister 181
Two Front Teeth 210
Two Orphan Vampires 191, 203
ultima preda del vampire, L' see Playgirls and the Vampire, The
Ultimate Vampire, The 160
Ultraviolet 207
Uncle Was a Vampire 22, 23, 124
Undead 214
Understudy: Graveyard Shift II, The 148
Underworld 207, 208
Underworld (film series) 37, 194, 220, 231
Underworld: Awakening 207
Underworld: Blood Wars 207
Underworld: Evolution 207
Underworld: Rise of the Lycans 207
Unholy, The 6
Until the End of the World 181
Upír z Feratu see Ferat Vampire
Upyr 101
V Wars (TV series) 37
Valerie and Her Week of Wonders 5, 9, 84
Vamp 147
Vampir Cuadecuc 77
Vampira 22, 23
Vampire 19
Vampire (1913), The 15
Vampire (1957), The 51, 55
Vampire (1991), The 101
Vampire and the Ballerina, The 5, 24, 58, 64
Vampire Bat, The 8
Vampire Circus 92, 104
Vampire Clan 38
vampire de la autopista, El see Horrible Sexy Vampire, The
Vampire Diaries (TV series), The 34, 35
Vampire Dog 28
Vampire Doll, The 5, 85, 89
Vampire Ecstasy see Devil's Plaything, The
Vampire Expert (TV series) 160
Vampire Family, The 101
Vampire Girl vs. Frankenstein Girl 4
Vampire Happening, The 93

Vampire Hookers 32
Vampire Hunter D 145
Vampire Hunter D: Bloodlust 145
Vampire in Brooklyn 187
Vampire in Venice 155
Vampire Is Still Alive, The 154
Vampire Journals 171
Vampire Lovers, The 4, 29, 86, 87, 90
vampire nue, La see Nude Vampire, The
Vampire of Düsseldorf, The 20
Vampire of the Opera 64
Vampire People see Blood Drinkers, The
Vampire Raiders: Ninja Queen 154
Vampire vs. Vampire 160
Vampire Who Admires Me, The 25
Vampirella 33
Vampires 195
Vampires (serial), Les 15
Vampire's Coffin, The 56
Vampire's Ghost, The 8, 48
Vampires in Havana 146
Vampire's Kiss 156
Vampires' Night Orgy, The 5, 107, 113
Vampires Suck 38
Vampires: Los Muertos 195
Vampires: The Turning 195
vampiri, I 21
Vampirina (TV series) 37
vampiro, El 52, 56, 60
Vamps 38
Vampyr 8, 43
Vampyres 119
Vampyros Lesbos 94
Van Helsing 228
Van Helsing (TV series) 37
Vault of Horror, The 29
Veil of Blood see Devil's Plaything, The
Velvet Vampire, The 5, 6, 95
venganza del sexo, La see Curious Dr. Humpp, The
Videodrome 6
Videoman 5
View to a Kill, A 147
viol du vampire, Le see Rape of the Vampire, The
Virgin Among the Living Dead, A 98
Visitor, The 6
Viy 22
Vlad 19
Vlad Tepes 19

Vlad's Legacy 19
Vurdalaki 101
Walking Dead (TV series), The 190, 216
Wampyr see Martin
Warlock 6
Watch Me When I Kill 6
Wave, The 217
Waxwork 153, 158
Wayne's World 66
We Are the Night 217
Welcome to Leith 232
Werewolf vs. the Vampire Woman, The 24
West Side Story 166
What We Do in the Shadows 230, 232
What's Love Got to Do with It 187
What's Up, Tiger Lily? 124
Whirlpool 119
White Reindeer, The 49
Who's the Boss? (TV series) 185
Wicked, The see Outback Vampires
Wicker Man, The 156
Willard 6
Wind, The 5
Wir sind die Nacht see We Are the Night
Wisdom of Crocodiles, The 196
Witchfinder General 92
Within the Woods 177
Wohi Bhayaanak Raat 161
Wolf Man, The 47
World of the Vampires, The 60
X: Night of Vengeance 172
X-Files (TV series), The 102
Yami no Teiō: Kyūketsuki Dorakyura see Dracula, Sovereign of the Damned
You Are Not My Mother 5
Young Dracula 123, 227
Young Frankenstein 133, 184
Young Hannah, Queen of the Vampires 23
Yūrei Yashiki no Kyōfu Chi o Sū Ningyō see Vampire Doll, The
Zinda Laash see Living Corpse, The
Zoltan, Hound of Dracula 28, 128
Zombie Lake 108
Zombieland 216
Zu: Warriors from the Magic Mountain 25, 205